The P.A.'s Handbook

The P.A.'s Handbook

Joan Moncrieff and Doreen Sharp

PAPERMAC

First published 1980 as *The Professional Secretaries Handbook* by
PAPERMAC
a division of Macmillan Publishing Limited
London and Basingstoke

Associated companies in Auckland, Dallas,
Delhi, Dublin, Hong Kong, Johannesburg,
Lagos, Manzini, Melbourne, Nairobi,
New York, Singapore, Tokyo, Washington
and Zaria

Second edition published 1983, reprinted 1984, 1985
Third edition 1986

British Library Cataloguing in Publication Data
Moncrieff, Joan
    The P.A.'s handbook.——3rd ed.
    1. Office practice   2. Secretaries
    I. Title   II. Sharp, Doreen
    651.3'741   HF5547.5

ISBN 0-333-42216-3

Printed in Hong Kong

CONTENTS

ACKNOWLEDGMENTS

The authors would like to thank the British Library, British Rail and SASCO for permission to use illustrative material, and the following for help and advice:

Appropriate Systems Ltd	Mr Henry Goldberg MA, BSc, MBCS
Banking Information Service	The Secretary
Barclays Bank Ltd	Mr Andy Cutter
British Library	Mr Malcolm Preskett
British Rail	
British Safety Council	Mr James Tye
British Standards Institution	Mr Michael Mann
British Telecom	
Bromley Central Library and West Wickham Branch Library	
Cable and Wireless Ltd	Miss Penny David
Mr Eric Crofts BSc (Econ), ACIS, AMBIM	
Equal Opportunities Commission	
European Association of Professional Secretaries	French National Group
Executive Connections	
Executive Services Ltd	
Fire Protection Association	Mr D. F. Gray
Gateway Building Society	
Hogg Robinson Travel	Mr John Simmons
Industrial Society	Miss Sally-Anne Hart
Institute of Public Relations	Mr J. Wild
Institute of Travel Managers	Mr Arthur Lyddall
Intercom	Mr Frank Legroux
International Computers Ltd	
Mr Alan H. M. Jutsum, ACII	
Kardex Systems UK Ltd	
Manpower Services Commission	Miss Michaela McCormack
Metropolitan Police Crime Prevention Service	Asst. Chief Inspector M. G. Parsons, Inspector Peter Jupp, Inspector Waddington
Midland Bank Ltd	Mr Martin Lockton

Muirhead Data Communications Ltd	Mr R. R. Wood OBE
NATFHE	Mr Jack Hendy and Mr Keith Scribbins
National Computing Centre Limited, Manchester	Mrs Jean Morris and Mr Steve Price
Mr Tom Pinder, Consultant in Speech-in-Management	
Professional Management Group	Mr Stewart Davis
SASCO	Mr Stephan Mercado
Mr Nicholas Sharp MA MBCS	
Shell UK Oil	
3M United Kingdom Ltd	Mr P. T. Williams
Travel Trade Directory	
WordPro Training and Recruitment	Mrs Rosemary Pratt and Mr Stephen Pratt

Although the authors have made every effort to trace their sources they cannot be held responsible for unacknowledged material.

INTRODUCTION

The authors are aware that business management and secretarial textbooks, in the main, fall into two completely separate categories; yet it is a fact that good secretaries are able to relieve their employers of many management-type duties, and also that young managers themselves need guidance to certain routine business techniques, which are not always included in their training courses.

In addition the authors have taken into consideration the fact that the range of subjects in top Personal Assistant/Secretarial examinations has now extended far beyond that of only a few years ago. With this in mind, the chapter contents have been carefully selected to cover the requirements of the present high-level business and secretarial examinations.

The authors feel that an augmentative handbook of this kind is urgently needed and long overdue, to bridge the gap not only between earlier examination-syllabus content and the wider aspects required today, but also between a career secretary's 'secretarial duties' and the young manager's 'business techniques'. Besides these two bridging operations there is a third aim, and that is to suggest to senior executives, who may not always recognise the latent capabilities of their staff, ways in which this potential may be realised to the full.

It is also hoped that this book will be of help to all qualified personal assistants and secretaries who intend to acquire a confident and polished professionalism, and who wish to make an interesting and meaningful career for themselves in the world of business, whether in the U.K. or abroad.

Joan Moncrieff
Doreen Sharp

June 1986

JOB DESCRIPTION

The following Job Description may be of interest to all manage-ment staff in general, professional secretaries and personal assis-tants in particular. It was issued by the French Group of the European Association of Professional Secretaries.

EXECUTIVE SECRETARY – or, according to the complexity of tasks and degree of autonomy – EXECUTIVE ASSISTANT

Secretary technically qualified and capable of:

– drafting correspondence with or without instructions, estab-lishing a filing system, setting up and maintaining a planning board, organising internal and external meetings;

– examining and synthesising material, assembling and keeping up to date relevant documentation, composing press reviews according to the needs of the job;

– heading a team of senior secretarial support;

– being delegated to transmit the boss's directives to his heads of division and ensuring their follow up;

– serving as intermediary between the boss and the staff in resolving personnel problems.

The Executive Secretary or Assistant receives unrestricted infor-mation from management and enjoys a certain autonomy.

As a collaborator she* is able, in the absence of her boss, to assess the degree of interest and/or urgency of a task and to establish the necessary liaison with those concerned. She is capable of assuming the responsibility of organising meetings of the directors and of the board, of attending such meetings and writing up summary records. She is expected to display, by her behaviour and appear-ance, her role as public relations officer both inside and outside the company.

Hierarchical position: Management.

JM & DS

---

* It should, of course, be understood that 'she' is used purely for convenience throughout and that many secretaries and personal assistants are male.

1 BANKING FACILITIES AND SERVICES

> *Accounts; bank draft; Banking Information Service; cash card and dispenser; cheque card; cheques; credit card; credit transfer; direct debiting; executorship and trusteeship; income tax; insurance; international services; investments; loans and overdrafts; movement of cash; night safe; open credit; safe deposit and strongroom; standing order; stocks and shares; travel facilities*

The services which banks can offer their customers vary from ordinary current and deposit accounts to financial transactions of a very complex nature. The major clearing banks – Barclays, Lloyds, Midland, National Westminster and the Royal Bank of Scotland – have arisen largely from mergers of many small regional banks some of which can trace their origins back to the sixteenth century. They are now amongst the largest companies to be found in the world.

It is impossible to write about branch banking without mentioning the manager, the man around whom all the services revolve. Since a bank manager will have spent the greater part of his career dealing in money and finance, the wide knowledge and experience which he will have gained can prove of great assistance to his customers. Using his expertise the manager has to make decisions on whether or not to lend money to people, quite a daunting task when you consider that requests can range from a private individual wishing to borrow money to buy a car, to a large public company requiring cash to finance a multi-million pound project.

Although a manager may have wide financial knowledge he still works very closely with the other companies in the group, consulting them if he requires specialist information, and he may direct customers to the specialist companies if their requirements are beyond the scope of branch banking.

Since the world of finance has grown very sophisticated there are some types of finance, particularly finance for industry, which are too complex for branches to deal with, and this has led to the formation of companies designed to cater for such specialist forms of lending as hire purchase, leasing and factoring.

An alphabetical summary of the banks' most popular services is
given below:

ACCOUNTS

Budget account (personal outlay)   This type of account is
available at some banks. The customer gives his bank a list of all his
regular bills, such as rates, gas and electricity, season tickets and
subscriptions to societies, and the total amount including any charges
involved is divided into twelve equal monthly amounts. This sum is
transferred each month from the customer's current account to his
budget account, so that he can be confident of being able to meet the
bills when they come in.

Current account   A current account is a working account maintained for personal use. Cheques are made out to pay bills or
withdraw cash and a statement is sent to the customer at intervals
showing the transactions in and out of the account and the final
balance to date. It is not economical to keep too large a credit balance.
The National Girobank has operated a free banking service for several years but now all the High Street banks have abolished their
current account bank charges for customers who keep their accounts
in credit. However, those whose accounts become overdrawn will
find themselves paying more heavily in order to compensate for this
free banking service. A joint current account can be held (eg husband
and wife) and either may sign any cheques. For security reasons a
company or club may require two or more signatures on any cheque
which authorises payments from its account.

Deposit account   This is a reserve account for customers who
wish to deposit money not wanted for immediate use; this earns
interest at declared rates which vary according to the economic
situation. A short notice is required before withdrawals can be made.
Money can be transferred from a deposit account to a current account
and vice versa. Larger sums can be deposited for 'fixed' periods,
eg two years, during which term this money cannot be withdrawn;
or 'notice' periods, eg one month's notice to be given by the customer.

BANK DRAFT

A bank draft is in effect a cheque drawn by a bank on its own head
office, or on another branch of the bank or even on a foreign bank. A
bank draft is used as a means of transferring money, in the same way
as a cheque, both in the UK and overseas. If funds are being sent
overseas a draft can be drawn on a bank in a foreign country in that
country's currency.

BANKING INFORMATION SERVICE

The Banking Information Service is an educational liaison organisation sponsored by most of the High Street banks. Its main objective is to help teachers and their students become more aware of the role of banks within the community by producing a wide range of educational resource material, and providing a comprehensive careers information service. Information is available from The Manager, BIS, 10 Lombard Street, London EC3V 9AT.

CASH CARD AND DISPENSER

Most banks and some building societies provide cash card and dispenser facilities whereby the holder of a cash card can obtain money at any time during the day or night, throughout the week. Many branches have cash dispenser units set into a convenient outside wall of their buildings. The customer taps out his personal code number on the small keyboard attached to the dispenser. Providing the code number is correctly given and the balance of the customer's account is sufficient to meet the amount required, the cash card is returned to the customer and the banknotes are passed out to an open drawer in the dispenser.

CHEQUE CARD

The possession of a bank cheque card entitles the holder to cash a cheque up to a permitted amount at any branch of any bank within the cheque card scheme in the United Kingdom and Ireland. On production of this card, retailers will accept cheques of up to £50. A cheque issued in this way cannot be countermanded by the drawer. The 'Eurocheque' scheme extends this facility to a number of European countries.

CHEQUES

A cheque is an order in writing from a bank account holder to his bank to pay out a sum of money from his account to a named person or company. It is an excellent way of transferring money from one account to another. The bank should be notified immediately if a cheque book is lost or stolen so that any cheque from that book, fraudulently presented, will not be honoured. A colourfully presented gift cheque, designed to mark a birthday, anniversary or other special occasion, is a feature of some banks.

CREDIT CARD

The possession of a credit card, eg Access, American Express or Barclaycard, entitles the holder to sign for goods and services bought at many shops, garages and restaurants, quoting his credit card account number. The proprietor then claims payment from the bank. The card can be used by the holder to obtain cash advances at a bank. A Barclaycard can also be used as a cheque card. Most cards can be used in many countries throughout the world, wherever the relevant card symbol is displayed. Each card holder is notified of his credit limit, ie the maximum amount that he may have outstanding at any one time. Once a month the credit card company sends him a statement showing the total of all bills for that month; one cheque to the bank may thus be used to cover several purchases from different shops.

CREDIT TRANSFER (BANK GIRO CREDIT)

The credit transfer system of payment can be used for settling a list of debts through any bank in the United Kingdom. A bank's customer can pay any number of bills by one cheque made out to his bank covering the total amount on all credit transfer slips. The bank then arranges for the creditors' accounts to receive the amounts due. The creditors must first have accepted this arrangement. People who do not hold a bank account may make a credit transfer payment in cash over the bank counter.

DIRECT DEBITING

This is a variation of the standing order. The customer gives his bank a written instruction to meet payments as they fall due. The organisation named in the instruction presents the payment and the bank deducts from the customer's account. There are two methods of direct debiting; one provides for payment of fixed amounts and the other provides for payment of unspecified amounts where the amounts due may vary, eg rates or club and association subscriptions.

EXECUTORSHIP AND TRUSTEESHIP

A customer can arrange with his bank for them to be appointed executors of his will and to administer his estate after death. This is one way of ensuring that, at a time of stress for his family, these duties and responsibilities are carried out by experts.

INCOME TAX

Income tax departments of banks will advise customers, or act on their behalf, regarding tax problems. They will prepare tax returns, check assessments, claim refunds and deal with capital gains.

INSURANCE

Many banks give advice and arrange insurance cover over a variety of personal, family and property risks, to safeguard individuals or businesses.

INTERNATIONAL SERVICES

All the clearing banks have international divisions which maintain a network of branches and representative offices throughout the world (for instance, Barclays, Britain's largest international bank, is represented in over 75 countries). They are well placed, therefore, to assist and advise on all aspects of international trade and travel.

There are many ways of settling international debts arising from the import and export of goods. These range from the simple collection of cheques drawn in foreign currency and payable abroad to the somewhat complicated papers and documents associated with a documentary credit. The latter, when arranged between a bank and its correspondent bank in a foreign country, enables an exporter to obtain payment for his goods when they are put on board the ship. The shipper gives the exporter a bill of lading, which is a certificate of ownership, and the exporter can obtain payment from his bank in exchange for the bill of lading. The bank then sends this to the importer overseas via the correspondent bank so that he can exchange it for the goods when they arrive.

Banks have teams of experts available to assist in the complexities of overseas contracts. Assistance can be sought by large or small companies on many matters such as overseas market reports, contract guarantees and the effect of overseas law, insurance cover against risks and currency deals where decisions have to be made as to the best method of payment and forward dealing.

Their wide knowledge of the economies of foreign countries enables banks to give advice to would-be exporters and they can obtain credit information on companies resident abroad.

Personal customers also make use of the bank's world-wide connections when they wish to send money to relatives abroad. This is done by telegram or by ordinary mail depending on how urgently the money is required.

INVESTMENTS

Banks offer a very wide specialist range of investment services for individual or corporate bodies and can offer professional advice to all investors. Banks will undertake the complete management of investment portfolios.

LOANS AND OVERDRAFTS

Bridging loan   This is a temporary loan for 'bridging the gap' between the buying of one asset or property and the selling of another.

Business loan   Banks will assist both large and small businesses to expand and develop by lending them money to suit individual circumstances, for such purposes as extending existing buildings, acquiring new plant and machinery, office or factory premises, etc. Borrowers range from self-employed persons and small traders to giant international companies with branches all over the world. Some large firms have seconded specialist staff to help and advise those starting up small businesses under Government schemes.

Overdrafts   By special agreement, customers may be allowed a temporary overdraft up to a specified limit. Interest is charged on amounts overdrawn, and the rate of interest may vary during the period of the overdraft, according to the bank's individual base rate.

Personal loan   A personal loan, tailored to suit a special need, can be obtained by agreement with the bank manager for such items as the purchase of a car or alterations and extensions to houses. Interest is charged, and the loan is repaid over a fixed period in agreed monthly amounts, usually by standing order. Larger loans may be granted against the security of property or other possessions for the purchase of more costly items. In some cases loan interest may be considered eligible for tax relief.

MOVEMENT OF CASH

The task of maintaining a smooth flow of bank notes and coin and of distributing them evenly throughout the country is important and expensive. Often taken for granted, it is a genuine service to the whole community, not only to companies and institutions such as large department stores, supermarkets and the Post Office, but to anyone at all who handles money. Cheques, credit cards, bank giro credits, standing orders and direct debits are all ways of transferring money without using actual notes and coin, but nevertheless about six thousand million pounds of cash is at present in circulation in the UK. This requires a very sophisticated banking system to ensure that sufficient currency always arrives at the right place at the right time.

NIGHT SAFE

A night safe, accessible throughout the twenty-four hours of the day, may be set into the outside wall of a branch bank. The customer possesses a key to a trap in the bank wall and uses a wallet in which he locks his cash and cheques. He unlocks the trap, places the wallet inside and locks the trap up again. The wallet slides down a chute inside the bank for safe keeping. As early as possible next morning the customer will call at the bank, unlock his wallet and deposit the money in the usual way over the counter. This facility, available at most branches, provides a convenient method of lodging money safely outside normal banking hours and is widely used by shop-keepers to avoid leaving cash in their tills overnight and at weekends.

OPEN CREDIT

Instructions to pay cash from a customer's current account can be sent from the customer's bank to any branch of a bank in the UK, together with the customer's specimen signature. Withdrawals of money can then be made at these branches up to a specified limit.

SAFE DEPOSIT AND STRONG-ROOM

All bank customers, whether individuals, companies, firms or associations, can deposit important documents or other articles such as deeds, wills, share certificates, jewellery, works of art, etc for safe keeping in lockable containers in specially constructed strong-rooms. Most branch banks have facilities which include deed boxes or private safes fitted with compartments. The customer has sole access to his individual safe and may keep his valuables in the bank permanently or for a few weeks while he is away on business or holiday. Items held in this way are not always insured against theft but extra insurance may be arranged if required.

STANDING (OR BANKERS) ORDER

An order can be given to the bank to make regular fixed payments on behalf of a customer monthly, quarterly or annually, for items such as rent or hire-purchase payments. This standing order is completed and signed by the customer and the bank programs its computer to make regular specified payments into the creditor's account until such time as the order is amended or withdrawn by the customer.

STOCKS AND SHARES

Banks are able to give their customers general advice, or obtain advice for them, on all aspects of the various types of investment that are available. These include stocks and shares, National Savings Certificates, Premium Savings Bonds, government securities, local authority bonds and many others. They can also arrange for all investments to be purchased or sold on behalf of customers.

When purchasing stocks and shares the banks use an independent firm of stockbrokers which deals directly on the Stock Exchange. These stockbrokers can also give up-to-date advice on the specific stocks and shares the customer is considering.

Many banks also have their own Unit Trusts, eg Barclays Unicorn and Midland Drayton. These are large portfolios of various shares bought by the unit trust managers into which people can buy a share. This helps to eliminate the effects of the large fluctuations sometimes seen in the share prices of individual companies.

For large companies the banks are able to give specialised financial advice through the merchant banking divisions. Their detailed knowledge of the financial affairs of the company, together with a considerable experience in this field, enables merchant banks to advise on share flotations, mergers, bids, rights issues, etc.

TRAVEL FACILITIES

Foreign currency   With only a few days' notice, business travellers or holiday makers can obtain foreign currency at the current rate of exchange for most of the countries of the world. Some countries which have money import restrictions offer facilities for cashing travellers' cheques at border points and airports.

Insurance   Many banks will arrange travel insurance for customers while they are abroad. The risks covered could include medical expenses, accident or injury, loss of baggage or money and possible cancellation of the trip.

Passports and visas   Arrangements regarding passport and visa applications can be made through some banks. They will also supply information regarding the latest customs regulations.

Telegraphic or telex transfer   Money sent by telegraphic or telex transfer through banking channels will await collection at a named bank. Proof of identity must, of course, be produced before collection is permitted.

Travellers' cheques   As an alternative to using a credit card, many people prefer to take travellers' cheques rather than carry large amounts of foreign currency. These are available in denominations of £5 to £100 and in certain currencies other than sterling if preferred. Travellers' cheques must be signed at the time of purchase and again, with the same signature, when cashed. They are accepted at many large hotels, restaurants and shops and can also be cashed at most banks in the UK and abroad. Unused cheques can be credited on return to the UK. It is possible to claim a refund for lost or stolen travellers' cheques from the issuing bank.

2 COMMUNITY AND PUBLIC RELATIONS

*The necessity; the resources; services
offered; who is concerned? Duties of a
PRO; PR agencies and consultants;
market research; planning a PR exercise;
press releases; press visits; press
conferences*

The work of the public relations officer (PRO) is to spread
information, and this work may not only cover the immediate and
exclusive needs of his or her firm, but help to fulfil the needs of the
community as well, to their mutual benefit. If a secretary is aware of
the aims and scope of community and public relations, she will be
able to use her own initiative in helping to plan and carry out PR
work for her employer.

Any business concern has relationships with three different groups
of people. These are:
   its own employees
   its customers, clients and business associates
   the community around it.
The employees relate to the firm through:
   working conditions
   salaries and wages
   training, career structures and promotion prospects.
Customers, clients and business associates relate through:
   personal business relationships, ie contact with management
      and staff
   response to advertising and the presentation of goods
   response to the reliability of products and services
   use of after-sales service.
The community is influenced by the firm's ability to:
   make itself a useful and acceptable part of the district
   cultivate useful and friendly contacts with local government and
      local traders
   show a practical concern for people within the area.
An important part of PR work is to see that business relationships
with all these groups – employees, customers and the community –
are friendly and mutually profitable.

PUBLIC RELATIONS – THE NECESSITY

There may be a few companies who wish to avoid the limelight for their own special reasons, but for most firms this would spell disaster. Industry needs the appreciation and support of the public, but if a company were to depend for recognition solely on the reliability of its goods or services, however excellent they might be, its publicity would only spread slowly and over a limited area.

It is surprising that, in this ultra-competitive world, there are still many firms who do not clearly recognise the impact and advantages of a public relations campaign. Well planned publicity can present the firm in a favourable light so effectively that public acceptance and approval will be forthcoming immediately, practically overnight in some cases. To achieve this a company must deliberately take the necessary steps to 'sell itself' to the public.

Publicity may also be necessary for purposes other than marketing. A firm can be very vulnerable to outside influences, some of which may prove detrimental. A change in the management or the resignation of a key figure, for instance a member of the board, may start damaging and completely unfounded rumours. Unfavourable comments and opinions may then develop in the press or on television and on the business grapevine that runs through the Stock Exchange and other parts of the City, and this may do much harm to the firm's good name. If the media are supplied by the PRO with correct information of the right sort at the right time these rumours need never arise. If they have arisen, then they may be promptly corrected by the issuing of accurate information refuting all misconceptions.

The functions of good PR work may be seen as follows:

1. Creating and maintaining a good national reputation for the firm and promoting confidence in its products.
2. Increasing business by the advertising of goods and services over a wide area.
3. Establishing good financial standing, which makes the firm attractive from an investment point of view.
4. Building up public approval and support by the presentation of new projects and policies in the most favourable light.
5. Issuing definite and accurate information either for a positive and specific purpose or to counteract any detrimental rumours or criticisms.
6. Improving and maintaining good morale among the firm's own employees.
7. Creating a good reputation within the local community by publicising and selling good products and services, also by showing a genuine desire to help the public in an active and practical way.

PUBLIC RELATIONS – THE RESOURCES

The twofold aim of external PR work is to obtain profitable publicity for the firm and at the same time establish a good rapport with the general public and the local community. This may be done by:

> the recommendation of the firm's goods and services by advertisements via the media
>
> services to the community, such as provision of sports, arts or other needed amenities, and/or sponsorship of charitable causes.

Publicity may be general, or directed to specific groups and sections of the community, or issued to cover certain special areas. Typical channels of communication are:

1. The national press, which will accept direct advertisements and 'copy' and will also follow up items that appear in local and provincial newspapers.

2. The local and provincial newspapers, which are always interested in local news and stories.

3. Magazines, both the general publications for leisure reading and the specialised trade journals. The firm's own house magazine may also contain material of interest to the general public, and if this is so it may be printed in greater quantities to allow for outside distribution. Extra copies could be issued to places where the public will notice them, such as library reading rooms, local government offices and cinema foyers.

4. News agencies, which will undertake the task of distributing your news items for you through suitable outlets.

5. Television and radio, which will feature items as part of a news or 'interest' programme or produce them as a 'commercial'. Short commercial films and radio features will require the special techniques and expertise of a publicity agency.

6. Notices and posters on selected sites, inside and outside the firm's premises. Leaflets, handouts and brochures may also be printed for distribution, either through the post as direct mail individually addressed to names taken from a mailing list, or by hand at strategic distribution points, such as a busy shopping area.

7. Special offers, promotion campaigns, free samples of goods, an attractive stand or stall in supermarkets and department stores with an eye-catching display and a salesman or demonstrator in attendance. Competitions with prizes, coupons for goods at reduced prices or 'two-for-the-price-of-one' offers are also popular publicity and selling techniques.

8. Exhibitions and demonstrations. The renting of a stand at an established trade fair, such as the Ideal Home Exhibition, the Motor Show, the Boat Show, etc, will give good publicity. Alternatively a firm may use its own premises and stage an 'open day' when the public may see over workshops, laboratories or training centres and learn about the work done there. A recruitment and careers convention could be staged in conjunction with an open day, with talks and lectures for the general public about the company and the advantages of working within it.

COMMUNITY RELATIONS

Under this heading the work of the PRO has wider and more outgoing implications. The purpose of service to the community, seen as a public relations exercise, is not of course wholly altruistic; the intention is that the firm should also benefit itself. Therefore not only is the service to be done but it must be seen to be done – to benefit from any community PR exercise the firm must blow its own trumpet loudly and continuously and blow it where most of its likely customers and other members of the public will hear. There is no point in being modest in this competitive commercial world, but this need not give rise to cynicism. It is perfectly reasonable for a business to expect to get some compensating value for the money it spends, while the community benefits at the same time.

Ways of serving the public can always be found and the following are typical examples:

1. The provision of something needed by the community, such as a new library or community centre, a pleasure park or children's corner, seats for the elderly at strategic places, or the purchase and preservation for the public of a building of special attraction or historical interest.

2. The loan of equipment, facilities or services. A firm of accountants could offer its services as auditors to a club or society, a printing firm could print leaflets at no charge or at cost price for a good cause; many firms could suggest their own specialised help of some kind. An offer to lend premises, such as a clubroom or hall, might be a godsend to a group having difficulty in finding a place of its own. Some firms may have information or advice of use to the Citizens' Advice Bureau or some of the welfare services. Several firms could get together to make a corporate effort in giving local help and service, and local government officials might be able to make useful suggestions of other ways of giving service and assistance.

3. Sports and arts groups are often in need of financial or practical help. Financial assistance in sponsoring a concert or an art

exhibition might be welcome, or the creation of art or music societies, drama groups, football teams or teams for any other sporting events, or the loan of a sports ground to a local club. Meetings and matches may be arranged with similar groups within the community. There may be wine clubs, swimming clubs, pop groups, photographic societies that could meet together for contests and social events. Many well-known industrial names come to mind, such as Foden's Motor Works Band and the Stock Exchange Dramatic Society, while the *Daily Mail*, Benson & Hedges, Tate & Lyle, Gillette, Colgates and a host of others have all been linked publicly with promotion of the arts or of sporting events.

4. A firm may initiate or support sponsored walks or swims for charity, or organise and decorate a float for the local carnival procession or a fête; if there is a dramatic or musical society in the firm a special performance may be staged for charity. Money collected could provide special equipment for the local hospital, the handicapped or the elderly, or toys for a children's home at Christmas.

5. Donations of money to charity may be made by direct covenant, which carries certain income tax advantages – although as this is not of so much benefit to the donating firm from the publicity point of view donations may perhaps be made as part of a wider scheme of community benefit.

To sum up, a company with a public relations fund at its disposal and a sense of concern and responsibility for the community will find, if it takes a little trouble to investigate, that there are plenty of opportunities for useful and positive public spirited action.

INDUSTRIAL PUBLIC RELATIONS

Staff We all express opinions, with facial expression as well as in words and in our behaviour, and in this way PR work is unofficially carried out by everyone in a firm's employ, whether they realise it or not. From the newest junior to top management, everyone is in some degree involved in public relations. If the firm is a good employer and its staff appear to be happy, the word will spread around the community and there will be no lack of applications from people wishing to work within it. If the firm's policy is sound there will be an air of confidence amongst staff and this also will increase the firm's good reputation. Sound management and policy, good products, a happy atmosphere, are all part of good public relations, and some of the most important PR representatives on the staff are the secretaries and PAs, who are in constant communication with other people, inside and outside the firm.

The Public Relations Officer and team   Effective publicity needs co-ordination, and this means efficient departmental teamwork from the chief PRO and his entire section. If the PRO is required to organise and supervise large-scale publicity for a company, he or she should have managerial status and full authority over his department. He should not just be, for instance, a subsidiary member of the sales team. He needs to have a comprehensive overall view of what is going on throughout his firm before he can 'sell' it to the public. Therefore he needs all the direct information he can obtain from senior executives, and should have access to all departmental managers. He should be able to meet the management team both informally and formally. He must know about the firm's new products or services, research projects and changes of policy. His information must be accurate and up to date; he should not suffer the embarrassment of being corrected by an outsider on matters concerning his own firm.

The senior secretary or PA   He or she will be quite capable of planning, supervising or carrying out a publicity campaign on a moderate scale, alone or with secretarial/clerical help, although for a large scale exercise outside assistance might have to be brought in.

DUTIES OF A PUBLIC RELATIONS OFFICER

Publicity and the press   As publicity is a two-way exercise a PRO must be able to handle incoming enquiries from the press, as well as take the initiative in giving information. This may involve interviews with reporters, preparing press releases or material for specialised television and radio features, organising demonstrations and exhibitions at which the press will be present and generally co-operating with them to the best of his ability.

External company liaison   If your company has other branches and subsidiaries the PR staff will need to maintain good liaison between them. The parent company's chief PRO will have overall PR duties, the others will deal with their own separate local publicity. Keeping in touch with each other is vital in order to co-ordinate activities and to avoid any possibility of unintentional overlapping. Close contact should be constantly maintained between PROs of home and overseas branches.

Internal company liaison   An assessment of the results of a publicity campaign may be gained from opinion surveys and a study of press comments, and reports from other branches. The PRO will analyse these reactions from the public, and will make a report to the management accordingly.

PUBLIC RELATIONS AGENCIES AND CONSULTANTS

With the development of the media a whole new network of expert professional PR agencies and consultants has rapidly grown. These firms offer specialist advice and services relating to most aspects of publicity: television, radio, films, trade photography, advertisements, mail order lists, press releases. They have equipment and facilities that the average business will not possess or that cannot be spared for the organisation of a large-scale campaign that is intended to use all the media available.

A professional PR firm will be able to co-ordinate different methods. For example, they may send direct mail publicity out to coincide with a period of special offers in the shops, with a simultaneous backing of newspaper advertisements and television commercials. They will probably also be able to assess and analyse the results on a broader basis than the firm's own internal staff.

MARKET RESEARCH

This can yield valuable information, for instance:
>   how a new product has been received
>   the reasons for its popularity or unpopularity
>   whether there is a special need for that product in any specific area where goods need more or different publicity to make them sell.

This information can be gleaned from questionnaires, High Street interviews or reports from retailers, followed by careful analysis. On the basis of the results obtained a company can decide whether to reorganise its future marketing policy or not.

PLANNING A PUBLIC RELATIONS EXERCISE

Anyone intending to plan a publicity campaign might do well to note the following steps to take, although the order may vary:

1. Decide on the precise aim of the campaign (sales promotion, dissemination of news, community service, etc.).
2. Decide on the image to be presented to the public.
3. Consider the present standing of the firm and decide whether publicity is required generally or from one special aspect.
4. Decide which section or area of the public is to be reached.
5. Decide what information they are to be given.
6. Check that, if the exercise is for the community, it will be welcomed.
7. Decide on the best medium, or combination of media, by which to communicate.

8. Decide on the most effective approach to attract the public's interest and attention.
9. Decide when to mount the campaign and whether it is to be short- or long-term.
10. Estimate the available resources and the cost.
11. Arrange to monitor and reappraise the scheme while it is in progress.
12. Make arrangements to hold a 'post mortem' afterwards at which, as far as possible, the financial advantage and degree of public approval and general interest will be assessed and appraised.

Many firms have started modestly with small publicity campaigns and then gone on to community and public relations on an immense scale. Examples of firms who have done this in the past, among many others, are Lever Brothers, with their Port Sunlight community area with all its amenities, and Cadbury's, with their housing and manufacturing complex at Bourneville.

PRESS RELEASES

Preliminaries   Before starting to write a press release, consider:
    the precise subject
    who is to receive it
    when it is to be received
    the length – check with the agency or editor if there is any doubt about the acceptable number of words.

Appearance and layout   A press release should be well presented, as appearance is very important. (See also section on Preparation of Material for the Printer.) A cover page is recommended for speedy identification (see Figures i and ii). On this page will be the title, the author or source of the material, and the approximate number of words. The addition of the name and address of the originating firm and its telephone number tells the editor whom to contact if further information is required. All this information should be set out neatly and attractively, clean and unsmudged.

The paper on which the release is typed should be strong, white and of good quality. The typing should be on one side of the paper only, with generous margins. Type should be tidy and accurate, in double spacing, with extra separation between paragraphs, which will enable the editor to insert sub-headings if he wishes. Paragraphs should not be split over two pages, as the sheets may go to two different typesetters for setting up.

To ensure that the printer is aware of continuation pages, 'mf' meaning 'more follows' should be typed at the bottom of each sheet that finishes with a complete paragraph. At the foot of the final page type 'ends'.

THE COST OF LIVING
by
P. J. PERKINS

From

P J Perkins
(give address)

Tel. No.

Approx. 450 words

Figure i

THE COST OF LIVING

From the
IMPERIAL STATISTICS DEPT.,
BRISTOL.

From K Richards, B.Sc., Econ.,
Chief Research Officer
Imperial Statistics Dept.,
Bristol.

Tel:

With pictures (2).

Approx 450 words.

Figure ii

Press Releases: Alternative cover pages

If an illustration is to accompany the release the cover should be marked 'with picture', and the picture or photograph should be marked on the back with a suitable caption to link it with the article. An identifying reference should also be made in the margin of the typescript at the place to which the picture relates.

Order of presentation An acceptable press release contains facts, not opinions, and the treatment requires a certain technique. Make an impact in your opening paragraph, starting with an attention-getting sentence. Set out the most important and dramatic points first, follow these with secondary matters, finishing with the least dynamic material. A study of newspaper and magazine reports of all kinds will show many instances of this order of diminishing importance. The editor can then see at a glance where he can cut material, as he has a right to do if he wishes, and the reader will have his attention caught and held from the opening sentence.

Style of writing If you intend your release to be published, the style is of vital importance. You would not expect to find a 'leisure magazine' style of writing in a highly technical journal, nor vice versa. Any subject can be treated in a dozen different ways, and it is up to you to find the most suitable angle for your selected publisher and to frame your release in the most acceptable style possible. On *The Cost of Living*, for instance, a women's magazine might accept a piece written from the human interest point of view of household shopping, while a financial paper would give factual information with figures and statistical comparisons, and perhaps an accompanying graph or chart. The daily tabloid papers accept a more informal style of writing than that which appears in the more traditional heavy-weight papers.

Imagine that you are an editor, and press releases and articles arrive on your desk, on all kinds of subjects, every day. Which ones would you accept? There would not be room in your paper to print them all. Editors are busy people and they do not favour submissions in a style that does not suit the paper, or those which look messy and untidy or which are not crisply written in good English. Wording should be clear, economical, precise and workmanlike, because paper and space are expensive. An editor will certainly not have time to alter the style or correct spelling and grammar. He will, however, welcome those releases that arrive looking as if they are submitted by someone who knows just what he wants, which is why a study of the varied styles used by the press is so important.

Accuracy It cannot be overstressed that accuracy is of the utmost importance, and any material submitted for publication should be checked and double-checked before it leaves your office. From time to time mistakes do occur in published articles, and when this happens the PRO must immediately take steps to have an apology and a correction printed.

Types of release   Your press release will probably be one of four varieties – News, Features, General or Background.

A *News Release* has urgency, and must arrive in the editor's office at the right time for publication, or it will become stale and will not be printed at all.

A *Features Release* is not likely to be urgent, being a general article on a subject of interest to the public; it may be necessary to collect material and do some research before writing it. Papers and magazines have their own Features Editors, eg Home, Finance, Motoring or Sport, to whom a features release should be sent.

A *General Release* consists of perhaps 2–300 words and gives a general summary of the subject (perhaps an announcement of a conference or the production of a new car or the visit of an important public figure) and this will be followed by the full story in more detail later. Alternatively the full story may be submitted at the same time, as a separate special feature.

Information or Background Releases are not for publication at all but are intended to give the editor brief details about the firm, such as its business, the names of the directors and the PRO, and basic facts about its products and policies, for his records. The editor then has background information to which he can relate any releases submitted to him. These brief details should be renewed and updated as necessary.

Embargo   It will be assumed that press releases sent in are for immediate publication, even if 'For Immediate Release' is not typed on the cover page. There are occasions, however, when some delay is necessary, for example when the text of a speech is submitted to the press before the speaker has actually delivered it, or the publicity material about the opening of a new building or launching of a new product is issued before the event. In this case an 'embargo' is imposed, meaning that an interval must elapse between acceptance by the press and actual publication. The words 'EMBARGO: Release for publication not before . . .' must be typed clearly on the article. The time of day may also be added, as evening papers have to be considered, eg 'Not before 12.30, Wednesday, January 3rd'. One advantage of an embargo is that it enables the typeface to be set up in advance, ready for prompt printing when the time is ripe.

PRESS VISITS

It may be that one morning you will find a reporter in your office, asking for information. It cannot be overemphasised that *no* information should be issued unless it is authorised by a responsible official. In most cases this will be the chief PRO. 'I'm sorry, I cannot comment on this just now' is a useful formula; do not let yourself be persuaded or tricked into saying any more. One unguarded word could do incalculable damage and newspaper reporters who, after all, have their job to do, will not relax their efforts if they think there is any hope of your letting them have a 'story'.

On the other hand, it is good policy to cultivate the press and make friends with them. On the majority of occasions you will welcome them and give them all the help you can. The PR office should be at their disposal, publicity leaflets and photographs handed to them when they call, and on special occasions a folder full of helpful information may be given to them to take away. They may appreciate an escort or guide to take them round the firm and introduce them to those they wish to see, and to assist in arranging or lighting a subject to be photographed.

The press will usually respond to an invitation to visit your firm, but it must be in the pursuit of a good sound story; they are busy people and will not thank you for wasting their time. If you wish to call them in for publicity reasons at some interesting function, make arrangements as early as possible and send out invitations to the names on your press list, giving them brief information as to why you think they will be interested. Arrange for enough reliable staff to be available to answer their questions when they arrive, and give them every assistance.

PRESS CONFERENCES

The section on Conference Planning will give the background arrangements for setting up a conference and welcoming delegates, but there are several ways in which a press conference is distinctive.

The main object is to give out information that is to be passed on, so your delegates will be publicity 'middlemen'. There are various ways in which you can help them.

1. A press conference should be held as early in the day as possible, as the times when editions of a paper 'go down' or 'go to bed' have to be considered. Your delegates will have work to do in their offices after leaving your conference and before they can submit their material for publication in the daily or evening papers. Late afternoon or evening would be unsuitable for meetings of this kind.

2. Delegates should be briefed in advance about the location of telephone booths and telex facilities; if possible these should be available nearby, in the same building.

3. Plenty of time should be allowed for questions and answers.

4. Catering, if provided, should be of good standard. It will probably be best to leave this to a first-class outside caterer, so that your firm's own staff are left free to circulate during breaks, answer queries, and be generally helpful to the press. Slipshod service or second-rate refreshments are not likely to enhance the reputation of your firm or predispose anyone to give you good notices.

As a press conference may prove to be time-consuming and expensive, it is an economy to give out publicity by alternative means if possible. On the other hand a conference does give reporters an opportunity to ask questions, to obtain directly as much further information as they want, and to meet other press representatives and the company's PRO and staff.

Press list　　Who is asked to your press conference depends on the nature of your publicity, but a standby list might be made out on the following lines:
> the chief news agencies
> the national daily and evening newspapers
> the local and provincial press
> trade and technical journals
> radio and television services
> representatives of organisations similar to your own and any other people who may have a special interest in the theme of the conference.

If preliminary information is sent out with the invitations it should be brief and do no more than indicate the purpose of the conference. You do not want to give away too much beforehand. Additional details may be printed as background notes, to be distributed on arrival.

A verbatim report should be made during the conference of any speeches, with questions and answers, against which to check the accuracy of any published accounts of the occasion, and a report should also be sent to those who wished to come but were not able to attend, a copy also being kept for the firm's own records.

International Contacts　　Press releases, reports and advertisements can of course be placed in overseas publications, and any good Public Relations agency will advise on the best contacts, the cost and the probable results.

3 CONFERENCE PLANNING

*Clarify the objectives; check the costs;
choose the chairman; decide on delegation of duties; venue; confravision; finding suitable accommodation; guest of
honour; speakers and visual aids; programme planning; invitations, acceptances, refusals; press and publicity;
conference staff; conference folders;
aftermath; post mortem*

When the Managing Director remarks, as casually as he asks for a
cup of coffee, that the directors have decided to hold an important
conference and that you are to help him mastermind the plan of
campaign, the main thing is to keep a steady nerve. Make sure,
however, that you will be allowed sufficient time to complete the
organisation thoroughly and that you will be given adequate help.

Where do you begin? Start by discussing a suitable plan of action.
This will vary, of course, according to the type of conference which is
to be held. The first things to be done are to:

clarify the objectives
check the costs
choose the chairman
decide on delegation of duties.

When the above have been settled:

decide the venue
inspect and reserve accommodation
invite the guest of honour
check on the availability of speakers and the visual aids that they
     may need.

The last four points will have to be carefully co-ordinated as
regards dates and times. Then:

work out the programme in detail
despatch the invitations and programmes
arrange for press coverage and publicity
engage adequate staff for conference duties
start a conference folder for your records.

CLARIFY THE OBJECTIVES

A firm will not embark on an expensive, complex, time-consuming campaign such as a conference without very good reasons and the aims and objectives should be quite clear from the start. A conference can be a way of giving and exchanging information, of fact-finding and/or problem-solving. It can build up morale, influence policy-making and give excellent opportunities for starting and renewing business and personal contacts. It may be intended as a good public relations project, with useful publicity for those concerned, or be a combination of any or all of these.

CHECK THE COSTS

It is essential to know the sum of money which will be available for the conference and a running check must be kept on expenditure to ensure that the budget is not exceeded. It is always wise to keep a reasonable contingency fund for unexpected items.

CHOOSE THE CHAIRMAN

It is very necessary to have a first-rate person in the chair, as the chairman's duties are of vital importance to the success of the conference and for this reason it is unwise to over-persuade someone who genuinely does not wish to do so to take on the chairmanship. He or she must be well informed about the firm's business and the exact purpose of the conference. The ideal person is someone with a good platform presence, who possesses a sense of humour without being an amateur comedian.

At the opening of the conference it is the chairman's duty to welcome delegates and also to announce any changes in the printed programme. He or she will re-state the special subject of the conference, introduce the speakers, and after lectures have been delivered will open the meeting for questions.

It is the chairman's duty to see that each session does not run beyond the allotted time, to keep questions and discussions to the point, and to make sure that the subject does not stray from the main theme. Finally he should thank the speaker and close the meeting without appearing hurried or abrupt. He should be unobtrusively, pleasantly and firmly in control.

DECIDE ON DELEGATION OF DUTIES

It should be obvious that no person alone can efficiently see to all the organisation required for a large conference, and you will need a considerable amount of help. Conferences differ very much, but the following points set out a possible breakdown of departmental help, although different firms will delegate responsibilities in different ways, depending on their staffing structure.

Managing Director
Supervising and taking responsibility for the campaign and its overall
  policy
Arranging special contracts.

Works Manager or General Manager
Setting up displays and demonstration models
Dealing with matters involving manufacturing processes and new
  products, technical research and laboratory work.

Sales Manager
Liaising with the Managing Director over the type and length of the
  programme
Clarifying the general aim of the conference
Selecting the venue and facilities required
Checking and booking accommodation
Establishing liaison with the public relations staff over publicity
  matters.

Chief Buyer
Ordering special brochures and leaflets, display material, etc
Making arrangements with coach and car hire firms
Setting up a special 'Conference Account' for expenses
Liaising with the Managing Director over the signing of cheques and
  special contracts.

Chief Accountant
Fixing the budget limit with the Company Secretary
Arranging special insurances.

Public Relations Officer
Organising publicity material in consultation with the Sales
  Manager, Reprographics Department and Chief Buyer
Making catering arrangements, including flowers and any special
  dieting restrictions
Contacting the press
Arranging to meet delegates and to make introductions and personal
  contacts as required
Arranging social functions
Engaging extra caretaking staff, etc, as necessary with the Personnel
  Manager.

PA to Managing Director
Attending to invitations
Making inspection visits and booking accommodation
Arranging menus and refreshments
Booking visual aids
Attending to letters of thanks after the conference is over.

Of course none of these personnel will be working in isolation; there will have to be a continuous process of mutual help and interchange of information.

Outside assistance   There is also an army of outside services available in the fields of catering, publicity, secretarial work, printing, electronic equipment and translation agencies. One simple and comprehensive solution to the conference problem would be to send a clear schedule of requirements to one of the many excellent firms of conference organisers. These firms would then take over the whole project and settle everything down to the last detail but they would, of course, present your company with a very large bill.

VENUE

It is possible that you already have suitable conference facilities in your own business premises or there may be other places you have used previously which have proved entirely satisfactory. In this case you are on familiar ground and your task is straightforward, but remember to reserve the boardroom, executives' dining room and/or conference room in plenty of time.

If your catering staff are in attendance, see that the manager is clear about special requirements and the hours involved and that the caretaker and his staff understand their extra duties. If an outside catering firm is brought in, whether for coffee, drinks, light refreshments or full meals, make sure tactfully that there will be no friction with your own resident kitchen and maintenance personnel and that the separate allocation of duties is clearly understood by all parties concerned.

If your firm's own premises are not suitable and an outside booking is necessary, the choice is wide. Many large towns, and a number of smaller ones, offer purpose-built conference accommodation with the co-operation of hotels and guesthouses in the locality.

On a smaller scale, many organisations and local authorities have their own training centres in converted mansions and country houses and these can make very good settings for conferences, having residential and catering facilities on the spot and staff available by arrangement.

Many universities offer conference accommodation during the long vacation and the atmosphere of history and tradition found in the older college buildings is a great attraction, particularly to overseas visitors. The catering arrangements in halls of residence may not compare with those of a five-star hotel but they are usually quite good and much cheaper. It must be taken into account, however, that meal times are likely to be firmly fixed and staff may not be on duty in the evenings.

Holiday camps have good amenities and can be booked in the off-peak season when they are closed to holidaymakers. They often provide good concert halls and ballrooms, with chalet-type accommodation for guests.

If there is no special priority for the area you choose, why not select somewhere known for its beautiful surroundings, in the country or by the sea or with good historical traditions and sight-seeing possibilities to add to the interest of the occasion? It is not even essential to keep your feet firmly on the ground. Conferences have been held most successfully on cruise ships and even on jumbo jet airliners.

CONFRAVISION ·

Confravision is British Telecom's public videoconferencing service, linking meetings between groups of people at different locations by way of television screens.

There are obvious advantages in savings of time, travel and hotel accommodation. Meetings and discussions can be carried on between videoconferencing rooms, with individuals and groups of people linked by sound and vision on television screens, with almost as much convenience as if they were all together in the same room.

Videoconferencing rooms are located in London, Bristol, Birmingham, Manchester, Glasgow, Aberdeen, Belfast and Ipswich (Martlesham). International videoconferencing is available to the USA, Canada and West Germany; other distant locations are also available on special request.

Full and up-to-date information about Confravision is available from your local Telephone District Office or from Confravision Marketing on 01-357 3982.

FINDING SUITABLE ACCOMMODATION

It is advisable to write to selected hotel managers and caterers well beforehand to ask for details of rooms, prices, available menus and any special services they can offer. Make a short list of the most suitable possibilities and visit the premises to make an inspection. Points to bear in mind are:

cleanliness
heating and ventilation
clean kitchens and bathrooms
comfortable bedrooms and lounges
adequate cloakrooms and car-parking facilities.

If other hotel guests are to be present, make sure this will not cause any difficulties.

Any good hotel manager will welcome a visit and be happy to discuss your requirements in the light of your budget, and to answer your queries.

For the principal events of the conference you will require a hall with adequate seating and with a platform large enough for the speakers to move around on without stumbling over microphones or other equipment. Smaller rooms may also be needed for separate discussion groups. An exhibition hall for the display of products may be a requirement and it is essential to have a comfortable lounge where coffee and other drinks can be served and also a dining room for formal lunches or dinner. Different rooms can often double for different functions if time is allowed for a changeover. For example, a talk or demonstration can be given in a hall that is to be set out later for dinner or dancing.

Modern buildings, sound-proofed and double-glazed, give good protection from outside disturbances but, in the summer, when people like to open windows, the quietest site is obviously the best one. It is good sense to check that the premises are not too near a school playground, a goods yard or a building site. Internally, nearby kitchens may prove to be noisy.

Fire precautions   All hotels and public buildings are subject to strict fire regulations, but check that escape routes are clearly signposted and that emergency doors are never likely to be locked during your period of occupation.

The speakers   The speakers deserve consideration. They will appreciate a clock at the back of the hall, as strict timing is important. See that they do not have to address people separated by a very wide centre aisle; they would then have to look from side to side to take in their audience like someone watching a tennis match from a point midway down the court. Two side aisles would be a more considerate arrangement, or indeed no aisle at all, providing the rows are not so long that it is awkward for people to move to the centre seats.

The audience   Not only should the audience be able to hear clearly, they must be able to see clearly as well. Have you ever been to a concert and had to sit behind a pillar? This should not happen to anyone, especially not when you are the organiser. If there are pillars, see that nobody is seated behind them.

Do not allow people to sit too near doors which will be draughty and distracting when opened. Inspection should be made beforehand to see that windows can be opened if the room becomes stuffy, that heating is adequate and that the lighting is strong enough without being glaring, and that seats are comfortable. Hard seats make even the most interested audience restless and impatient.

There is one other point to consider, and that is the floor level on which your conference is taking place. In the normal course of events this should cause no difficulty but, should there be a number of elderly guests or anyone physically handicapped, do make sure that their difficulties are minimised as far as possible. An understanding management may be able to arrange short ramps over steps or provide extra staff to help at awkward places such as swing doors and lifts which might be difficult to negotiate.

Smoking   Most speakers will, understandably, object to this, but some people in the audience may wish to smoke. One solution is to request people not to smoke during lectures, but to make clear where and when it is permitted. This may be mentioned in the programme, and notices could be put up in the conference rooms. In the smoking area there should, of course, be an adequate supply of ashtrays, and someone should be delegated to empty these from time to time.

Formal Dinners   If there is to be a formal conference dinner, the catering manager will need a list of those expected to attend and a seating plan in order to make out place cards. Seating arrangements require tact and consideration, especially if there is to be a top table for the chairman and guest of honour and an order of precedence is to be followed. Menus should be printed after consultation with the catering manager. The names of the after-dinner speakers, and toasts, should be included and the menu card may be set out to form an attractive little souvenir of the evening.

GUEST OF HONOUR

If there is to be a guest of honour make sure that he or she is invited well in advance and that the acceptance is confirmed in writing. In the case of guest celebrities it may be necessary to contact their agents.

SPEAKERS AND VISUAL AIDS

When the speakers have been chosen, write or telephone them well before the conference dates to find out whether they are available and if they wish to accept the invitation. If so, confirm all details to them in writing. Keep a reserve list of alternative speakers in case of emergency.

Ascertain the speakers' exact requirements regarding any visual aids they will need for their talks and, if necessary, arrange for the hiring of equipment.

Ideally the lecture hall should be accessible the day before the conference begins so that any special equipment can be set up beforehand. If films are to be shown, black-out arrangements may need to be checked. If equipment does have to be put into place on the actual day it is needed, arrange for the doors to be unlocked sufficiently early for the electricians to finish their work before the conference is due to start. You might wish to engage experienced operators as well as equipment, and the hire company will need to know when they may dismantle their equipment and take it away again. Ask them to make sure that there are adequate spares of anything that might go wrong. Conferences have been known to come to a grinding halt for want of a handy technician with a spare electric plug or length of fuse wire, or even just a spare screwdriver. Good planning is a matter of attention to detail.

If the hall is designed for lectures there should not be any difficulty over acoustics, but if there is any doubt at all try it out yourself with a colleague. A clear speaking voice should carry easily from the platform to the back of the hall without the speaker having to shout. Lofty rooms can distort sound, however, and some halls are so large that an amplifier is essential. This should be checked beforehand as the equipment may need to be adjusted, modified or extended.

PROGRAMME PLANNING

The printed programme should give precise details of where the conference is to be held and how to get there. A small simple sketch map would be helpful, showing the location in relation to the main roads in the district, the nearest railway station, airport or bus terminal, and the recommended car-parking area for those delegates coming by car.

The programme will probably commence with a welcoming assembly, followed by formal talks, lectures, discussions, seminars, demonstrations, films or workshops.

Suitable dates   If the conference is to be run over two or more days, consider whether it would be better to hold it over a weekend or during the week. Try to avoid peak working periods of the year when the firm may be unusually busy, avoid religious festivals, bank and public holidays and any competitive conferences scheduled for close or overlapping dates.

Events   Each day's events must be clearly defined in the printed programme, giving details of the time, place, the name of the speaker and the topic. The words 'at leisure' indicate that delegates are free to follow their own devices and, if no set excursion has been arranged, suggestions might be given for interesting places to visit.

Every part of the day throughout the conference should be covered, but the working schedule must not be overloaded. People do not like to be rushed and need time to move from place to place. Even with careful planning unforeseen delays can occur and a talk or demonstration might be late in starting or finishing.

Meals   Details should be given regarding times of breaks for tea and coffee, also luncheon and dinner arrangements. Advance notification must be given if any formal dinner is a feature of the conference.

Excursions   If the conference extends over several days, entertainments and excursions may be organised through coach firms to local beauty spots, places of interest or a theatre. Running concurrently with lectures and business meetings, these excursions could provide a diversion for delegates' wives or husbands who are temporarily free.

Additional information   Helpful details may be included on the printed programme, such as the shopping facilities in the area, early closing days, railway and bus routes, location of churches and local places of general interest.

Hotel list   A list of suitable hotels, close to the conference centre, could be included giving details of the grade of hotel and the cost of accommodation.

Cost   The overall cost to the delegates must be specified and also any extra charges for excursions or other subsidiary items. People attending can then accept for the main conference events and for any additional social arrangements in which they have a special interest.

Printing   As soon as the programme is finalised a leaflet can be designed and printed which will serve as both announcement and invitation, with a detachable section or separate acceptance slip to be completed and returned to the organiser as soon as possible.

INVITATIONS, ACCEPTANCES, REFUSALS

When the list of names has been compiled, invitations should be sent out and a record kept of acceptances and refusals as the replies come in. It might be advisable to keep a 'reserve list' of extra names in case there are a number of refusals but this will depend on circumstances and the amount of accommodation available. The record could be set out as follows:

Delegates to Conference on (date)

Name	*Status*	*Name and Address of Company*	*Tel.No.*	*Acceptance or Refusal*

PRESS AND PUBLICITY

The press   If press coverage is desired, write to the local and/or national papers enclosing a copy of the programme and invite them to send a reporter, who should be given every facility for making notes and taking photographs. Supply a press table and sufficient publicity literature and appoint a responsible member of staff to answer any relevant questions they may wish to ask. Make sure too that the press are included in the catering arrangements. (See also section on Community and Public Relations.)

Publicity   A business organisation may like to take the opportunity offered by a conference to disseminate printed information about itself regarding its origins, history, present organisation and future policy. Booklets and pamphlets of this kind could be distributed to delegates on arrival, or arranged on a stall for people to help themselves. This stall could carry extra programmes and maps or plans of the building complex, showing the different halls, exhibition rooms, dining rooms, cloakrooms, etc. Advertising literature about the firm and its range of products might also be made available, and the opportunity taken to give information about immediate staff vacancies, training schemes and matters of general interest.

CONFERENCE STAFF

See that there will be sufficient staff to answer enquiries and look after lost property, find a taxi, send or receive telephone messages, produce a sticking plaster or aspirin, and give directions to those who have lost their way.

Never forget that you are not just setting up a programme, but dealing with people. Guests should be met on arrival at their hotel or the main conference building. VIPs coming from a distance should be met at the railway station or airport. They should be taken to their hotel and later personally introduced to the chairman. At the reception selected members of staff should move tactfully around to introduce people who wish to meet each other and generally look after those who otherwise might feel neglected.

CONFERENCE FOLDERS

It is the usual practice to supply each conference visitor with a folder which will include a copy of all the relevant documents, a list of delegates and any 'handouts' the firm wishes to supply. At the same time visitors can be given name badges to wear.

'Appraisal Forms' are sometimes issued to Delegates, so that they may comment later on the conduct of the Conference. Their opinions on the value of the occasion to them, with reasons why they found it a success (or not) can be very useful to the organisers when arranging similar future events.

AFTERMATH

The farewells have been said, the cars have all driven away, the rooms are deserted, the flowers wilting, you are exhausted and your feet are killing you. Brace yourself for a last heroic effort because there are still staff on the premises and you have not finished yet.

Did you remember about tipping? This is important as you do not want your firm to appear to be cheeseparing. What about the kitchen staff and the porters and the caretaker and the telephone operator and all the behind-the-scenes personnel who have put in long hours and without whom you could not possibly have managed? Staff should be personally thanked and tips discreetly distributed. For this you will need a little store of banknotes, in envelopes, made ready beforehand. Appreciation should be warmly shown in a practical manner. It is much better done on the spot, at the time, than left until the next morning or even later.

Prior arrangements should be made to ensure that everywhere is shut up safely when the last weary helper has gone home, and that the keys are in safe custody.

As soon as possible after the event send out written acknowledgements of help, letters of congratulations and general courtesy 'thank you' notes. These should be sent off promptly, so give them priority. If in doubt, send a 'thank you'. It will be appreciated.

POST MORTEM

As soon as practicable after your conference, arrange a follow-up meeting of those concerned to see if anything went wrong and, if so, why, and how to avoid a similar mistake another time. If the conference was a success there will be things you will wish to repeat on another occasion. Keep your conference file open a little longer and add a final analysis of names of guests or delegates, numbers attending, general points of interest, names of suppliers and caterers, with recommendations or otherwise, as all this information will be useful for future occasions. When they appear, include cuttings of the press reports and photographs.

After all, it may not be long before the Managing Director remarks, as casually as asking for another cup of coffee, that the last conference was organised so successfully that the directors are thinking of making it a regular event.

4 DICTATION AND TRANSCRIPTION

Taking shorthand dictation; using a dictating machine; ideal audio dictation; transcription; remote control; British Standard Guide for Typewriting

TAKING SHORTHAND DICTATION

A senior secretary may have to advise juniors on the ways in which they could organise their shorthand notes. Instructions might contain some or all of the following points:

1. Use a shorthand notebook with hard covers, good quality paper and spiral binding.

2. Fasten an elastic band round the used pages of shorthand notes so that the notebook will open at a fresh page.

3. Write with a fountain pen or use special shorthand pencils. Keep the pen filled and pencils sharpened in readiness for taking dictation at any time. Notes written in ink are easier to read and form a more permanent record; a properly designed shorthand pen will have a good flexible nib and will hold the ink supply for longer than the average fountain pen.

4. Enter the current date at the bottom of the page for ease of reference.

5. Develop a suitable system for inserting small corrections, such as leaving a wide left- or right-hand margin. For long substitutions or reminders it might be preferable to use a form of footnote.

6. Make a note at the beginning of any item of correspondence of the number of copies to be made and any special instructions.

7. Write NOO which stands for 'Not On Original' against any dictated note which is to be typed on the copies but is not to be included on the top page.

8. Make a careful note regarding 'blind' copies, ie where certain items on the top page are to be excluded from the copies.

9. Follow the established 'house style' in regard to outgoing correspondence and also to internally distributed memos, reports, etc.

10. 'Flag' – with an asterisk or dagger – any urgent or important items which must have priority.

11. Number separately each piece of dictation and annotate any supporting papers or documents with the same number for speedy identification.

12. Draw a horizontal line right across the shorthand page after each item of correspondence.

13. Practise turning over pages of the notebook quickly and quietly. When getting near the foot of one page, turn up the bottom left- or right-hand corner, ready to flip over to the next one.

14. Make use of any opportunities given by pauses or interruptions in the dictation – when the telephone rings or there are callers – by reading through the shorthand notes, inserting punctuation, amending outlines etc so that 'keying-in' the dictation, when it continues, will be smooth.

15. Follow the sense of the dictated material and try not to take notes completely automatically, which could hinder the speed of transcription.

16. Raise any queries at the end of an item of work rather than interrupt the dictator's concentration while he or she is speaking.

USING A DICTATING MACHINE

The main advantages of using a dictating machine may be summed up as follows:

1. A machine saves time as personal shorthand dictation may be interrupted by incoming telephone calls.

2. It enables the dictator to record while travelling in a car, on trains or planes, late in the evening, during lunchtime and at home.

3. A continuous flow of work can be maintained which increases daily and weekly output, as pre-recorded work can be shared and more evenly distributed between several typists.

4. Recordings are easily mailable, eg from an executive on a business trip to his secretary in the office.

5. Interviews, talks and telephone conversations can be recorded verbatim for subsequent transcription.

IDEAL AUDIO DICTATION

All executive secretaries will be capable of using a dictating machine to transcribe recorded correspondence but they should also be able to dictate and record material on to a machine for junior typists to transcribe. Often considerable practice is necessary to acquire a really good dictating technique. Poor dictation can cause considerable difficulty for the transcriber.

Ideal dictation could be achieved if the following rules were applied:

1. Insert tape, cassette, disc, sheet or belt correctly into the dictating machine.

2. Plug in the microphone and hold it a few inches away from the mouth; too close and the speech will be blurred, too far away and words may be lost.

3. Record, if possible, in a room free from noises or interruptions.

4. Keep the voice low, speak clearly, distinctly and not too fast.

5. State exact requirements before beginning to dictate each piece of correspondence, eg number of copies, name of addressee, layout instructions, any special paper requirements, and probable length of material such as 'short letter', 'long report', etc.

6. Play back the first sentence to ensure that the machine is recording correctly and adjust volume if necessary.

7. Switch off the microphone while pausing to think, speak to a caller or answer the telephone.

8. Indicate the commencement of new paragraphs, give punctuation marks when necessary and give clear instructions for headings, underscoring and capital letters where required.

9. Spell out any unusual personal names, place names or foreign words/phrases which may not be familiar to the transcriber.

10. Dictate numbers, prices or amounts of money with particular clarity. Use the 24-hour clock wherever appropriate.

11. Make erasures and substitute amendments according to the type of recording machine used.

12. Mention any necessary enclosures and hand all supporting papers or files to the transcriber with the recording.

13. Indicate length of all items of correspondence on the index or reference slip.

TRANSCRIPTION

From shorthand notes   Again it may be necessary to give the following guidelines to junior staff:

1. Keep adequate stocks of stationery of all types and sizes, paper-clips, carbon paper, envelopes and dictionary close at hand.

2. Transcribe the most urgent and important work first.

3. Check each page against the shorthand notes before removing it from the typewriter.

4. As soon as a letter has been completed, type the corresponding envelope. Do not leave all the envelopes until last.

5. Draw a diagonal line through each page of shorthand notes after the work has been completed.

6. Mark the place reached in the shorthand notes if typing is interrupted.

7. File fully-used notebooks for at least six months in case reference has to be made to them. Mark period of time covered on the outside.

From a dictating machine

1. Keep adequate stocks of stationery of all types and sizes, paper-clips, carbon paper, envelopes and dictionary close at hand.

2. Transcribe the most urgent and important work first.

3. Put on headset and plug in foot control pedal.

4. Adjust volume control.

5. Select the right size of stationery from instructions given either at the start of the dictation or on the index or reference slip.

6. Take careful note of all preliminary directions given by the dictator and follow any instructions given regarding spelling or punctuation in the text.

7. Check each page before removing from the typewriter.

8. Type each envelope as it is required.

9. Be methodical in arrangement of material awaiting transcription and in disposal of material already transcribed.

REMOTE CONTROL

Some organisations have installed a remote control system for audio dictation. Dictation is given over an internal telephone or through a specially wired microphone to a central pool of dictating machines. The supervisor in charge of the centre will re-load machines when necessary and decide priorities when allocating work to the various typists, each of whom will have her own transcription machine. The supervisor will also see that transcribed work is checked and returned as promptly as possible to the originator, for signature.

BRITISH STANDARD GUIDE FOR TYPEWRITING

This British Standard gives guidance on typescript presentation suitable for office documents, including general office correspondence and masters for multiple copies. It applies to work produced on word processors as well as on conventional typewriters. A copy of the British Standard Guide for Typewriting can be obtained from the British Standards Institution, 2 Park Street, London W1A 2BS.

5 EFFECTIVE COMMUNICATION

*The spoken word; typing and printing
processes within the firm; external services in communications; telecommunications; Videotext; effective selection;
the personal touch*

In a busy office communication is unceasing; from the moment the
mail arrives and the telephone and telex operators come on duty
information flows constantly in, out and sideways. Most incoming
business communications belong to one of the following categories:
   those requiring immediate action by the recipient
   those to be passed on to someone for attention
   those to be set aside until the right time for action
   those to be filed away safely as part of a system of records.
   When an outgoing communication is initiated there are other
considerations as well. It should be remembered that:
   all messages should be worth hearing
   they should be comprehensible to the hearer
   they should go by the shortest and most suitable route
   they should arrive at the right destination at the right time.
   There is a variety of choice and permutation of choices for effective
communication today. At your disposal are:
   the spoken word
   typing and printing processes within the firm
   external reprographic processes of various kinds
   the specialised services of publicity companies
   television and radio
   telecommunications (telex, datel, etc)
   electronic aids (word-processors, etc)

THE SPOKEN WORD

There is plenty of scope for the spoken word and consequently there
is every reason for cultivating an audible, distinct and pleasant voice.
It is the cheapest method of communication, all that is needed is the
speaker, a little care and attention, and the hearer. There is, however,
one important disadvantage from the business aspect and that is that
there will not necessarily be any record of what has been said.
Nevertheless, in the right circumstances, there may be nothing better

than direct conversation as a way of exchanging ideas and solving problems. Consider the following:

    face to face personal communication
    internal or external telephone systems
    tape or cassette recordings, or desk call units (intercom)
    loud speaker or public address system
    public speaking at meetings and conferences
    radio communication.

It is important to cultivate tact. Speak naturally, on the wavelength of your hearer. You might say 'Hi, George, how did the meeting go?' to a colleague, but to the chairman this would probably be translated as 'Good morning, Sir George, I hope the meeting went well'. Newly engaged staff in particular should be advised to use caution; it is better, when in doubt, to appear a little more formal rather than over-friendly.

Good manners are always important; even if you are in a hurry it is possible to say 'I'm sorry to bother you, but . . .' or 'Would you mind . . .' and sound as if this is really meant, rather than 'Get me – so and so' or 'I must have . . .' which is likely to arouse unnecessary resentment.

Not only should there be care in the tone of personal conversation, it is just as important to judge *when* to speak. Even the most easy-going and relaxed member of a firm may have traumatic periods when he or she is in no mood to listen. Use tact, gauge the atmosphere of the office, decide whether the time may be more auspicious later. Try to develop a sensitivity about when, as well as how, to communicate. Many a request has been refused for the sole reason that it was made at the wrong time.

Telephone communications   The telephone is not always a time-saving device whether used for external or internal calls, and delays are expensive and may lead to loss of business. Often outgoing calls are delayed because the line is engaged, and incoming calls are held up because the caller has to wait for an extension to be free. In the busiest departments of your firm the installation of one or two extra extensions may therefore prove to be an economy in the long run.

Conversations should be as direct and as short as possible, as telephone time is expensive. If there are several points to discuss, list them on a slip of paper before making the call. This will help to keep matters in the right order and ensure that nothing is omitted. If further information is likely to be required during the conversation, have the relevant files and papers within reach. Always keep a pencil and pad near the telephone; any points that need to be recorded should be neatly typed out after the conversation, together with the date and the initials of the member of staff speaking. Messages intended for other people must be passed on without delay, put on their desk or handed to a reliable messenger.

The telephone provides a great temptation to waste time with gossip and unnecessary chatting. When a conversation has served its purpose it should be brought firmly but courteously to a close. One useful formula is 'I mustn't keep you, I know you must be busy' or alternatively 'Forgive me, but I really must go, I have an appointment'. The appointment may only be with a pile of correspondence, but one must be sensible about priorities.

The cost of external calls can prove astronomical. It should be remembered that some calls, for instance those booking accommodation or making appointments, will have to be confirmed in writing and so the call may not really be necessary at all. On the other hand local calls will cost less than a letter, providing they are kept short, especially if they are made during the hours when rates are cheapest.

If the operator tells you that your contact is on another line, or cannot be found at once, leave a message asking him to telephone you when he is free, or alternatively ring later yourself; holding the receiver while you wait for an indefinite period wastes money as well as time. The extra fee charged for a personal call via the telephone exchange may well be worth while for long distance, as your contact will be found and brought to the telephone before your call begins to be charged.

It is an established fact that most people like to hear the sound of their own name. 'Goodbye, Mr Jones' gives a better impression than just 'Goodbye', which could convey the idea that you had not sustained sufficient interest in your caller to remember who he was.

Tape or cassette recordings   It is sometimes forgotten that as well as the normally accepted function of storing dictation for a typist, a desk recorder may be used as a useful stop-gap messenger service. Instructions may be left, for instance late in the evening when most staff have gone, for a secretary to play back on arrival next morning. The message might, for example, be something on the lines of 'Good morning, Miss Smith. I may be a little late in the office, so would you cancel my ten o'clock appointment and try to fix it for tomorrow instead? If you will type out the minutes of yesterday's meeting by mid-day I shall be able to show them to the chairman when I see him at lunch time.' A recorder can be a very adequate means of covering an unexpected gap in personal office contacts.

Desk call units or intercom   A desk call or intercom unit provides a useful and immediate flashing or buzzing signal, with or without microphone and speaker, giving a quick two-way link. It is a useful method of communication, but cannot be said to lend itself to subtlety. The most frequent messages conveyed by this device must surely be 'Please bring in your notebook', 'I'm ready for my coffee now' and 'Please bring in the next person waiting to see me'.

Call systems   (a) On-site: Staff perpetually on the move can be quickly located and called to the telephone to receive a message by means of lights that flash in a framework installed in a corridor or workshop, or by a 'bleeper' which can be carried round individually in a coat pocket, each person concerned having his own colour code or signal. This arrangement is particularly useful in such cases as a doctor doing his rounds in a hospital or a foreman moving around an extensive workshop area.

(b) Wide-area: The British Telecom Radiopager can be programmed to operate within any specified area of the British Isles, or nationwide. The holder can be dialled, free of charge, on his own special number, and the pocket pager will bleep. He can then go to the nearest telephone to collect the necessary message. The distance that can be covered by this system is considerable. It is no longer restricted to a building or group of buildings, as were the earlier models. An office in, say, Southampton, can bleep a director who at the time is on the golf course at St Andrews. In addition to the simple direct signal it is possible to have the following variations: patterns of bleeps to indicate the call's origin, a memory for storing bleeps, a numerical display to spell out the telephone number to be called, or a message in code, and more sophisticated models can also provide a written display of words and numbers.

Loudspeakers and public address systems   The user should have a clear voice and take special care to be concise and distinct, possibly speaking more slowly than usual. The disadvantage of such a system lies in the fact that it could be overpowering in an office, or might not be heard at all in a very noisy workshop. Out of doors acoustics may be difficult, especially in a high wind. Public address systems are most suitable in a large, reasonably sheltered area where there is not too much competing noise. The words 'May I have your attention, please' spoken once or twice should be sufficient to stop a buzz of conversation, and the message can then follow and be clearly heard and understood.

These systems are invaluable in emergencies such as fire or a bomb scare, but the speaker should at all costs sound calm and controlled to avoid the slightest risk of starting a panic. For this reason alone, only a person in authority should have access to and responsibility for the use of a public address system.

Radio communication   A radiophone installed in a car, linking the driver or passenger with the public telephone network, will maintain a useful personal contact during journeys. Also there are many businesses in which it is particularly important to have direct communication between a moving vehicle and a control point, enabling instructions to be given and a two-way conversation to be held while travelling. Taxi-hire firms, ambulance services and fire brigades are all dependent on mobile radio communications for on-the-job reception of messages.

TYPING AND PRINTING PROCESSES WITHIN THE FIRM

Internal memoranda   Memos are economical but tend to be overemployed, thereby adding to the volume of office paperwork. They do, however, have several distinct advantages as a means of internal communication:

1. They provide a visible record of the message.
2. Copies can be made to pass to others for action or information and for the reminder file for further follow-up.
3. The list of recipients' names on each copy informs each person who else has received the message.
4. For economy memos may be so designed that space is allotted for a reply to be added, so the original is returned to the sender with the answer.
5. Memos are a means of sending a message on its way when contact cannot be made by internal telephone.
6. Memos provide an economical means of communication between, for example, branches of a company, bank or multiple store. All branch memos from different departments of the firm are sorted into piles in the mail room, and each pile despatched in one large envelope to its separate destination.

Instructions conveyed by memo should be worded as carefully as for outgoing letters. Inexperienced employees, for example, may sometimes appear thoughtlessly brusque. It is always possible to get good results without being dictatorial, and a message on the lines of 'We need this information urgently, please can you help?' is more likely to produce the desired result promptly than 'Send us the information by tomorrow at the latest'.

The sender may receive a quicker reply if his telephone extension number is typed in beside his name.

Internal distribution   The internal messenger service should be so organised that everyone knows when to expect collections and deliveries. Deliveries to the in-basket and collections from the out-basket should be made at the same time, and the last outward collection of the day should be in time for any mail in it to be sorted and sent out from the mailroom to catch the evening post.

Letters   Appearance is of great importance. It is up to the secretary never to commit a spelling mistake, make an untidy alteration or allow an uncorrected error to pass through. The spelling of names is particularly important and, if a signature cannot be read on a letter to be answered, it may be possible to telephone the writer's firm and ask the switchboard operator to help. Guesswork should be avoided if at all possible.

The tone of a letter is just as important as the choice of words in conversation; it is not only a matter of what is said, it is also a matter of how it is said. Whatever the mood of the sender, a letter must be thoughtful, logical, clear and courteous.

When a letter involving complicated wording or complex statistical information has to be composed, it may be advisable to make a preliminary draft. This will help you in arranging the facts in the clearest and most readable way. All financial or statistical matter set out should be double-checked, even if the figures were not yours in the first place. If you find an error in calculations anywhere, make contact with the originator at once, who will thank you for discovering it before the information was despatched.

If extra copies of a letter have to be distributed, see that the names of all recipients are typed on each copy, underlining each name appropriately on the separate copies. Each person then knows who else has the information, at the same time being able to identify his own copy; the file copy will bear the full list of names for your records. It is tactful to list these names in order of precedence, if any, or, if in doubt, in alphabetical order.

When an original document has to be photocopied for distribution, the list of the recipients' names may be typed out on a small separate strip of paper, which is laid across the top or margin of the document before photocopying. These names will then appear on all the copies, where they can be separately underlined as required, while the original document remains unmarked.

When a letter has been typed and *before* it is taken out of the typewriter, read it through to make a final check on appearance and content; corrections are more easily made before the paper has been moved out of position. Make sure there are no discrepancies between the address on the letter and that on the envelope, and consider whether marking it for First Class mail carries any worthwhile advantage.

Reports   A report is a formal communication and should be set out clearly in concise intelligible language. Technical terms, if used, should not be beyond the understanding of the reader.

There must be clear terms of reference, that is, a definition of the reason for the report. A typical reason is to set out the findings resulting from a series of enquiries, or the suggested way of solving a problem, giving the reasons for the recommendation. A report may be an account of a business trip or the description and result of an experiment; it may simply be intended to bring together and analyse factual information.

The main heading will state the purpose of the report and set out the subjects to be covered, and a sub-heading will name the author or the team or company initiating it. Sub-headings and paragraphs will follow each other in logical sequence, numbered or lettered, and in a long report these may be indexed. At the end of the paper will be set out the conclusions reached, or a summary of the findings and recommendations, according to the purpose of the report. The date of issue should be added last of all.

Précis and extracts of material   It is important to be clear about the difference when asked to set out one or other of these. A précis takes the main points of a report, article, chapter in a book, letter or similar material, and presents this information in a shortened form, condensed to the minimum length consistent with keeping the original sense. It should give the salient points, sufficient for the purpose but pruned of all extraneous information. If a précis is required to be of a specific length (eg for a publisher) a little careful re-wording may be necessary.

An extract, by contrast, will keep strictly to the original wording, and is lifted out of the context, leaving behind the material not relevant to the purpose.

At the end of a précis or an extract, reference should always be made to the source of the material, the author, the publication and the date and reference number if any. It is very important always to identify the original work.

Financial statements   Within any office, financial statements of varying size and complexity will appear and these should be set out so that the figures are clear and calculations may be followed through and checked with the minimum of difficulty. Any financial statement should be thoroughly checked for accuracy, then dated and signed or initialled before being issued.

A company's annual official financial statements will be professionally prepared, audited and printed for circulation. A firm of security printers will ensure that the information to be printed does not leak out before the authorised date for release. (See section on Preparation of material for the printer.)

Route cards   A single issue of a magazine or periodical for internal circulation may be guided by a route card (a list of names attached to the front cover) to be ticked and passed on, in turn, by each person named. A copy of this list should be kept for reference, in case there is a delay and the holder needs to be reminded to pass the publication on to the next person. Below the last name should be 'Return to . . .' for filing or storage.

EXTERNAL SERVICES IN COMMUNICATIONS

Unless your firm has a large public relations department of its own, communications to cover a widespread area may best be organised by a publicity agency, which will advise on methods and costs. This is discussed more fully in the section on Community and Public Relations, but procedures that could be considered include:

> announcements and advertisements in the press, on radio and television
> printed papers for direct mail
> posters for hoardings and notice boards
> brochures, handouts, leaflets and house magazines
> printed form-letters and postcards.

Radio and television   Time bought on radio and television networks is expensive, but the cost may be well justified in terms of public response, if it is carefully chosen to reach the widest and most suitable audience. The visual impact on the public can be strong and effective, but consideration will have to be given to the time of day or evening for which publicity space is purchased. Early evening during weekdays, when people are likely to be at home, would be more profitable than a Saturday morning when they are more likely to be out.

Press announcements and advertising   The national daily and evening papers, your local newspaper and your firm's particular trade journals all carry advertisements. A well-composed paragraph or display in one or more of these should bring in a good response.

Direct mail   We are all familiar with the printed letters, postcards or leaflets that come uninvited through our letterboxes, often beautifully produced and sometimes with our own name and address skilfully incorporated as if the letter was intended for us alone; this individual approach is intended to bring out a greater response than less personalised circulars. Any firm can compile its own mailing list for this purpose, selecting names from the Yellow Pages in the telephone directory as well as from any trade or professional journal, according to the kind of market to be covered. Names could also be taken from a list of customers or people who have sent in enquiries. A specialised direct mail agency can be of assistance in starting up a project of this kind.

Posters for hoardings and notice boards   These provide a forceful way of conveying a message, if well designed and strategically placed. Bright colours and a bold layout help to attract attention. Small print is unsuitable, unless the notice is placed where people are likely to linger.

Simple basic messages drawing attention to a particular place or instruction should be placed at the actual site, such as PRIVATE, NO SMOKING and FIRE EXIT. More detailed general notices, such as an announcement of a Christmas Staff Dance or an appeal for blood donors, should be placed where most people congregate, in a main hall, canteen or rest room. Special noticeboards are sometimes maintained for special purposes, such as staff vacancies, social activities, or trade union matters. The position in which a notice-board is placed should be chosen with care.

Brochures, handouts, leaflets and house magazines   A firm's own reprographics department may be able to produce all these very efficiently. If not, an outside printing firm will be needed. Distribution throughout a company can be made by internal messenger service or on a 'help yourself' basis at selected points. Small notices can be slipped into wage packets when the wages are made up in the accounts department.

House magazines will probably be issued at set intervals, and these are an excellent channel for internal business and social matters. They can carry announcements of future events, reports of past functions, advertisements of all kinds, photographs, notices of retirements and new appointments, policy statements and so on. They are not only of great help in keeping staff up to date with matters of general concern within the company but also in keeping them in touch with each other.

Printed form-letters and postcards   These provide a time-saving means of routine communication. Spaces are left in the pre-printed wording for the insertion of special words or figures, for example the sum of money in a routine reminder for payment, or a date on a postcard acknowledgement of a letter. Form-letters can be quickly completed and individually addressed for posting; in many offices these are now processed by computer.

TELECOMMUNICATIONS

Telex   This fast, accurate, twenty-four hour service provides a virtually instantaneous worldwide form of communication. Each subscriber to this public teleprinter network is given an individual call number and an answer code, the message is typed out on the sending unit and copies are printed simultaneously at both the sending and the receiving terminals. Typed 'conversations' can be carried on, question as well as answer appearing on each feed-out paper as they are typed by the operators at either terminal. Each person thus has an identical visual record of the message and a confirmatory letter is usually unnecessary.

A particular advantage is that the installation can be left 'open' when unattended, so that one-way messages can be received overnight and read in the morning. This cuts down unnecessary delay in the exchange of messages between countries with different time zones.

Statistics and complex tables, too intricate or lengthy for convenient typed transmission, can be converted to punched paper tape, fed into the telex sending unit, and rapidly reproduced at the other end and reconverted to the original layout of tabled figures.

A further advantage is that messages in an unfamiliar language are more easily understood when received visually. Most people would prefer to read a printed telex message rather than hear a foreign voice on the telephone.

More and more firms are becoming telex subscribers and the Telex Directory is now a very substantial publication. Charges for European calls are based on the actual time taken, so a short telex call may be cheaper than telephoning. Most calls can be dialled direct, but some distant overseas calls may have to go through the Telex Exchange and are then subject to a minimum time charge of three minutes. In this case short messages may be cheaper by telephone, but against this must be set the fact that there is no visual record of a telephone call, and a reply cannot be received as quickly as by telex.

Confravision   See section on p. 27 under Conference Planning.

Teleprinters   This simple form of telex, suitable for internal use within a firm, can link up widely dispersed sections or departments and, in the same way as the wider telex network, provide an automatic visual record of messages sent.

Datel   This is a British Telecom system whereby information (data) can be sent from a data station or terminal (or a number of terminals), over any distance, to a central computer where the information (input) is processed. The central computer is not only able to store this information, but will also have analysing and problem-solving capabilities. The processed information will therefore be retrievable from this central computer in the required form, immediately on demand.

The equipment used for translating data into a form suitable for transmission from the terminal to the computer is known as a 'modem' (short for 'modulator/demodulator'). Modems are housed in neat grey cabinets, which can be stored in special racks and can be added to when the customer's business expands. The Datel Network Control Systems (modems, racks, cabinets, control units etc) are known as DNCS.

Datel services operate over the British Telecom circuits, that is, the Public Switched Telephone Network (known as PSTN). Private circuit systems can also be obtained through British Telecom and British Telecom regulations must therefore always be observed.

Each business customer wishing to subscribe to and install datel services will have different needs. Each custom-designed scheme will, however, have the same basic principle, ie the fast accurate processing of the input information for rapid retrieval in the required form.

The advantages of datel services are that they are fast, accurate, and absolutely up-to-the-minute; there is no limit to the distance over which the information is sent, and there can be any number of terminals linked to the central processing/analysing computer.

Typical users are managers in control of stocks who monitor deliveries and withdrawals over a number of warehouses; personnel and payroll officers supervising the fluctuating records of staff in various companies and their subsidiaries; or scientists and engineers submitting, extracting and analysing specialised data. Virtually any business or profession can set up their own scheme of requirements for input and retrieval of data.

Several types of datel are offered by British Telecom, varying according to:

> speed of transmission (transmission takes place at speeds calculated as 'bits per second', a 'bit' being short for 'binary digit')
>
> whether the circuit is a private or public one
>
> sophistication of equipment; incoming and outgoing data can be transmitted simultaneously (duplex working), or a special channel may be required for backward transmissions
>
> whether unattended answering services and automatic calling are required, allowing the equipment to be left 'open' without an operator being present
>
> systems of retrieval; data can be received by way of visual display units, line printers, card readers, punch tape readers, and remote job entry terminals.

International Datel transmits to most of Europe, USA, and many other countries, over PSTN.

Any telephone sales office will be able to supply the address and telephone number of the enquiry point for your area, where full details and sales literature on datel will be available on request.

Electronic aids, word-processors, etc.   See Chapter 6 on
Electronic Offices.

VIDEOTEX AND TELETEXT

In other industrialised countries (eg France, Italy, Germany,
Canada and Japan) also Singapore, as well as in Britain, these
visual information services are still expanding and developing. In
the United Kingdom the British Telecom *Videotex* service is
'Prestel', and 'Oracle' and 'Ceefax' are the television information
services covered by *Teletext*. Any of these may be received in the
home just as easily as in an office, the information called up being
displayed on a television screen. The differences and similarities of
these two main systems are described below.

There are two main systems in the United Kingdom:

1. **Prestel**, which is a British Telecom computer-based
   information service, known as *Videotex,* whereby the
   customer can call up the information 'pages' he wishes to see.

2. **Ceefax** and **Oracle**, which are both direct one-way television
   services. Ceefax is the name of the service put out by the BBC
   and Oracle is that coming from ITV.

   Ceefax and Oracle are known as *Teletext*, and any teletext
   adapted set can receive both (and in most cases Prestel as
   well).

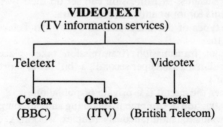

VIDEOTEXT
(TV information services)

Teletext   Videotex

Ceefax   **Oracle**   **Prestel**
(BBC)   (ITV)   (British Telecom)

1. **Prestel**   This service comes via a connection with the Telecom telephone installation, and with a monitor and keypad
the customer can call up the information 'pages' he requires. A
visible index of the available information can be obtained on the
screen. There is also available a directory of subscribers who have
taken page space, with their page numbers. Many of these are
well-known organisations. The extra telephone charges incurred
are added to the normal telephone account, and a separate account
is rendered for the Prestel information service, based on the time
taken.

As an example of the information available, you or your chief could call up, by selecting the appropriate page numbers on the keypad, any or all of the following:

Stock Exchange prices, updated several times a day; investment figures; foreign exchange rates and international monetary market information; government statistics; tax guides; information about leading companies; export information; legal information; property; Good Food Guide; cinema and theatre guides; hotel, holiday and travel information; travel timetables, standby flights; job agencies and managerial opportunities, etc.

An immediate booking or purchase can be made, orders given, transactions carried through, services organised, all at the press of the appropriate button.

Prestel subscribers can send *Videotex* Greetings Messages to each other (by electronic Mailbox) from a selection which includes 'Happy Birthday' and 'Get Well Soon', amongst others.

Prestel is referred to in Chapter 6 on Electronic Offices.

2. **Ceefax and Oracle**　These provide a public service of televised information, constantly updated to the immediate moment by the Teletext organisation concerned (BBC or ITV respectively). A Teletext set can be rented, or an existing ordinary set adapted to receive teletext information, as well as the usual broadcast programmes. This is not as comprehensive a service as Prestel, and is less expensive. There is no page charge. Amongst the categories of information available are:

News (up to the minute); weather reports; travel information; food prices; theatre, film and book reviews; sports results; games and competitions; horoscopes; general information of all kinds.

Oracle also has an added commercial facility, ie for advertising. Ceefax and Oracle also provide subtitles for the hard of hearing.

EFFECTIVE SELECTION

Obviously a confidential message would not be passed by way of a public address system, nor would a complete workforce be contacted efficiently by means of a little noticeboard set up in a dark corner. Not only the possible method, but the people concerned have to be considered. What sort of people are you contacting? Where are they? How many of them are involved? Your communications network is a complex one and different permutations of methods will have to be selected for different occasions. You should be able to make a sensible selection from the following lists to fit any situation:

1. Exclusively internal methods are:
    personal conversation, the internal telephone system, recording and dictating machines, lectures or meetings, public address

system, teleprinters, desk units or intercom, call systems, bleepers.

2. Methods suitable for internal or external use:
   letters and memoranda, reports, minutes of meetings, précis or extracts of more detailed material, financial statements, house magazines, leaflets and handouts.

3. Exclusively external channels:
   external telephone system, telex, conferences and outside meetings, direct mail, facsimile transmission, press announcements and advertisements, radio communications, radio and television.

With a knowledge of all the available possibilities it will soon become second nature to choose the best combination for each purpose. Your choice will depend on a blend of speed, appearance, safety, accuracy, economy, the number of recipients, whether a permanent record is required, and any other special considerations. If communications are to be in a foreign language, for instance, a little extra time may have to be allowed for the services of a translation bureau if you do not have a linguist on your own staff.

One or two typical office situations will show how a variety of communicating methods naturally blend together.

A. New staff need to be recruited.
1. You will use the internal telephone system to call the department concerned to ask for their exact requirements.
2. They will send you an internal memo setting out the qualities and experience necessary for the post.
3. You will compose an advertisement and send it to the editor of the local paper or the national press, with a covering letter, and you will keep copies of these for your records.
4. You will also make out a clear notice giving details of the vacancy for the staff notice board.
5. When the applications come in, a form-letter of acknowledgement will be sent to each applicant.
6. Printed application forms will be sent to those short-listed.
7. Individual letters will be typed and sent to those selected for interview.
8. Duplicated or printed notes will be sent to those who are unsuccessful, regretting that the post is filled.

B. A member of your staff has just become a father. You would then:
1. Personally convey your warm congratulations, either face to face or on the telephone, and ask his permission to put an announcement in the house magazine.

2. Type out the announcement and send it via internal messenger service to the magazine editor, with a covering typed note, asking him to print it in the next issue.

C. Your overseas branch is late in sending in its quarterly financial statement, and one of your subsidiary companies urgently requires certain figures from it.

1. You send a telex message asking for the statement to be sent as soon as possible.
2. When it arrives (by facsimile transmission) you make an extract of the required figures and key this in to your data processing centre.
3. You telephone your subsidiary company to inform them that this has been done.
4. They will then retrieve the required information from the data processing centre without further delay.

THE PERSONAL TOUCH

Lastly, and because business communications should never become too remote from the human situation, remember the catchphrase 'Say it with flowers'. This is not completely out of place in a business office, or anywhere else for that matter. Just a small vase of fresh flowers on your desk can say 'Have a good day' to everyone who sees them.

More formally, flowers can convey thanks, apologies, get-well-soon messages, congratulations, anniversary or birthday greetings. They are prettier than a letter and they smell nicer. They convey a personal message in a warm and special way, and you are sure to come across occasions when sending flowers to someone is exactly the most acceptable and effective means of communicating.

Bibliography

John Markham: *Successful Business Communication* (Witherby and Co. Ltd., 1977).

Barry Maude: *Practical Communication for Managers* (Longman, 1974).

L. A. Woolcott & W. R. Unwin: *Mastering Business Communication* (Macmillan Ltd, 1983).

6 ELECTRONIC OFFICES

Cost justification; selection of suitable hardware and software; assessment of education and training requirements; employment of staff; health and safety; data security; word processing; electronic mail; facsimile transmission; viewdata information systems; teletex; voice systems; networks; glossary of terms

(NB   A glossary of terms used in this section will be found, starting on page 62).

With the introduction of microelectronic technology, electronic or automated offices are being set up. The office revolution is likely to develop rapidly through the next decade. Microcomputers containing small silicon chips are being used both in the office and in the home.

Converting a conventional office into an automated one may appear to be rather daunting but it need not be a traumatic experience if the innovations are carefully planned. A number of factors have to be taken into account, such as:

> cost justification
> selection of suitable hardware and software
> assessment of education and training requirements
> employment of staff.
> health and safety
> data security

COST JUSTIFICATION

The costs of office supplies, office space and labour are all rising steadily. Office work is mainly concerned with communication of information both internally and externally; paper work of all kinds has increased enormously and so has the cost of despatching it. To be able to function effectively while remaining competitive, firms are replacing the manual handling of huge quantities of information on paper by the use of computer controlled equipment. Text, statistics and diagrams are input, stored, processed and distributed on word processors, and on micro, mini and mainframe computers, which are able to communicate with each other over electronic telecommunications links.

Reduction in the costs of computer hardware has meant that equipment using computer technology is now being vigorously marketed directly into all offices, not just into special computer rooms. More and more applications become feasible as the cost of this equipment continues to fall. The responsibility for the acquisition of computerised equipment rests increasingly with the non-computer manager and consequently the full potential is perhaps not realised. Management's primary concern must naturally be with the cost benefits to the company of any new systems and equipment, but in these competitive times it may be that a firm's future growth and development will depend upon the introduction of the new technology. The cost of buying equipment bit by bit may be easier to justify initially but could result in a collection of disjointed systems which do not easily integrate.

No matter how technically sophisticated a machine is, the success or failure of an installation will in no small measure depend on the abilities of the operators and supervisors involved in the day-to-day running.

SELECTION OF SUITABLE HARDWARE AND SOFTWARE

Sound advice should be sought on the choice of equipment and programs in the ever-widening scope which is offered as it is essential that any new hardware and software which are to be introduced must be tailored to fit the firm's specific requirements. Moreover, if systems are to function effectively, selection of machinery should go together with the training of operators and other staff involved (eg originators of work). Management has to appreciate the variety of systems which are becoming available and select equipment which will ensure a smooth continuing work flow, and accommodate any anticipated increased work load.

ASSESSMENT OF EDUCATION AND TRAINING REQUIREMENTS

Experience of working in an electronic office is still comparatively limited. Consequently the intending user finds a distinct shortage of sound, impartial advice on matters such as training requirements, equipment selection and optimum utilisation of equipment. It is essential that any innovations are seen in perspective against the background of business objectives and that they evolve to meet changing requirements.

All levels of staff will become directly involved with the use of electronic equipment, and roles within a firm may undergo some changes. Some skills will inevitably diminish in importance while others will become more valuable. Staff training and/or retraining will have to be very carefully assessed. Some machine operators may require specialist knowledge but it is not essential for all operators of new machinery to have an in-depth knowledge of them. For example, the caterer in the canteen, using a dishwasher which has a microelectronic control system, does not need to have an intimate knowledge of microelectronics in order to get her washing-up done; the secretary answering her telephone does not have to know precisely how the computerised switchboard operates. What is important is that all staff should understand what the equipment is capable of doing and be able to use it intelligently to its fullest potential. They also need clear instructions regarding the operational procedures to be followed in the event of a machinery breakdown. A really efficient operator of a business machine needs an appreciation of the communicational, organisational and logical thinking skills involved. There will be changes, however, in job content, skill values and work patterns. These changes must be carefully controlled and should be anticipated by awareness training, skill training and re-evaluation of jobs and career structures.

EMPLOYMENT OF STAFF

Current and future developments in an electronic office, in which most of the processing, storage and communication of information are electronically controlled, could considerably affect the employment of staff. There are, of course, some grounds for fear of job displacement because of the curtailment of routine tasks and repetitive typing. There is little doubt that, with properly used automated equipment, fewer people would be needed to cope with a specific workload. However, it is equally likely that the introduction of word processing and other electronic systems might stimulate much greater output and increase profits, thus cutting the need for making drastic reductions in the labour force, provided staff can adapt to the new techniques. Real efforts have to be made to develop an appreciation of the possible impact of the work of an automated office and to train staff to be flexible in coping with changing methods.

HEALTH AND SAFETY

Any electronic equipment, and the way in which it is used, must comply with the Health and Safety at Work Act 1974 (see pages 67–8 under Employment Legislation).

DATA SECURITY

Access to confidential information must be limited to authorised persons and data must be protected against accidental or deliberate falsification or destruction. This usually requires appropriate procedures to be followed by the staff and facilities built into the equipment. (See also page 71, Data Protection Act 1984.)

WORD PROCESSING

The introduction of a word processing system is one of the first steps towards the formation of an electronic office. Word processing describes the electronic equipment used in the preparation, editing, storing and retrieval of text. In a relatively short time technology has progressed from basic automatic typewriters, using punched tape or card, to flexible systems which can print out at several hundred words a minute in a variety of type styles. There is a tremendous variety of word processors on the market.

Stand alone system   The most basic word processor consists of an input keyboard, a printer, a storage facility usually in the form of a floppy disk or diskette, and a microprocessor, which is the nerve centre of the computer system. All this equipment comprises a single work station. Display for proof reading purposes may be in the form of hard copy (ie on paper), but the addition of a VDU (Visual Display Unit) on which the characters typed on the keyboard can be displayed on the screen, extends the facilities considerably. The size, shape and capacity of a VDU screen varies according to the make and manufacturer of the word processor. *Thin-window display* is only capable of showing the last two or three dozen characters typed; *part-page display* shows about 20 to 30 lines at a time; *full-page display* may show as many as 70 lines. Some manufacturers offer alternative formats on the same screen. Text which requires revision, including re-arranging of paragraphs, margin adjustment, insertions, deletions and layout adjustment, can be accessed, displayed on the screen, edited and merged.

The automatic printer, for output of final copy, generally uses a 'daisy wheel', and produces good quality output at 45–55 characters a second. Any number of error-free copies can be made of an original text. Each version is obtained by playing through the recording which was made while the original was being typed on the keyboard.

The word processing operator handles the printing as well as doing the keying and is likely to be responsible also for the storage of all the floppy disks.

The stand alone system is fairly easy to install into established office procedures.

Shared logic system   The shared logic system has a more powerful central processing unit (CPU) and associated storage devices to which a number of input keyboards and VDUs can be attached, thus allowing a larger volume of work to be handled at one time. More complicated text work can be achieved by groups of operators who can enter or input text from work stations in various different places. A large number of input stations enables intensive use to be made of fewer printers. This system is particularly suitable for installing an efficient typing centre with a supervisor in charge of printing and storage of disks. (See diagram.)

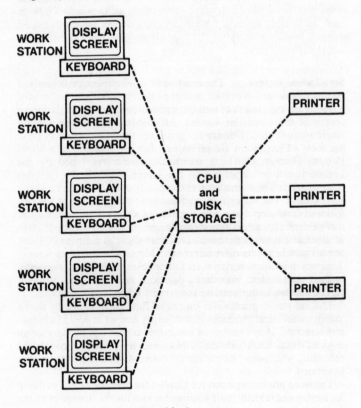

Shared logic system

The installation of a shared logic system might entail considerable re-organisation but additional work stations could be added once the basic system had been installed.

The CPU of a shared logic system need not be solely concerned with word processing but can be linked at the same time with other computer applications.

ELECTRONIC MAIL

It is likely to be some while before electronic mail completely displaces traditional paper systems, but the sending and receiving of mail by electronic means is a natural extension of word processing. It involves the use of computers, with their ability to receive, store and transmit messages, without any need for the framework of the present postal system. Electronic mail could:

    replace a major part of business mail
    substitute for many telephone calls
    replace inter-office memoranda.

Text, prepared on one processor and sent by telecommunications to another, would be filed on tape or disc and printed out or displayed on a screen for viewing. The concept of an almost 'paperless office' begins to emerge.

However, the growth of technology involving these communicating text processors will be limited until agreement is reached on international standardisation of appropriate 'communications protocol'. The process whereby one computer communicates with another is analagous to a telephone conversation between two people. First the number is dialled, then the caller identifies himself and ascertains that the correct person has been contacted. The information which necessitated the call is exchanged, the conversation is concluded and the receiver replaced. The 'mechanics' of the call (ie dialling, establishing identities, confirming that the exchange of information has been completed and the replacing of the receiver) are all part of the 'communications protocol'.

Forms of electronic mail such as telex and facsimile transmission are well established, viewdata information systems can be used to send messages, and teletex is in use (see page 61).

Telex   See section on pp. 47–8 under Effective Communication.

FACSIMILE TRANSMISSION

Anything from a short printed message to a complicated map, diagram or photograph can be rapidly relayed across the country, or across the world, by facsimile transmission. The expense of installing transmission equipment would be offset by the advantage of obtaining high-speed, accurate, round-the-clock communication. An exact copy of any document can be transmitted between two terminals. The original document is inserted into the sending equipment and a copy of it is produced in the receiving installation. As the original document remains with the sender there is no risk of its being lost in the post, and the expense of stamps and stationery and the delay involved in posting are saved.

Systems of facsimile transmission can be custom-designed to suit the needs of any particular organisation and the following are typical examples of the uses of this method of communication.

1. Weather stations transmit weather charts to airports, ports and ships at sea. Ships can also receive contour charts of the sea bed, etc.

2. Newspaper offices relay copy pages to regional printing presses, so that they may all begin issuing simultaneously.

3. Fire Brigades transmit information to fire-engines on their way to a burning building, telling the firemen where to find exits and entrances, fire escapes, etc. (Receivers are fitted into the vehicles.)

4. Medical records are sent between laboratory and hospital groups when the delays of post or messenger service might prove fatal.

5. Main airports transmit data on passengers and cargo, storage space, loads, etc, which can change right up to the last minute before flight clearance.

6. Mobile police vehicles can receive identikit pictures and fingerprint records.

VIEWDATA INFORMATION SYSTEMS

In 1979 the world's first public viewdata service, known as Prestel, was launched (see also Chapter 5, Effective Communication). This is a telecommunications system which enables people to call up information over their telephones from a central computer and have it displayed in words and diagrams on modified televisions, either at home or on their office desk.

The information, which can be called up in seconds by the subscriber when he presses the buttons on a key-pad, ranges through such items as stock market prices, sports results, weather forecasts, travel timetables and tourist information.

Through the Prestel service, subscribers can purchase goods or properties which are offered for sale. A customer may be interested, for instance, in the purchase of a new car. He will request the car market section of the computer-stored advertisements to display on his screen the information as to where he may find a car of a particular make, within a certain price range. A list of those dealers holding cars within this category will be shown on the screen. The customer selects a dealer, signals his choice to the computer and asks for further details. He may then choose a car and indicate his wish to purchase it. The computer acknowledges his offer and enquires about payment. On sending in the number of his credit card the deal is completed and details of the car that he has just purchased will then be deleted from the classified list. All he has to do now is collect his car or have it delivered.

For office use, a special keyboard unit has been designed which provides an interconnection with the telex system. Incoming telex messages are routed directly on to a television screen or held in store if necessary. A light on the machine shows that a message has come through and the subscriber has only to press a button to receive it.

Large organisations might well be considering the possibility of becoming 'closed users' of the Prestel service. In this case a number of terminals are connected to the service and each has access to the others and to the information store. The circulation of information is restricted and no-one outside the individual organisation has access to this information. 'Closed user groups' could also be established by organisations who wish to limit the availability of information to nominated users, eg product information to established customers.

There are various associated information systems, such as Teletext which is used by television broadcasting agencies, Fintel which gives business information from the Financial Times, and Extel which supplies special information in regard to share prices and company developments and general financial information.

TELETEX

This is a text communicating system similar to telex but it does not need a dedicated terminal (ie one reserved for exclusive use) and is much faster. A word processor can be used as a teletex transmitter-receiver. International standards have been established, making inter-company communications easier.

VOICE SYSTEMS

Voice recognition   Although research is still in its early stages, it is possible for computers to recognise, and therefore respond to, the human voice. A use of this speech device might be as follows: A manager wishes to write a letter. Currently he would probably dictate it directly to his secretary or to a dictating machine. In future he might have on his desk a small computer, a keyboard, a VDU and a microphone. He would dictate his letter into the microphone. The computer would recognise the words and display them on the screen and the manager, using the keyboard, would correct any errors. The letter would then be ready for output on a printer or for immediate transmission to a similar machine in the addressee's office.

Voice response   Computers can now produce a replica of human speech. This facility might be used by a sales representative to telephone his orders for immediate processing by his firm's computer which would have been suitably programmed to receive information by means of the numeric codes 0–9 from a push-button telephone. Such a telephone generates a unique tone for each button and the computer recognises these sounds. The same effect can be simulated on an ordinary (dial-type) telephone by a 'touchtone' device. The computer acknowledges verbally, detects obvious errors and reads the order back as a check.

NETWORKS

Various devices may be linked together in different ways to form a variety of networks.

Local area networks (LAN) can be installed in one building or complex of buildings, allowing computers, peripherals, telephones, facsimile transmission etc to be interconnected simply by plugging in so that they can all communicate speedily and effectively with one another – and with equivalent devices on other networks.

Wide area networks (WAN) enable various devices to be linked together over telecommunication lines provided by the appropriate PTT authorities (eg British Telecom). A suitable WAN can link devices on opposite sides of the globe and it can also link together two or more LANs.

GLOSSARY

COMPUTER	Electronic equipment for processing information according to a stored sequence of instructions.
CENTRAL PROCESSING UNIT (CPU)	Main part of a computer containing the control unit and arithmetic unit; separate from the main store where the programs are kept whilst they are running.
DAISY WHEEL PRINTER	A printer in which the typeface is held on arms radiating from a small wheel which can be interchanged in order to select different typefaces. Daisy wheel printers are often bi-directional, ie they print one line forwards and the next backwards during the carriage return.

DISTRIBUTED SYSTEM	Word-processing or general-purpose computer system where individual work stations have access to shared storage devices and printers via a local area network.
DOT MATRIX PRINTER	A printer in which each character is formed by a rectangular pattern (matrix) of dots. Technologies used include impact, thermal, and ink jet. (See also Near Letter Quality.)
FACSIMILE TRANSMISSION	The scanning and despatch of an exact copy of a document between two terminals.
FILE STORE	Any device or medium capable of receiving and retaining information and allowing it to be retrieved and used when required.
FLOPPY DISK OR DISKETTE	A flexible magnetic disc for storage and rapid access of data and programs. It can store many pages of text and allow random retrieval of text for editing purposes.
HARDWARE	Electronic or electro-mechanical equipment associated with a computer.
INFORMATION RETRIEVAL	The extraction of information from a file or files.
INPUT (verb)	The process of transferring data from an external store or peripheral device (eg magnetic tape or VDU) to an internal store (eg main store of the computer).
INPUT (noun)	The data itself.
MAINFRAME COMPUTER	A large computer that receives data from a network of smaller systems.
MEMORY	A device for accepting information which can be recalled when required.
MICRO-COMPUTER	Very small computer, based on a microprocessor and associated circuits.
MICRO-ELECTRONICS	The general term given to the technology of integrated electronic circuits.
MICRO-PROCESSOR	Central processing unit of a computer contained on a single silicon chip.

MINI-COMPUTER	A medium power computer with considerable storage and processing capacity.
MODEM	Device to enable computers to communicate data over telephone lines (MOdulator DEModulator).
NEAR LETTER QUALITY	Mode of printing offered by some dot matrix printers to improve character quality. (See also Dot Matrix Printer.)
OUTPUT	The process of producing the required data from a CPU via peripheral equipment.
PERIPHERAL	A piece of equipment attached to a CPU to make up a computer system. It includes magnetic storage devices (eg floppy disks), printers, keyboards and VDUs.
PRESTEL	British Telecom computer-based viewdata information service.
PROGRAM	Detailed sequence of instructions to the computer to perform a particular task (see Software).
PROGRAMMER	Person who prepares a program.
SHARED LOGIC SYSTEM	Word processing or general purpose computer system where a number of individual terminals have access to one CPU and frequently to shared storage devices and printers.
SILICON CHIP	A complex electronic circuit, constructed on a tiny piece of silicon, which may perform most or all of the functions of earlier large computers.
SOFTWARE	Programs associated with a computer system.
STAND ALONE SYSTEM	Word processing or general purpose computer installation which is a self-contained single work station.
TELETEX	A text communicating system.
TELETEXT	A broadcast TV information system operated by the BBC (Ceefax) and ITV (Oracle). See also page 50.
TERMINAL	Work station for inputting and retrieving information from a computer system.

TEXT EDITING

Revision, both in content and layout, of recorded draft text.

VIEWDATA
(VIDEOTEXT)

Video information transmission systems which supply data, via a telephone line, to modified televisions. See also page 50.

VISUAL DISPLAY
UNIT (VDU)

A television-style device which displays text either input from its associated keyboard or sent from the computer to which it is connected.

WORD PROCESSOR

Electronic equipment used in the preparation, editing, storage and retrieval of text.

Bibliography
Books and magazines on all aspects of the Electronic Office are continually being produced and updated. Reference libraries are able to advise on the newest publications.

7 EMPLOYMENT LEGISLATION

> *Equal Pay Act 1970; Employment and Training Act 1973; Health and Safety at Work Act 1974; Sex Discrimination Act 1975; Race Relations Act 1976; Employment Protection (Consolidation) Act 1978; Employment Act 1980; Data Protection Act 1984*

Every employee should be aware of his or her rights and duties under the various employment acts, and employers must be aware of their statutory obligations.

Croner's Reference Book for Employers provides information on the Acts of Parliament relating to employment and a monthly amendment service is provided in order to keep the information up-to-date.

Employment legislation in the 1970s included:

Equal Pay Act 1970 (Revised January 1976)

Employment and Training Act 1973

Health and Safety at Work Act 1974

Sex Discrimination Act 1975

Race Relations Act 1976

Employment Protection (Consolidation) Act 1978 – individual rights

EQUAL PAY ACT 1970

This Act became fully effective on 29 December 1975. Its object is to eliminate discrimination between men and women with regard to pay and conditions of employment. Men and women, working for the same employer and doing broadly similar work, are entitled to the same rates of pay and terms of employment. Where a woman's job differs from that of a man but has been given equal value under a job evaluation scheme, she is entitled to equal rates of pay and terms of employment.

The Act applies to all kinds of work everywhere – manual and non-manual, full-time and part-time, in offices, shops and factories.

In the event of a dispute and if agreement cannot be reached with the employer, either through the trade union or otherwise, an individual can refer the matter to an industrial tribunal. An industrial tribunal is an independent body which considers complaints about such matters as equal pay, unfair dismissal, redundancy payments or other questions relating to employment.

Bibliography
Barbara Dyer: *Implementing Equal Pay* (The Industrial Society, 1976).

EMPLOYMENT AND TRAINING ACT 1973

The Industrial Training Act 1964 had three main objectives:
> to ensure an adequate supply of properly trained men and women at all levels in industry
> to secure an improvement in the quality and efficiency of industrial training
> to share the costs of training more evenly between firms. It also provided for the establishment of Industrial Training Boards (ITBs).

The Employment and Training Act 1973 amended the Industrial Training Act 1964 and the law relating to employment, making some changes in the way the Boards operated.

The 1973 Act also provided for the establishment of the Manpower Services Commission (MSC) to run the public employment and training services. The general function of this Commission, according to the Act, is 'to make such arrangements as it considers appropriate for the purpose of assisting persons to select, train for, obtain and retain employment suitable for their ages and capacities and to obtain suitable employees'. It is specifically stated in the Act that arrangements should be included 'for encouraging increases in the opportunities available to women and girls for employment and training'.

HEALTH AND SAFETY AT WORK ACT 1974

Employer's duties   These are stated in the Act to be as follows:

1. To provide and maintain safe plant and work systems.
2. To ensure safe using, handling, storing and transporting of articles and substances.
3. To provide information, instruction, training and supervision to ensure the health and safety of employees.
4. To provide a safe working environment without health risks.
5. To provide adequate facilities for their employees' welfare at work.
6. To ensure that the public are not exposed to risk as a result of the employer's enterprise.
7. To make no charge for anything provided for the employee's safety which is required by a specific law (eg goggles).

8. To provide a safety policy and bring it to the notice of employees.
9. To consult Staff Safety Representatives and establish Safety Committees.
10. To prevent noxious or offensive fumes entering the atmosphere.

Employees' duties

1. To take reasonable care regarding health and safety for themselves and others.
2. To co-operate with the employer so far as necessary for the execution of the employer's duties.
3. To refrain from intentionally or recklessly interfering with or misusing anything provided for their health, safety or welfare.

The functions of the Health and Safety Commission as established by the Act:

1. To take action appropriate to furthering the purposes of the Act.
2. To promote research and training.
3. To provide information and advice (eg via the Employment Medical Advisory Service).
4. To carry out major investigations or inquiries (usually via the Executive).
5. To establish an Executive whose main function is the enforcement of the law and advisory work on the means of complying with it (mainly via the Inspectorate).

The functions of the Inspectors

1. To enter premises to make investigations.
2. To serve improvement notices (these tell the employer to improve something within a time period, the employer having a right of appeal to an industrial tribunal).
3. To serve prohibition notices. These are issued where there is a risk of serious personal injury; they can have immediate effect but a right of appeal exists.
4. To seize and destroy dangerous articles and substances.
5. To give information where necessary regarding matters of health, safety and welfare to the representatives of employees.
6. To initiate action, if necessary, which might lead to prosecutions for contraventions of the Act.

Bibliography
Health and Safety Executive: *Health and Safety at Work – Basic Rules for Safety and Health at Work* (HMSO).
C. Curson: *Health and Safety at Work in the Public Services* (Councils & Education Press, Longmans).

SEX DISCRIMINATION ACT 1975

The Sex Discrimination Act 1975, which applies to the whole of Great Britain but not to Northern Ireland, makes sex discrimination unlawful in employment, training and related matters (discrimination against married persons is also dealt with in this context), in education, in the provision of goods, facilities and services, and in the disposal and management of premises. The Act gives individuals a right of direct access to the civil courts and industrial tribunals for legal remedies for unlawful discrimination.

The Act established an Equal Opportunities Commission to help enforce the legislation and to promote equality of opportunity between the sexes generally. The Commission has a general responsibility for advising the government on the working of the Act and of the Equal Pay Act 1970, and it is also a principal source of information and advice for the general public about the Acts. The Commission has discretion, where there are special considerations, to assist individuals who consider that they may have been discriminated against.

The Commission's address is Equal Opportunities Commission, Overseas House, Quay Street, Manchester, M3 3HN

Bibliography
The Equal Opportunities Commission has published a number of leaflets which can be obtained from the Commission or from Citizens Advice Bureaux.

RACE RELATIONS ACT 1976

To the Race Relations Acts of 1965 and 1968 has been added a third Act of 1976 which creates powerful legal machinery for tackling racial discrimination. The major provisions cover:

1. Definition of racial discrimination both direct and indirect.
2. Discrimination by employers with regard to recruitment, terms of employment, promotion prospects and dismissal.
3. Discrimination in the areas of education, public services, housing, social clubs and associations.
4. Discriminatory practices and advertisements.
5. Exceptions to the Act, where discrimination can be made in favour of a racial group, eg provision of English language or pre-apprentice training courses.
6. Establishment of a Commission for Racial Equality.

Bibliography
Dr M. A. Pearn: *A Guide to the Race Relations Act 1976* (Industrial Society, 1976).

EMPLOYMENT PROTECTION (CONSOLIDATION) ACT 1978

This Act consolidates the previous legislation which dealt with the individual rights of employees under the following:
Redundancy Payments Act 1965
Contracts of Employment Act 1972
Trade Union and Labour Relations Acts 1974 and 1976
Employment Protection Act 1975
The major provisions cover:

1. Written statements to be supplied by employers giving normal hours of work, rate and method of calculation of pay, and the main terms and conditions of employment.
2. Guarantee payments to a full-time employee who is laid off work or put on short-time working.
3. Payment of employees suspended from work on medical grounds.
4. Reasonable provision of time off work for trade union and civic duties.
5. No victimisation or penalisation for union activities.
6. Rights to maternity pay and the right of return to work after pregnancy.
7. Entitlement to minimum periods of notice and written statement of reasons for dismissal.
8. Legal protection against unfair dismissal including compensation and interim relief.
9. Re-instatement and re-engagement orders.
10. Redundancy payments including payment of money owing to an employee on the insolvency of an employer; written explanation to be received indicating how payments have been calculated.

Bibliography
Joan Henderson: *A Guide to the Employment Protection (Consolidation) Act 1978* (Industrial Society, 1978).

Employment legislation in the 1980s included:
Employment Act 1980
Data Protection Act 1984

EMPLOYMENT ACT 1980

This Act amends some sections of the
Trade Union and Labour Relations Acts 1974 and 1976
Employment Protection Act 1975
Employment Protection (Consolidation) Act 1978

The major provisions of the 1980 Act cover:
Section
1–3. Trade union ballots and Codes of Practice.
4&5. Exclusion from trade union membership.
6–10. Unfair dismissal.
11–13. Maternity.
14&15. Other rights of employees.
16–18. Restrictions on legal liability.

DATA PROTECTION ACT 1984
The 1984 Data Protection Act provides that all people who hold personal information about others on computer must register with the data protection registrar in order that individuals may have access to the material held on them.

The right of individuals to claim compensation for damage caused by loss or unauthorised disclosure of personal data became effective in September 1984.

Bibliography
APEX: Data Protection – Guidelines (November 1985).

8 FORM DESIGN

Paper; printing; spacing and general layout; envelopes; copies; instructions; methods of completion; drafting; summary of guideline points

It has been said that the only certain things in life are birth, death and taxes, and it could have been added that none of these things are allowed to occur without the necessary form being completed. There are also plenty of other intermediate occasions for form-filling.

To join a club, enrol on a course, apply to go on an organised holiday, the chances are that a form must be filled in. If you own a dog or a television set or wish to drive a car, you are required to fill in an application form for a licence; a form has to be completed for an insurance claim, an application for benefit, to ask for gas or electricity services and to request a mortgage. In fact, in business, forms are as essential a part of communication as the telephone, and they have the extra advantage of being a visible and tangible record of information carried from A to B and even further.

The function of a form is to convey information, and if it is badly designed, perhaps by someone with insufficient understanding of its special purpose, it can, instead of being helpful, prove a hindrance, causing delays and confusion. If forms are allowed to become so numerous that they impose a heavy burden on the filing and mailing system, the firm will lose money through wasting time, labour and postage.

A well-designed form is not likely to be the result of a few hurried sketches on the back of an envelope. If a form is intended to show certain specific information, set out clearly and in a certain order, there are a number of factors to be considered before it can be suitably drafted and produced.

It is also advisable from time to time to consider whether an existing form has become redundant and should be discontinued, or it may be posible for an old form to be merged with a new one, so that one will do the work of both. If an existing form is proving unsatisfactory it may be possible to make it usable by slight adaptation. All forms in use should be subjected to regular appraisal, with these points in mind.

For routine purposes pre-printed forms, which may well suit your requirements adequately, particularly in the accounting field (order forms, loose-leaf accounts sheets, etc), can be supplied in large variety by stationery firms.

A further reason for caution when deciding to add a newly designed form to your system is that, if only required for short-term purposes, it may soon become surplus to requirements. However, if you cannot adapt an already existing form and cannot make use of inexpensive pre-printed stocks, and if you need sufficient quantities to make the expense worth while, then you will be justified in initiating a new custom-designed document.

Your form may be a single unit (eg an application for membership of the firm's sports club) which will probably have no special restrictions regarding style. On the other hand if there is a close link with other forms, it is advisable to keep the size and layout of each similar to the others, as, for example, in the natural sequence of quotation, invoice and statement of account. A third consideration is the advantage of a two-in-one design, with a perforation across the paper forming a detachable section, as for an invitation with a tear-off slip for an acceptance.

PAPER

Type of paper   Select the weight of paper carefully, with the following points in mind:

1. For many internal uses there is no need for top quality paper, eg for memos, stationery requisitions and message pads.
2. Light-weight papers are necessary if they are to be interleaved with sheets of carbon, but not so light that they tear easily.
3. A strong quality is needed for papers intended for loose-leaf filing.
4. When entries are likely to be handwritten a smooth matt surface is best.
5. Papers to be passed round different departments or handled by a number of people need to be of strong quality; workshop records in particular often receive rough treatment.
6. Ease of folding has to be considered in some cases, eg for outgoing mail.
7. Good quality paper of attractive appearance, used in outgoing forms to other business contacts, will enhance the standing and prestige of your firm.
8. Forms intended for long term use, or for a particular kind of filing or indexing system, may more conveniently be printed on light card, but this will cost more than sheets of paper.
9. Packs of forms making up manifold sets are usually printed on NCR (no carbon required) or Idem paper.

Your printing firm or wholesale stationer will advise on suitable types of paper for your purposes; the cheapest grades are not always the best and may turn out to be a false economy.

Size of paper   It is not economical to plan for large sheets if smaller ones will suffice, but the allowance of space for entries should not be restricted so that the information to be entered is cramped or inadequate. The internationally accepted paper sizes (A4, A5 etc.) are universally stocked and are therefore the most economical to purchase; specially cut sizes will involve extra cost.

For outgoing forms the size should be chosen that will best fit into the standard envelopes used by your firm. Paper sizes should also conform to the firm's existing filing folders, and it is not advisable to order paper that is wider than the average typewriter carriage, unless there is some special reason for doing so.

PRINTING

A good printing style enhances the appearance of a form, and the cost of prestige work for outgoing papers is usually well worth while from the advertising and public relations aspect.

A consistent type-style is desirable. Two type-styles may be combined to give contrast, but no more than two should be used unless a special section of the form needs particular prominence or distinction. Emphasis may be made by heavier type or larger letters, or by an area being shaded or stippled. Any printing firm will advise on suitable typographical styles and will produce samples from the many varieties of type face to help in your choice.

A special symbol or logo identifying your firm can improve the appearance of the form as well as having a functional purpose. Good contemporary examples are shown in Figure i:

Figure i

Colour   Colour printing makes a form look attractive and interesting and can help quick identification of sections and special areas by means of shading or a distinctive border. It is worth remembering that simply printing in, say, red rather than the standard black is not normally any more expensive; it is multi-colour printing that adds to the cost. A small amount of colouring in headings or trademarks can add distinction, but may not be very effective on a dark background.

Colour coding assists in quick identification; when a form is one of a sequence or set of forms an instant signal to the eye may be given by a bold block or band of colour.

To distinguish between forms in manifold sets, however, tinted paper is usually preferable to colour printing. Tinted paper may also have advantages for more general use, as pastel shades can provide an attractive background to dark lettering, and buff paper is actually cheaper than white.

Tumbler printing   This is the printing of matter which continues from the bottom of one side of a card or sheet of paper on to the other side, the bottom edge of page 1 becoming the top edge of page 2. The paper is therefore turned bottom to top when the reverse side is read. This sometimes saves time in handling, but is not suitable for papers which will eventually be put away flat in a file.

SPACING AND GENERAL LAYOUT

There should be no doubt about the purpose of the form. There should be a main identifying title or heading, distinctively printed horizontally across the top, eg APPLICATION FORM, QUESTIONNAIRE, CLAIM FORM, ORDER, centred or against the left-hand margin. If there is a serial or code number for filing purposes this is usually placed in the top right-hand corner.

Give consideration to the likely answer when allocating space after a printed question. Some questions may be worded to bring out only the word 'Yes' or 'No'. A small space will be sufficient for a telephone number but several lines are needed for an address.

Allow plenty of space where 'free' wording is required. On a claim form for instance (where lost property, or an accident, may have to be described) space for a sketch as well as the wording may prove helpful.

Whenever possible entries should be made in a natural sequence and from left to right, which is the easiest way for the majority of people to follow. Related entries should be grouped together.

If several departments have to insert or extract information from the same form, the sections should be clearly differentiated and each area kept compact.

Figures
Figures to be added or subtracted should be arranged vertically in columns. If figures are to be entered by hand, faint ruled or printed guidelines will keep the completed column tidy. Double lines, or lines in heavier print, may be used to separate groups of columns and will make the overall arrangement clearer to the eye. See Figure ii. In order to differentiate particularly narrow columns, ten per cent screening can be used in alternate columns to give a lightly stippled effect as in a computer print-out.

Week No.	Pay in Week	Total pay to date	Total taxable pay to date	Tax deducted or refunded
	£	£	£	£

Figure ii

In some cases, eg within a paragraph, a space for words as well as figures may be a safeguard, eg £5,000 (five thousand pounds).

Perforations   If a form is designed to do two jobs, ie with a tear-off portion, the necessary perforations should be arranged to run across the shorter edge of the paper.

Margins   Printing should not be taken too near the left side as this side may be partly covered when the paper is eventually filed, although there is no disadvantage in placing punched holes in this area, for loose-leaf folders.

Printing should not approach too close to the bottom edge of the paper, particularly if the form is likely to be completed on a typewriter. This would not apply, however, to forms printed as part of a sheet of continuous stationery, when the paper is fed into the typewriter in the form of a long strip, each section divided by horizontal perforations.

Columns   Columns should have clear headings or captions, and these headings should be printed horizontally if at all possible. The width may be reduced by using double lined headings, or by abbreviations, as in Figure iii.

VAT	Jan	Feb	Mar

Invoice No.	Date of Completion	Delivery Date

Figure iii

When headings are wide compared to a narrow column of figures beneath, a diagonal or vertical arrangement will save space, as in Figures iv and v, the latter being preferable because it is easier to read.

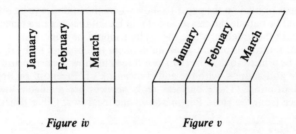

Figure iv   *Figure v*

It is not advisable to save width by misleading abbreviations, as in Figure vi, which to some people might read Percentage, Deduct Allowances, Gross Monthly Tax and Net Amount, but to many others would be merely confusing.

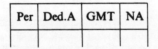

Figure vi

When allowing space between vertical lines for calculations, remember that the total figure is usually the amount taking the greatest width. Therefore, when additions are to be made, this should be your key in estimating the column width required. It is better to allow too much space than too little here, as figures should not be cramped, particularly when handwritten. An extra column to the right, for sub-totals, may make the final appearance clearer, and will help towards any analysis to be made from the figures.

ENVELOPES

If envelopes are needed, the time spent in typing each name and address may be saved by designing the forms to slip into window envelopes. The exact area for the name and address on the form itself should be indicated by marking the four corners or ruling in the rectangular space before submitting the draft for printing.

Folding   Forms to be sent through the post, providing they are not confidential, may be designed to fold with a tucked-in flap or gummed edge in order to save the expense of envelopes, but the paper must be strong enough. When folded, the corner bearing the stamp or franking mark should be between two folds, not against an open edge.

Lines printed on the paper to show where the folds are to be made should be outside the crease, and it is helpful if they are numbered to indicate the order in which the folding should be done.

For returnable papers, as an inducement to a prompt reply, forms may be printed so that they can be refolded to show the firm's printed name and address, with the added incentive of 'Freepost' or Reply Paid printing. (These business reply services are available under licence from the Head Postmaster of the local Post Office district.)

COPIES

A completed form is a record in itself and, if extra copies of the form are required after it has been filled in, photocopying will probably be the most convenient method of making them. In some cases forms may be sent out in duplicate, with the request that both should be completed and returned.

Manifold sets   When several departments need a copy of a form or a transaction follows several stages, sets of forms in 'manifold' pads are used. The layout of each page matches that of all the others and the pages are sometimes differentiated by differently tinted papers, for instance a blue delivery note, yellow invoice form, white statement of account, all referring to the same transaction. A customer might be issued with a white rental form for hiring a car; at the same time and from the same set a pink copy of this would be made for the car hire firm's accounts department, and a blue copy would simultaneously be made for the insurance company.

Manifold pads are usually printed on Idem or NCR paper, lightly gummed together at the top edge to hold the set together. On selected pages within the sets an area may be masked, preventing the full information entered on the top copy being transferred through to a particular page. In this way figures typed in the columns of an order, giving the precise cost of the goods, could be masked on the Goods Received sheet which goes to the storeman for him to use when checking that all the goods are being delivered.

INSTRUCTIONS

Instructions printed on a form should be simple, clear and kept to the minimum. Paragraphs of crowded small print should be avoided and any questions should be worded concisely. Bear in mind that what can be misunderstood probably will be.

Instructions are of several kinds. They may explain how to complete the form, eg 'Block letters' or 'Sign on the dotted line', and directions of this sort should be placed as near the relevant entry as possible.

Instructions may indicate what is to be done with the form after completion, such as 'Tear off and return the coupon', or draw attention to a point, eg 'See Note 2 overleaf' or clarify a request, as 'Delete items not applicable'.

Instructions may therefore be printed at the appropriate section, or placed at the head or foot of the form as required. Figure vii shows examples of both types of instructions.

APPLICATION FOR SUPPLY OF GAS
This form should be returned to the District Controller
for your area (See list of addresses overleaf).

PLEASE COMPLETE IN BLOCK LETTERS

Name ———————————————————————

Address ——————————————————————

Date supply required (give three days' notice) ———

Do you wish to pay by standing order?
     (please tick)   Yes ☐ No ☐

Name and address of Contractor
  (See condition 5 overleaf)   —————

                            —————

Please give the address:
a) to which accounts should
      be sent   —————

                            —————

b) at which you were last
     responsible for payment
     of gas accounts   —————

                            —————

(Please read the conditions overleaf)

Figure vii

Choice and preference   Consider the following:
   How do you wish your goods to be sent? . . . . .
This is too vague and may bring forth the reply 'by special messenger'
which is not convenient to the sender of the goods. The following
layout would be preferable:

   Do you wish your goods to be sent by Rail . . . . .
                                        Air . . . . .
                                       Road . . . . .

However, this could produce one 'Yes' and two 'Nos' and still take up
more space than is needed to get the correct answer. Either of the
following arrangements would be more compact:

   Do you wish delivery to be by Road . . . Rail . . . Air . . .
   (Please tick as appropriate)
   or
   Do you wish goods to be sent by Road/Rail/Air
   (Please delete as appropriate)
Both these methods take a minimum of space and will bring in a
clearer response to the question, in accordance with the available
delivery services.

   Information in more depth may be required; consider the following
example of an enquiry to a prospective customer:

   Please state colour and size of garment . . . . . .

This may bring in an imprecise reply, or a request for a colour or size
that is not in stock. The following is preferable:

Please mark colour in Red ☐ Blue ☐ Green ☐ Yellow ☐
order of preference
Please tick size   10 ☐ 12 ☐   14 ☐   16 ☐
required

Here the customer will be able to give a clear indication of what is
required, within the available size and colour ranges, by the use of
pre-printed wording and small blocks.

METHODS OF COMPLETION

The form may be intended for only one person or for several people; it
may be meant for departmental entries, to show a sequence of stages
or operations, being marked or ticked at intervals or having wording
added to it until a programme is finally completed. In this way a form
can constitute a useful progress chart.
   If the form is a link between different people and processes it may
be associated with computers, punched card systems, accounting
machines or otherwise stamped or overprinted. Entries may be made
by machine or by hand. If by hand, plenty of space should be allowed

for entries, as handwriting takes up more room than type. If entries are to be typed in, or completed by computer, there are technical points to remember.

Vertical ruling, if any, should be spaced to conform with the type-spacing on a typewriter (eg twelve spaces to the inch for machines with élite type). If vertical lines do not correspond with typewriter spacing requirements the tabulator stops cannot conveniently be used and time will be wasted by constant adjustment.

Similarly, if ruled or dotted horizontal lines are planned to correspond with the spacing on a typewriter, ie in multiples of one sixth of an inch, a typist making the entries will find it quicker and easier to complete the form than if the lines were set at a variety of different distances apart; this latter would mean constant adjustment of the variable line-spacer.

Make	Model	Salesman
Year	Month	Reg. No.
Mileage	Colour	Price

Figure viii

In figure viii the box titles in the top left hand corner of each block give the maximum space for entries, and typewriter tabulator stops can be used with ease; the variable line-spacer need not be used at all. By contrast the layout in figure ix would take longer to fill in on the typewriter, and the boxes have less space for entering the information owing to the central position of the headings:

Make	Model	Salesman
Year	Month	Reg. No.
Mileage	Colour	Price

Figure ix

DRAFTING

When it is decided that an old form must be adapted or a new one set out, make a full-sized draft for the printer, to scale. The following points should be made clear (see also section on Preparation of Material for the Printer):

1. The precise areas, width of panels and columns should be shown with all dimensions marked, also the size and position of punched holes or perforations.
2. If colour is to be used, state which colour and where, indicating where blocks of solid colour and shaded or stippled areas are required.
3. Show precisely the position and colour of ruled or dotted lines.
4. Specify the quality of paper required, and whether you need separate sheets, gummed-spine pads or continuous stationery.
5. State whether there is to be printing on one or both sides of the paper; if on both sides say whether or not you wish for tumbler printing. (Note that the draft should only be set out on one side of a sheet of paper, marked 'front' or 'back' accordingly.)
6. State whether or not Idem paper or carbon inter-leaving is required.

Ask the printer for prices and dates of delivery before ordering. The printer will follow instructions according to your specification, so it is important to get everything right before ordering.

When the draft is finalised, check it with those people who will use the form; check it also against any filled-in copies of similar forms now in use. Send the draft form on an experimental run through the system. Do not hurry this testing procedure; once a form is on order it can be a very expensive business to have something amended, and if a fault should show up after the forms are delivered and put into stock, it will be a constant source of irritation.

Order well in advance to allow for any unexpected delays in printing; rush orders are usually very expensive.

SUMMARY

A list of summarised guideline queries is set out below.

1. Is your form really necessary?
2. Who will originate it and what is its main function?
3. How many people will use it, and in what order?
4. What is to be entered on it?
5. Should it link up with other related forms?
6. Is it to be part of a manifold set?
7. How many copies will be needed and how should they be made?
8. What is the most suitable type and colour of paper?

9. Will the form be for external as well as internal distribution?
10. If the paper is to be folded, should fold-lines be indicated?
11. What is the best treatment of directions and headings?
12. Where should columns for calculations be placed?
13. How much space is required for each entry?
14. Which type style is preferred?
15. Is colour printing to be used?
16. Are symbols or logos to be included?
17. Are both sides of the paper to be used, and if so will tumbler printing be better than 'head to head' printing?
18. Has the draft form been tested under working conditions?

INTERNATIONAL PAPER SIZES

The standard sizes are as follows:

A0	841 × 1189mm	A4	210 × 297mm
A1	594 × 841mm	A5	148 × 210mm
A2	420 × 594mm	A6	105 × 148mm
A3	297 × 420mm	A7	74 × 105mm

Bibliography
British Standards (British Standards Institute).

9 MEETINGS

*The secretary's role and the chairman's
role in relation to meetings; terminology
at meetings*

THE SECRETARY'S ROLE IN RELATION TO MEETINGS

Type of meeting   It is essential for the chairman's secretary to be
thoroughly aware of the aims, objectives and terms of reference of the
council, board, committee, sub-committee or working party meeting
which is to be covered and to have a clear knowledge of routine
meeting procedures.

Notice of meeting   It is the secretary's task to send the notice of
the meeting to every member who is entitled to attend in accordance
with the organisation's standing orders or rules. This notice states the
type of meeting to be held, the place, date and time of that meeting
and the subjects to be discussed (the agenda). A formal notice is not
necessary when a committee always holds its meetings on specified
dates at specified times and places. However, when a future date is
arranged at a meeting, notification must always be sent to any
absentees.

Agenda   The secretary prepares the agenda in consultation with
the chairman. The agenda paper must be sent out well in advance of
the meeting so that members have plenty of time to consider the items
which are going to be discussed. The agenda and notice of meeting are
usually sent together. A customary order for agenda items is:

    appointment of chairman (if not already appointed)
    apologies for absence and any relevant correspondence
    verification of the minutes of the previous meeting
    any matters arising from the minutes
    notification of any other items of business to be discussed at the
       end of the meeting
    reports of committees and/or officers
    general business of the meeting
    date of the next meeting
    any other business

Items raised under 'any other business' must be of minor
importance.

There are various styles for presenting agendas but the method of setting out must be consistent throughout. One acceptable arrangement is as in Figure i:

---

5 May 1986

The eighth meeting of the Advisory Committee, which I hope you will be able to attend, will be held at 1430 hours on Thursday 29 May 1986 in the Large Committee Room, Smith Place, London WC2N 4BZ

Paula King
Secretary

AGENDA

1 APOLOGIES for absence

2 MINUTES of the seventh meeting held on 25 March 1986 (already circulated but further copy attached)

3 MATTERS ARISING from the Minutes

4 NOTIFICATION of any other items of business

5 GENERAL WORKING PARTY
To receive report from Mr Hill – AC/86/Paper 1 to follow

6 CONFERENCE ARRANGEMENTS
To receive preliminary report from Secretary – AC/86/Paper 2 attached

7 DATE OF NEXT MEETING

8 ANY OTHER BUSINESS

Figure i. Notice of Meeting and Agenda

Chairman's agenda   The secretary can assist the chairman in the
conduct of the meeting by setting out for him an extended version of
the normal agenda circulated to the members. This will include
additional details, such as action which has been taken since the
previous meeting or investigations which are pending, which will
enable him to amplify items without necessarily having to refer to
other documents or papers. The chairman's agenda should have a
very wide right-hand margin so that he can make notes which will
help later in the compilation of the minutes.

Minutes of previous meeting   Although members will have
already received a copy of the minutes of the previous meeting with
the agenda paper, further copies are usually made available at the
meeting.

Supporting papers and documents   Wherever possible copies of
all supporting papers and documents are sent to members by the
secretary with the agenda so that they can be studied by them in
advance of the meeting. If a supporting paper is not ready in time for
despatch, reference such as 'to follow' or 'to be tabled' should be
made against the agenda item. In any case further sets of papers
relevant to the meeting should be held in reserve.

Preparation of meeting room   Most firms and organisations have
a board room or special committee room which is set aside for
meetings. It is essential to ensure in advance that there is adequate
seating, lighting, heating and ventilation and a sufficient supply of
notepaper and pencils, water and glasses. If the meeting is a large one
the chairman may wish to use a gavel.

   It may be convenient for newly formed committees to have name
cards, lettered on both sides, put in front of each member's place. The
lettering must be clear enough for all members round the table to be
able to distinguish the names of their colleagues at a glance. Name
cards are also beneficial to the secretary who will need to identify the
speakers when recording the minutes. A 'Meeting in progress' notice
should be placed outside on the door when the meeting is about to
start.

Telephone calls   Liaison with the switchboard operator should
ensure that telephone messages will be routed elsewhere during the
meeting, although a certain amount of discretion must be exercised in
the case of urgent communications.

Refreshments   Arrangements will have to be made with the
catering staff for refreshments to be served at convenient times. In
addition to coffee in the morning and tea in the afternoon there is the

question of lunch. A light and attractive buffet is often preferable to a 'sit-down' meal as it enables members to circulate freely for discussion.

Receiving both new and regular committee members   Remember to have a preliminary word with the receptionist in order that new members may be directed to the correct floor and room number. Alternatively an indicator board in the foyer may be used to give adequate information and directions.

Many chairmen like to have a few brief words with any newly joined committee members before the start of a meeting. The Chairman will need to introduce new members to the whole committee. If the secretary has prepared a short background note on any newcomer this can be included in the notes on the chairman's agenda.

She should try to become familiar with the names of all committee members as rapidly as possible so that she can receive them by name as they arrive for the meeting.

Attendance sheet or register   All members present at the meeting will sign the attendance sheet or register as they arrive and the secretary must ensure that the list is complete for recording in the minutes.

Minute book   For record purposes, all organisations should keep one official copy of each set of minutes bearing the chairman's signature. It is useful for the minute book to have an index, or alternatively a separate index list can be maintained. This enables quick reference to be made to any special item dealt with at an earlier meeting or meetings.

Recording the meeting   The secretary must concentrate on the important task of assisting the chairman in his duties; she normally sits on his right-hand side. She may be required to take a full record of the meeting from which she will later draft the minutes but at an important meeting, where the secretary needs to concentrate wholly on assisting the chairman, a minuting secretary may also be appointed. However, the responsibility for the accuracy of the final minutes still rests with the chairman's secretary. The chairman must play his part by ensuring that all motions and decisions are clearly made and that the final wording of resolutions is precise and unambiguous.

Preparing the minutes   Each item on the agenda will be recorded as a separate minute. This official record of the business discussed at a meeting, the decisions reached and the resolutions made should be drafted as soon as possible after the meeting. It must be in reported speech and, except at formal meetings, it is not necessary to name the proposers and seconders when recording a motion; however, the name of a member presenting a report should be noted. A decision in favour of a motion is recorded as being 'agreed' or 'resolved'.

The minutes must be shown to the chairman for his approval before they are duplicated and circulated to all committee members.

Following up   One copy of the agenda, supporting papers and the official copy of the minutes must be filed carefully and safely. Occasionally the auditors may ask to see the authority for certain items which have appeared in books of account; the tax inspector can, if he wishes, ask for an extract from the minutes of a meeting. In some cases minutes may be submitted as legal evidence.

It is important to keep a circulation list of those who should receive copies of the minutes of meetings, and a note should be made of any necessary follow-up action which is required to be taken by individual committee members or administrative staff. When a member has agreed to take certain action on behalf of the committee it may be sensible to send a reminder in time for him to take the appropriate steps before any subsequent meeting. The secretary should check that the chairman has also taken any appropriate follow-up action which he has promised.

THE CHAIRMAN'S ROLE IN RELATION TO MEETINGS

The chairman must be well informed about the function of the committee and ensure that the meeting has been properly convened. He must also:

> ensure that the minutes of the previous meeting are correct and sign them
>
> keep order at the meeting
>
> ensure that the discussion keeps to the point of the business in hand
>
> formulate proposals and amendments on which members will be asked to vote
>
> give decisions on points of order and on other incidental matters which may arise during the meeting
>
> be responsible for taking votes and declaring results
>
> close or adjourn the meeting
>
> make decisions, in consultation with the secretary during the intervals between meetings, and agree the minutes
>
> take any appropriate follow-up action which he has promised.

TERMINOLOGY AT MEETINGS

ab initio	From the beginning.
ABSTENTION	Members of a committee not wishing to vote 'for' or 'against' a motion may abstain, ie refrain from casting a vote at all.

ADDENDUM	An addition or alteration to a proposed motion.
ADDRESS THE CHAIR	Any committee member wishing to speak must first address the chairman . . . 'Mr Chairman' or 'Madam Chairman . . .'
AD HOC COMMITTEE	A committee formed to deal with a single unit of work; upon completion of this task the committee disbands.
ADJOURNMENT	A meeting may be adjourned and re-convened at a later date to complete un-finished items on the agenda.
AMENDMENT	(See Addendum)
ANNUAL GENERAL MEETING	A statutory meeting, held once a year, open to an organisation's whole membership.
BALLOT	A written, secret vote conducted in accordance with the Constitution.
BOARD MEETING	A management meeting of the board of directors of a company.
CASTING VOTE	In the case of an equal number of votes 'for' and 'against' a motion, the chairman may be allowed a second or 'casting' vote.
COMMITTEE WITH ADVISORY POWERS	A committee with advisory powers can only make recommendations.
COMMITTEE WITH DELEGATED POWERS	A committee with delegated powers can take action on its own without referring to any other body.
CONSTITUTION	This document, which describes the objects of an association, should also define the powers which it has delegated to its committees.
CO-OPTED MEMBER	One who has been invited to serve on a committee by a majority vote of existing members.
ELECTED MEMBER	One who has been elected by the votes of the other members of the organisation represented at a meeting.

en bloc	Several committee members can be re-elected 'in one lump' by the passing of a single resolution.
EXECUTIVE COMMITTEE	A committee which carries on the actual management of an organisation.
EX-OFFICIO MEMBER	One who is invited to attend a committee 'by virtue of office' but without voting rights, eg the official secretary to the committee.
EXTRAORDINARY GENERAL MEETING	A meeting of members to deal with one specific urgent problem or an emergency situation. Notice has to be given according to Standing Orders.
IN ATTENDANCE	Those who are present on invitation to give expert advice, help or information.
in camera	In private – not open to the public.
in extenso	In full – without abridgement.
intra vires	Within the legal power or authority of the organisation.
JOINT COMMITTEE	The co-ordination of two or more committees to form one large committee.
LIE ON THE TABLE	A motion is said to 'lie on the table' when it is decided that no action will be taken on it at present.
MAJORITY VOTE	A vote taken with the greater number of members voting either for or against a motion.
MEMORANDUM AND ARTICLES OF ASSOCIATION	An official document in which the structure and internal management of an individual company are set out.
MOTION	A formal proposal, moved by a member, that certain action be taken.
MOVE THE CLOSURE	A phrase used to indicate that there should be an end to discussion on a particular motion, and a vote should be taken on it.
nem con	No one contradicting, ie no votes against the motion but some members may have abstained.
nem dis	No one dissenting.

ORDINARY GENERAL MEETING	A scheduled meeting of members held at stated regular intervals eg once every four months.
OUT OF ORDER	The chairman can rule a member 'out of order' if that member is not keeping to the point under discussion or is speaking improperly.
POINT OF ORDER	A query regarding possible infringement of Standing Orders, raised by a member during a meeting.
POLL VOTE	(See Ballot)
POSTPONEMENT	The action taken to transfer the holding of a meeting to a later date.
PROPOSER	A member who puts forward a motion for discussion at a meeting.
PROXY VOTE	A member may be appointed to vote by proxy, ie on behalf of another member who is unable to attend the meeting.
QUORUM	The minimum number of members, as specified in Standing Orders, who must be present before a meeting may be held.
RESOLUTION	A motion passed by a majority vote becomes a resolution.
RIDER	An addition to a resolution which has already been passed. Such an addition has to be proposed, seconded and voted upon.
RIGHT OF REPLY	The proposer of a resolution has the right of reply when the motion has been fully discussed and is about to be put to the meeting for a vote.
SCRUTINEER	An officer who supervises the voting at an election.
SECONDER	The member who supports the proposer of a motion prior to a vote being taken.
sine die	For an indefinite period.
STANDING COMMITTEE	A permanent committee carrying on day-to-day work; eg local government has standing committees for housing, education, welfare etc.

STANDING ORDERS	The rules of an organisation which regulate committee procedure.
status quo	As things stand at present.
STATUTORY MEETING	A meeting (usually of the shareholders in a public company) which must be held in order to comply with the statutes or laws of the country.
SUB COMMITTEE	A group of members from a main committee selected to form a working party to deal with detailed work which will be referred back later to the full committee, with findings and recommendations.
TABLED	This describes a document to be presented to a committee 'on the table' not one which has been included with the agenda papers.
TELLER	One who is appointed to count votes given by a show of hands.
TERMS OF REFERENCE	A statement of the work to be carried out by the members of a committee.
ultra vires	Outside the legal power or authority of the organisation.
UNANIMOUS VOTE	All votes in favour of or all votes against a motion.
VERBATIM REPORT	An exact literal (word for word) account.
VOTE OF NO CONFIDENCE	In the event of total disagreement between the chairman and members of a committee a 'vote of no confidence' in the chair can be taken.

Bibliography

Leslie Hall: *Meetings* (MacDonald and Evans, 1977).

P. J. C. Perry: *Hours into Minutes* (BACIE, 1983).

Michael Locke: *How to run Committees and Meetings* (Macmillan Press, 1980).

M. A. Pemberton: *A Guide to Effective Meetings* (Industrial Society, 1982).

10   PREPARATION OF MATERIAL FOR THE PRINTER

Copy preparation; proof correction

Any secretary may be called upon occasionally to prepare for publication material such as pamphlets, reports, articles, booklets or even a complete book. You may also be required to proof-read and correct such material before final printing.

COPY PREPARATION

Anyone who is going to prepare typescript copy for printing must be given clear and concise instructions before starting the work so that the style of presentation will be consistent throughout. All copy should be typed on one side only of good quality A4 paper, in double spacing, using a clear black ribbon and taking at least one carbon copy as a precaution against the loss of the original. The editor of a book may require several copies of a manuscript and the top copy should go to the printer.

Abbreviations   The general trend now is for open punctuation (no full points) for most abbreviations and acronyms, as follows: eg ie Dr BBC UNESCO or Unesco.

Corrections   Minor corrections or additions in ink can be made on a typescript but if there are substantial alterations the pages should be retyped or additional pages inserted.

Dates   These may be given as '1 December 1980', without punctuation, or 'in the 1980s', without an apostrophe. When used in tables or schedules the months of the year can be abbreviated to three letters.

Extracts and quotations   These should be rendered exactly as they appeared in the original and permission to publish, which is usually the responsibility of the author, must be obtained from the holder of the copyright, preferably in writing. Acknowledgement of any permission thus obtained should also be made in the publication.

Footnotes   Footnotes which provide additional information relating to the text may be placed:
  at the foot of the page on which the text reference appears

at the end of a chapter
as an endnote at the end of the whole work
at the foot of a tabulation.

A single footnote appearing on a page or in a tabulated schedule is often indicated by an asterisk. Numerous footnotes are usually indicated in the text by superior numerals, with or without brackets, running serially throughout an article or chapter. The signs *, †, ‡ and § are sometimes used in preference to superior numerals where the text contains mathematical characters.

Headings   The style to be adopted throughout the work in regard to main headings, shoulder headings, side headings and sub-headings must be decided upon and used consistently. The relative importance of each type of heading must be made clear to the editor and printer.

Illustrations   These are usually kept separate from the main typescript but an indication must be given as to the place where diagrams and illustrations should appear in the printed work, although the need for economy may restrict the freedom of arrangement. Photographs will be damaged if they are folded, written on or clipped to a manuscript and they should be packed carefully with a stiff card reinforcement for posting.

Latin expressions   The following is a list of some of the most common expressions formed from or consisting of Latin words:

AD – *anno domini* – in the year of our Lord
ad infinitum – without limit
ad valorem – according to the value
am – *ante meridiem* – before noon
bona fide – in good faith, genuine
c or ca – *circa* – approximately
cf – *confer* – compare
compos mentis – of sound mind
de facto – in fact
eg – *exempli gratia* – for example
et al – *et alii* – and others
etc – *et cetera* – and so forth
et seq – *et sequentia* – and the following
ibid – *ibidem* – in the same place
id – *idem* – the same
ie – *id est* – that is
loc cit – *loco citato* – in the place cited
modus operandi – manner of working
modus vivendi – manner of living
MS – *manuscriptum* – manuscript (plural MSS)
NB – *nota bene* – note well

non compos mentis – of unsound mind
non seq – *non sequitur* – not following logically
op cit – *opere citato* – in the work cited
passim – throughout or here and there
per se – by itself
pm – *post meridiem* – after noon
pro tem – *pro tempore* – for the time being
PS – *postscriptum* – postscript
qv – *quod vide* – which see
sic – thus (confirming accuracy of what precedes)
sub rosa – secretly
v or vs – *versus* – against
v – *vide* – see
vice versa – the reverse
viz – *videlicet* – namely

Margins   Margins should be kept uniform from page to page so that a quick estimation can be made of the number of words per page or per chapter. It is usual to have a much wider left-hand margin than right so that the editor and/or the printer can annotate with instructions for printing where necessary.

Mathematical and scientific symbols   Great care must be taken when using mathematical and scientific formulae. If it is not possible to type the exact symbols then they should be carefully inserted by hand.

Metric system   Nearly every country in the world is now using the metric system, or is in process of changing to it. Most Standards Authorities have adopted the 'Système International d'Unités' – S I Units.

The following schedule gives some of the most commonly used units and the symbol for each:

QUANTITY	UNIT	SYMBOL
Length	millimetre	mm
	centimetre	cm
	metre	m
	kilometre	km
Area	square millimetre	mm^2
	square centimetre	cm^2
	square metre	m^2
	hectare	ha

QUANTITY	UNIT	SYMBOL
Volume or Capacity	cubic centimetre	cm^3
	cubic metre	m^3
	millilitre	ml
	centilitre	cl
	litre	l*
Weight or Mass	gram	g
	kilogram	kg
	tonne	t
Temperature	degree Celsius	^oC†
Speed	metre per second	m/s
	kilometre per hour	km/h
Pressure	pascal	Pa†
Frequency	hertz	Hz†
Energy	joule	J†
Power	watt	W†

* The typewritten 'l' for litre can be confused with the figure 'one' and it is better to handwrite the 'l' for litre rather than type it. A recommendation has been put forward for approval to use the capital 'L' but this has not yet been agreed.

† Where the symbols are derived from the names of actual people (C for Celsius, P for Pascal, H for Hertz, etc) capital letters are used.

The names of units can be made plural (eg metres, hectares, tonnes etc) but symbols are never given in plural form (eg 10 m).

A space is always left between a figure and its symbol and a full stop is not used after a symbol, except at the end of a sentence.

When a number is less than one, the decimal point should be preceded by a nought.

Pages   A preliminary page should be included giving the name and address of the author(s) and the title of the article or book. Pages (folios) should be numbered consecutively through the typescript at the top right-hand corner. It is preferable for the complete manuscript to be 'hole-punched' and threaded on a tag rather than stapled. It should never be pinned together.

Punctuation   Punctuation marks and symbols must be used consistently according to personal preference or house-style. Single quotation marks can be used for quotations and double quotation marks reserved for a quotation within a quotation (or the exact reverse of this system may be followed if preferred).

Spelling   Many dictionaries and books on English usage give alternative spellings for certain words but there should be a consistent choice in the use made of words throughout any one piece of work.

Time   It is becoming increasingly common to use the 24-hour clock wherever possible.

PROOF CORRECTION

Galley proofs   The first printed proofs sometimes appear in the form of 'galleys'. (The word 'galley' originated from the long, shallow metal trays into which lines of type were placed as they came from type-setting machines). These take the form of long printed strips and are not divided into pages at this stage. These proofs have to be read carefully and checked word for word against the original manuscript for errors.

Page proofs   The printer then converts the 'galleys' into page lengths and produces page proofs. These page proofs are first corrected by the printer's proof readers, who will mark any literal errors and any queries they have for the author. The editor and the author will then check the proofs and mark any further printer's errors they may find. Any alterations or corrections made by the author should be done in a different colour from that used by the printer. Although some minor adjustments can be made at this stage it is very costly to do so and alterations should be kept to an absolute minimum and should ideally be merely a matter of correcting any misprints.

Standard correction marks   Every proof correction instruction has to be indicated by a mark in the text with a corresponding marginal mark to signify or amplify the meaning of the instruction. (Some instructions have a combined textual and marginal mark). Where several instructions occur close together in a single line, the marginal marks can be divided between the left- and right-hand margins, the order being from left- to right-hand across both margins.

A classified list of the standard marks used for copy preparation and proof correction is issued by the British Standards Institution (BS 5261C:1976). The marks are classified into three groups:

A – General
B – Deletion, insertion and substitution
C – Positioning and spacing

An example of part of the classified list for Group C is given in Figure i. An example is also given in Figure ii of a marked proof of a title page setting, together with the revised version incorporating the corrections.

Return of proofs to printer   If the printer has asked for any particular points to be clarified, or raised any queries, these must be settled by clear written instructions on the proofs.

The printer must be told whether any further pages of proofs are needed or if the manuscript is now considered to be ready for printing; subject, of course, to the final corrections being incorporated.

Bibliography

F. H. Collins: *Authors and Printers Dictionary*, Eleventh revised edition (OUP, 1973).

Copy Preparation and Proof Correction (British Standards Institution) BS5261 Part 1 1975 (reviewed and confirmed 1983) – Recommendations for preparation of typescript copy for printing. BS5261 Part 2 1976 – Specification for typographic requirements, marks for copy preparation and proof correction, proofing procedure. (BS5261C 1976 – Marks for copy preparation and proof correction – extracted from BS5261 Part 2 1976). BS3763 1976 S I Units – International System of Units.

How to Write Metric (HMSO) – A style guide for teaching and using S I Units, intended for people in trade, industry, publishing, journalism, printing and education.

NOTE: The letters M and P in the notes column indicate marks for marking-up copy and for correcting proofs respectively.

Group C   Positioning and spacing

Number	Instruction	Textual mark	Marginal mark	Notes
C1	Start new paragraph			MP
C2	Run on (no new paragraph)			MP
C3	Transpose characters or words	between characters or words, numbered when necessary		MP
C4	Transpose a number of characters or words	3 2 1	1 2 3	MP To be used when the sequence cannot be clearly indicated by the use of C3. The vertical strokes are made through the characters or words to be transposed and numbered in the correct sequence
C5	Transpose lines			MP
C6	Transpose a number of lines		——— 3 ——— 2 ——— 1	P To be used when the sequence cannot be clearly indicated by C5. Rules extend from the margin into the text with each line to be transplanted numbered in the correct sequence
C7	Centre	enclosing matter to be centred	[ ]	MP
C8	Indent			P Give the amount of the indent in the marginal mark

Figure i

Revised proof of title page setting incorporating corrections

Mediaeval CO₂

A serio/comic
history of a
century's
invention and discovery;
by "ALCHEMIST"

Magic Press
London...........1975

Marked proof of title page setting

Mediæval CO₂

by ALCHEMIST
A serio comic
HISTORY
of a
and discovery invention
century

Magic Press
London 1975

Association of Legal Secretaries; Association of Medical Secretaries, Practice Administrators and Receptionists; Association of Personal Assistants and Secretaries Ltd; European Association of Professional Secretaries; Executive Secretaries' Club; Institute of Agricultural Secretaries; Institute of Qualified Private Secretaries

All established professional bodies have their own societies, associations or institutes. These organisations set and uphold high standards of ability and conduct for their members, and they form a focal point for their profession throughout the United Kingdom and beyond. Membership is open only to those who are suitably qualified.

Details of associations open to professional secretaries are given below. It will be appreciated that membership of any of these confers a certain *cachet* upon the holder, which is not merely satisfying in itself but carries a recommendation when a secretary or personal assistant is seeking a change of job.

ASSOCIATION OF LEGAL SECRETARIES

Object

To provide an organisation for men and women of education, ability and experience who desire to qualify as legal secretaries and to secure professional status.

To do all such things as from time to time may be necessary to maintain and advance the status and interests of the profession.

To provide opportunities for contact between the members of the Association and to form branches for that purpose.

To provide a bureau for members seeking employment.

Membership Qualifications

1. Fellowship   Elections to the highest grade of membership are made annually by the Council of the Association from persons who:
(a) are over the age of twenty-five years, have been a Member for not less than five years and are in a position of responsibility in a legal office; or
(b) possess such academic qualifications or experience that election as a Fellow would be in the best interests of the Association.

2. Membership   Applicants for this corporate grade should be over the age of twenty-one and:
(a) have been an Associate Member for at least one year and have passed the qualifying examinations of the Association or obtained exemption therefrom; or
(b) have such experience and status that election as a Member would be in the best interests of the Association.

3. Associate Membership   Designed for persons who hold the Diploma for Legal Secretaries or who have obtained exemption therefrom.

4. Student Membership   Open to persons who are pursuing or who intend to pursue a course of study approved by the Association leading to the Diploma or to exemption therefrom.

Publication   Quarterly Journal *Legal Secretary*

Enquiries   To Mrs A. Ibberson, Secretary General, The Mill, Clymping, Nr Littlehampton, West Sussex BN17 5RN

ASSOCIATION OF MEDICAL SECRETARIES, PRACTICE ADMINISTRATORS AND RECEPTIONISTS

Membership ensures continued expansion and updating of knowledge at branch, national and international levels – achieved by attendance at lectures, symposia, etc, and by the exchange of ideas with colleagues in all spheres of medicine.

Qualification for membership of AMSPAR is itself a hallmark of the first-class professional in the medical secretarial field. Membership of AMSPAR, which is a widely recognised body, is increasingly influential when applying for employment.

Apart from the maintenance of high standards and principles any category of membership affords the opportunity of social and professional contact among people with common interests and understanding.

Membership Qualifications

1. **Membership**   Open to those who have been successful in the Association's Diploma examination and have spent two years in qualifying employment, ie secretarial employment in any branch of medicine, which expression shall include employment with a medical practitioner, in the public health service or in a hospital, medical research laboratory, nursing home or other medical establishment.

2. **Associateship**   Open to those who have been successful in the Diploma examination or qualified for the Certificate, Letter of Recognition or the Reception Certificate.

3. **Affiliateship**   Open to those who have been continuously employed for a period of two years in the health field.

Students are warmly welcome to partake in all Association activities while engaged on the AMSPAR course of training.

Publication   Quarterly journal *The Medical Secretary and Receptionist*

Enquiries   To The Association of Medical Secretaries, Practice Administrators and Receptionists (AMSPAR), Tavistock House North, Tavistock Square, London, WC1H 9LN

ASSOCIATION OF PERSONAL ASSISTANTS AND SECRETARIES LTD

Aims and Objectives

1. To establish the status of the qualified Personal Assistant and Secretary within the management structure.

2. To offer professional advice and formal training to all members.

3. To publish a quarterly Newsletter, 'Secretary', the definitive voice of the profession.

4. To promote recognition and acceptance of the Association within industry, commerce and the professions.

5. To endeavour to ensure the professional development and success of its members.

Membership Qualifications

1. **Honorary Fellow**   Awarded for an outstanding contribution to the work of the Association.

2. **Fellow**   Awarded to persons whose qualifications and experience are outstanding, and who have at least five years' senior secretarial experience.

3. **Member**   Awarded to persons who have successfully completed a secretarial course, and have at least three years' secretarial experience.

4. **Associate**   Awarded to students who are undertaking a course of study for a private secretary's diploma, or persons who have completed this course within the last three years.

Publication   Quarterly Newsletter

Enquiries   To The Association of Personal Assistants and Secretaries Ltd., 14 Victoria Terrace, Royal Leamington Spa, Warwickshire.

EUROPEAN ASSOCIATION OF PROFESSIONAL SECRETARIES

Aims
To be the recognised voice of the secretarial profession in Europe.
  To spread throughout Europe the fact that the executive secretary is an essential element of the management team:
    by improving the status of the secretary
    by encouraging training of secretaries to a high level both before and during career development
    by implanting the idea of the secretarial career as a profession.
To encourage secretaries to develop their potential.
To form a nucleus of highly qualified European secretaries, able to advise on secretarial development.
To provide useful European contacts for business information.
To promote European fellowship, understanding and cooperation:
    by providing a forum for the exchange of ideas and practices between all those interested in the secretarial profession
    by assisting members who wish to work in another member country
    by holding international meetings of a business and cultural nature.

Membership Qualifications
1. **Full Membership**   Open to Executive Secretaries, defined as

those who have sufficient knowledge of their chief's activities and sphere of work to be able to have a considerable amount delegated to them. They are able to make decisions, give instructions and represent the chief on business occasions. They may have a junior secretary or shorthand-typist working for them. The Executive Secretary must be able to demonstrate at least three years' experience at this level, and be willing to further the aims of the Association.

Full Membership is also open to National Secretarial Associations. The Chief Executive Officers of National Secretarial Associations are *ex officio* members of EAPS during their term of office.

2. **Affiliate Membership**   Open to those interested in the efficient functioning of secretarial services, whether individually or on an organisational or corporate basis.

Publication   *EAPS Brief,* published four times a year

Head Office   Maison de l'Europe, Hôtel de Coulanges, 35/37 rue des Francs-Bourgeois, 75004 Paris

Enquiries (UK)   To the Membership Secretary, EAPS UK, 9–11 Kensington High Street, London W8 5NP. Telephone 01-937 9801. Telex 267009 METMAK G

EXECUTIVE SECRETARIES CLUB

Aims
To help secretaries achieve recognition as skilled members of the management team.
To achieve a realistic career structure for secretaries with appropriate salary levels and opportunities for promotion.

Membership Qualifications

1. **Full Membership**   Open to those who are executive secretaries, PAs and top management secretaries with at least five years' experience.

Meetings/functions are held three or four times a year.

Enquiries   To the Secretariat, 34 Chestnut Avenue, Gosfield, Nr Halstead, Essex CO9 1TD

INSTITUTE OF AGRICULTURAL SECRETARIES

Aims and Objectives

To assist and advise on education, training, research and all matters connected with the agricultural secretarial service:

To help the new entrant to the profession.

To help the practising secretary.

To help the agricultural industry.

To create a well informed public opinion on the subject of agricultural secretaryship and by its efficiency and integrity to earn a lasting and worthwhile place in the development of a modern agricultural industry.

Membership Qualifications

1. Fellowship   May be conferred by the Council of Management.

2. Associateship   By passing the Institute's internal examination.

3. Licentiateship   A licentiate must have:

a) successfully completed a two-year course and passed the BTEC National Diploma for Agricultural Secretaries or Scottish equivalent or the NCFS for Farm Secretaries, or passed such other examination for Agricultural Secretaries as the Council may approve.

b) spent not less than three years in qualifying employment after the age of 18 years.

c) be engaged in an acceptable ancillary industry.

There is a minimum age of 20 years for this grade.

4. Studentship   A student must be:

a) on a course recognised by the Institute at an Agricultural College, but not yet qualified.

b) engaged in qualifying employment in the agricultural industry.

c) under the age of 20 years.

Publications   Monthly Bulletin; Quarterly Newsletter.

Enquiries   To Mrs A Dymond, Secretary, NAC Stoneleigh, Kenilworth, Warwickshire, CV8 2LZ. Telephone Coventry (0203) 20623

INSTITUTE OF QUALIFIED PRIVATE SECRETARIES

Aims and Objectives
To establish the status of the qualified private secretary.

To obtain national recognition of the London Chamber of Commerce Private and Executive Secretary's Diploma, and any other such qualifications as the Council of the Institute may feel to have a like standard.

To stimulate the interest of employers in the Diploma or other recognised qualifications for membership of the Institute.

To seek the co-operation of employers and teaching staffs in encouraging their personnel and students to train for the Diploma or other recognised qualifications for membership of the Institute.

To offer advice and guidance to those wishing to train for a career as a private secretary.

To provide members with information on appropriate professional matters.

To promote a free exchange of ideas, opinions and experiences among members by organising formal and informal meetings.

Membership Qualifications

1. Full Membership   Open to:
(a) Holders of the London Chamber of Commerce Private and Executive Secretary's Diploma.

(b) Holders of qualifications comparable to the Diploma and approved by the Council of the Institute.

2. Associate Membership   Open to:
(a) Holders of the London Chamber of Commerce Private Secretary's Certificate.

(b) Holders of comparable qualifications as approved by the Council of the Institute.

3. Country Membership   Available to any member who is no longer in full-time employment.

4. Student Membership   Available to any person studying for the London Chamber of Commerce Private and Executive Secretary's Diploma or Certificate.

Publication   The IQPS Journal, published twice a year, is designed to provide an interchange of ideas, information and comment between members and the Council of the Institute.

Enquiries   To Assistant Secretary, 126 Farnham Road, Slough, Berks SL1 4XA

12 PUBLIC SPEAKING

> *Self-confidence; objectives; constructing*
> *your speech; summarising; delivery;*
> *reading a paper; question time; intro-*
> *ducing a speaker; thanking a speaker*

To be able to speak confidently and well in public, or introduce another speaker and publicly thank him afterwards, is a very great asset to anyone in today's world of business, and it is well worth while taking the necessary trouble to acquire it.

At the outset, however, let us dispel the popular image of a public speaker. The impression that probably comes to mind is that of an impressive figure, immaculately and formally dressed, holding forth from the platform of a large hall and speaking with measured and authoritative tones to a vast audience, each member of which hangs on his every word. This is only one side of the picture and in any case is not a very realistic one.

A more typical situation consists of someone talking to a group of people sitting around a boardroom table, giving a brief after-dinner address, or making a speech before opening a new hospital wing; examples can be endless. The common factor is that one person has something to say to a small or a large number of other people.

The setting may be formal or informal. The speaker may know the audience or they may all be strangers to him. However, it is most unlikely that any truly successful speech is ever an 'off the cuff' affair; it needs careful preparation beforehand. We are not at the moment discussing impromptu occasions.

SELF-CONFIDENCE

There need be nothing really alarming about the idea of speaking in public. If the idea seems terrifying at first, consider carefully what it is that appears frightening. You would not have been asked to speak if someone had not thought you were perfectly capable of doing so. If this is something that you have never done before, remember that there has to be a first time and that you may even enjoy it.

You always take care with your appearance, so there is no difficulty here. You know your subject or you would not have been asked to speak about it, and the audience are interested to hear what you have to say, or they would not be there. All that is needed is a certain amount of self-confidence, and with good preparation you know you can be a success.

OBJECTIVES

There are several ways to approach public speaking, and you will need to decide on your own particular goal before you can map out your route. The most important first step, therefore, is to clarify the reasons for your talk and know what result you wish to achieve. You will find that your talk will fall into one or more of the following broad categories:

> to give people information of some kind
> to air a problem and offer a solution or choice of solutions
> to bring people round to a particular point of view, which in some circumstances will lead to a decision on some kind of recommended action
> to amuse or entertain.

Depending on circumstances, visual aids can be of help, such as slides or an overhead projector, a demonstration model or an exhibit of some kind, which will give added interest.

To give information   This kind of talk requires a 'sequence', a time sequence for instance. This would come quite naturally if your talk were to be about some historical character. You would start by saying when and where he was born and then follow his career as the years passed.

If you are giving a 'how to do it' talk, such as 'How to prune an apple tree' you would start with what should be done first, then take the next step, and so on. An account of a journey would have a built-in time sequence, so would a talk about a firm's production record and the future policies to be based on it. It is usually not too difficult to find some sequence associated with the subject and to link up the different parts of your talk so that each idea flows naturally on to the next and your audience follows the theme through with you.

To resolve a problem   It is necessary to make quite clear at the outset the nature of the problem, how it started and the effect it is having. You might forecast what you think will happen if the problem is not solved. Then you can explain any suggestions that have been made to deal with the difficulty, what you see as the best course to take, the reasons why such a particular course should be taken and the advantages to be gained.

To persuade or convince   If your audience has to be won over, be as persuasive as possible, bringing in good reasons that they will be able to understand, showing why your choice of policy is the right one. This is where good preparation beforehand is particularly valuable.

If you expect there to be opposition to your ideas, anticipate the objections beforehand. Think of all the counter-reasons there may be, and put the other side of the question before such objections are even raised. If you include such sentences as 'You may say that the new computer will be too costly, but . . .' and proceed to show that it will really be an economy, or 'If you think that unemployment figures will go up because of this plan, I can show you that . . .' and prove the opposite, then you will cut the ground from under the opposition's feet before they have time to ask a single awkward question.

If you want to influence people to take some particular action you must convince them that there are good reasons for it. Explain how you see what the results will be. 'If we organise the Swimming Gala on the lines put forward, the expenses will be far outweighed by the proceeds and the Swimming Club will benefit enormously.' 'If we reorganise our staff selection procedures on these new recommendations we shall find ourselves with a much higher calibre of new recruits.' 'Vote for us and the first thing we will do when in power is to build you the recreation centre you need.' An excellent example of this kind of thing was Sir Winston Churchill's 'Give us the tools and we will finish the job'.

If possible bring in examples of how similar successful action was taken elsewhere. 'When the Town Hall organised a Swimming Gala two years ago on these lines it made a huge profit', the implication being that what other people can do well can also be done by your audience. You should have them all agreeing with you so whole-heartedly that they may well start cheering and saying 'When can we start?'

After a talk intended to inform or persuade it is a good idea to reserve one or two minutes at the end, to recap and sum up before coming to your conclusion. A short summary is a helpful winding-up procedure as well as being a reminder to your hearers of the main points.

To amuse or entertain   A talk of this kind, on the lines of an after-dinner speech, has to be happy and entertaining, but guard against any temptation to go on for too long. Collect a few funny (but never risqué) stories or anecdotes beforehand to use. Avoid any reference to politics, religion or racism. Bring in subjects to which your audience can relate, for example personal situations and problems that are common to everyone.

If you are to thank someone, or propose a toast to a particular person, do not omit to finish by actually doing it.

Ten minutes is usually enough for an after-dinner speech, especially if others also are speaking.

CONSTRUCTING YOUR SPEECH

When you have decided on the treatment of your subject, note down the main headings and marshall them into logical follow-through order. Then write out your whole speech, word for word. This will be time-consuming and will seem especially so if you are not used to it, but nevertheless it has to be done.

Not only does your speech have to have a clear objective, it must also have a definite 'shape'; a beginning, a middle and an end. Good speakers also pay careful attention to vocabulary and allocation of time.

Introduction   A good opening is very important, the speaker should catch the attention of the audience from the very first. If you feel that it is a compliment or an honour to be asked to talk to them, say so. There is nothing fulsome about doing this, it is a courtesy and it will be appreciated. Try to follow with an interesting statement, a question to be answered or, if the occasion is a light social one, an appropriate amusing story. A quotation is also a good starting point if you can select one that will lead you into your theme.

Conclusion   At the end of your talk, come to a definite finish. If you have made a neat summary of your main points you will then be able to conclude with a recommendation or solution, put clearly and firmly. If you are proposing a toast you will finish with the name of the person concerned. At all events, whatever the kind of talk you are giving, never tail off lamely but end on an emphatic and decisive note.

Vocabulary   When speaking to any audience bear in mind the type of people to whom you are talking and choose your words accordingly. A speaker giving a speech about a new technological breakthrough to a group of scientists would use technical terms, knowing that his audience would understand them; when giving a talk on the same subject to a group of school-children he would express himself very differently. A speaker must never talk down to his hearers, but it is just as much a fault to talk above their heads, assuming an expertise that they probably do not have.

Use the word 'we' rather than 'I' whenever possible, and remember that you must talk naturally, not pontificate.

Timing   You will probably have been told beforehand how long you should be speaking. If no-one has given you a time limit you will have to make your own estimation. Fifteen minutes may be a reasonable time for your subject, with perhaps an allocation of a few minutes' additional time for questions afterwards. Anything over twenty minutes without a break requires an experienced speaker, and even then he may be taxing the audience. It is quite possible for a good speaker to talk for half an hour and make his hearers feel it all went by in a flash, but if you are in this category you do not need to read this chapter.

Shut yourself away somewhere where you will not be interrupted and read your draft speech right through to yourself, at the pace you will deliver it, being careful not to go too quickly. Most people's normal conversational style tends to be fast and uneven. To talk to a group of people in a formal situation it is necessary to slow down slightly, to be very distinct, and also to use the technique of pausing from time to time. Time your reading, exactly, with a stop-watch.

Pausing   To pause occasionally need not be an indication that you have forgotten what you were going to say next. It is an attention-getting ploy and can keep the audience mentally cliff-hanging, anxiously waiting for what is coming. Mark a few strategic places where you can make a 'pregnant pause'. Lead up to a selected point and pause deliberately before delivering your special emphasis or punch line. Ask a rhetorical question and then wait for a second or two before continuing. Alternatively, give a firm statement and pause for the audience to absorb it. Many a good point has been thrown away because the speaker has raced on too quickly, leaving no time for his words to sink in. An audience becomes tired when following rapid and continuous speech and a tired audience is a bored one and a bored one gets restless and you will have lost them; then it is difficult to re-establish any rapport.

Trimming   You will probably find to your surprise that your trial run has taken too long. It is then necessary to prune it carefully, tightening up the sentence construction and altering some of the words to give greater emphasis or clarity. Read it through again, retiming it, and work in this way until your talk is about the right length when spoken at a pace that is not too fast for your audience, and allows an extra second or two here and there for those pregnant pauses for dramatic effect.

If you have access to a tape or cassette recorder it is a great help to hear your own speech when you have finalised it and trimmed it down to the right length. Be interested in your own talk, read the finished version to the recorder, get a little vitality and enthusiasm into your voice, and play it back. You may wish to re-record if you find there are stresses or intonations you feel should be altered. A recording of this kind is of great help in recalling your words when you are speaking later and can only refer to brief notes.

It is a good idea to have some material in reserve, just in case, in spite of all your careful planning, you find yourself – on the actual occasion – coming to your conclusion and there is still a little time over.

SUMMARISING

It is vitally important to realise that you should neither read your speech word by word, nor learn it by heart. Your talk must sound spontaneous and if you 'learn your words' there is great danger of its sounding stilted. You must appear to be thinking your way through your speech and it will not sound like this unless that is actually what you *are* doing. However, you will need a few notes to hold in your hand, to keep you from drying up and to help you to keep your themes in the right order. So go through your written out speech again, underline the vital key words, and rewrite it as a series of very short summaries of each theme or paragraph, following each other in natural sequence.

Reminder cards   At this stage, when summarised paragraphs are enough to bring to your mind the full substance of your talk, reduce them still further to a few clear headings on a card. A postcard is suitable, something smaller would be even better. You will probably need several of these and they can be held unobtrusively in the hand; it does not matter that you will be seen to refer to your notes. While giving your talk you can look down occasionally at your card, where the cue words and titles are written in bold lettering so that you can read them at a glance, and you will carry on with your speech without interruption, keeping to the logical sequence you worked out in the first place, and moving the top card to the back of the 'pack' as you go.

In this way you will not leave out anything and at the same time will be talking spontaneously, because you now know your theme thoroughly and at no time did you learn anything slavishly by heart to the point where it sounds dull and mechanical.

DELIVERY

Look at the members of your audience. They are the ones to whom you are speaking, not the ceiling or the windows or the back of the hall. Make contact with them through your eyes. Sometimes you can pick out someone by name, for instance you might smile at someone you know in the front row and say 'Bill will remember when . . .' or 'Jane will agree with me when I say that . . .'. Of course this depends on the circumstances of your talk and a quick assessment of who is in the audience.

Incidentally, never apologise – it is a sign of weakness in a speaker. The only exception to this would be an occasion when you were prevented from arriving on time and had to keep an audience waiting.

At all costs do not separate yourself from your hearers by an off-hand manner, for you do not wish to give the impression that you dislike talking to them. If you believe in what you are saying, can forget yourself and just concentrate on getting the message over, you will generate a warmth that your audience will feel and they will respond with attention and friendliness.

Stand easily without fidgeting. We have all seen speakers who jingle money or keys in their pockets, who pace up and down like caged leopards, who rub their noses and adjust their clothes. Relax and stand naturally, keeping movements quiet and controlled. Speak out clearly and confidently.

Smile. Enjoy yourself. You too can be a successful speaker.

READING A PAPER

When a speech is to be reported in the press or as part of a public relations exercise, it may be issued beforehand in the form of a press release or printed handout to news and publicity agencies. This enables them to set up their presses in plenty of time for prompt publication after the speech has actually been delivered. It is therefore essential that when the speech is made it corresponds exactly word for word with the issued printout. In this case the speech *has* to be read.

It may also be advisable to read out information containing detailed or complex facts and figures, when it would be unsafe for a speaker to rely only on memory.

With practice a reader will find that an occasional glance at printed words, which have been pre-rehearsed and underlined at key points, will enable him to keep good 'eye contact' with his audience without having to look continuously at the print he is reading.

QUESTION TIME

If question time after a talk does not naturally come to a stop within its allotted space, it is not too difficult for the chairman, or whoever has introduced the speaker, to bring it to a close by looking at his watch and saying firmly and distinctly 'I think we have time for just one more question'. He can then select someone with a question to ask, and bring the session to an end after the answer has been given by pointing out that there is regrettably no more time available. The 'Thank you' formula can then be brought in to wind up the proceedings.

INTRODUCING A SPEAKER

If you have ever listened to anyone introducing a speaker you will have noticed that the name is usually left until last. This is a good principle and worth following. There is a useful basic formula for these occasions, as in the following example:

'Ladies and Gentlemen, we are very fortunate to have with us this afternoon someone whose knowledge and experience of his subject is very wide indeed. He is going to tell us about recent developments in microprocessors.

For the past five years he has been on the staff of the Experimental Unit of the Imperial Micro-Processing Centre and has led the research team there. He is the author of those two well-known books *Smaller and Smaller* and *The Silicon File*. Ladies and Gentlemen, I have great pleasure in introducing . . .' and then give his name, and sit down. Look at him and smile and start clapping, and the audience will follow your lead and your speaker will then stand up and begin.

You have thus briefly identified the speaker's qualifications to speak, the subject of the talk and his name, at the same time giving the audience a minute or two to settle down quietly in anticipation.

THANKING A SPEAKER

Mr Tom Pinder, consultant in spoken and written communications, sets out the following useful strategic plan for thanking a speaker:

Listen carefully while he is speaking, have a pad of paper handy. Soon he will say something interesting on which you can comment. Write it down. When the time comes to thank him, rise to your feet and say 'Ladies and Gentlemen, I was very interested (or amused or surprised etc) to hear our speaker say (read out whatever it was in its exact words). This makes me think (or realise etc) . . .' and develop a warm and friendly comment. 'Thank you (and give the speaker's name and look at him) for a most delightful (or entertaining, interesting etc) talk'. Look at him and smile and start the clapping.

Bibliography
R. S. Lawrence: *Guide to Speaking in Public* (Pan, 1972).
Bartlett: *Familiar Quotations* (Macmillan Ltd., 1985).
Ivor Spencer: *Speeches and Toasts* (Ward Lock Ltd., 1980).
Clive T. Goodworth: *Effective Speaking and Presentation for the Company Executive* (Business Books Ltd., Hutchinson Publishing Group, 1980).

13 READING THE NEWSPAPERS

*Why you should read the newspapers;
what is in them; where to find different
topics; when do the newspapers appear?
how do they affect the businessman?*

To read an intelligent newspaper regularly is, in effect, to do one's business homework. From early schooldays it is all too apparent that people who do their homework get on better than those who neglect it, and there is no exception to this principle in later years.

WHY SHOULD YOU READ THE NEWSPAPERS?

For several very good reasons:

1. To keep abreast and informed about what is currently going on in business, in the City, in the country, in the world.
2. To develop a political awareness; to know what is going on in government, who has made a speech in Parliament, on what subject and from which angle, how the debate in the House of Commons went yesterday; to be able to follow political trends.
3. To be aware of recent developments in the arts, eg theatres, concerts and ballet, films and exhibitions.
4. To know about current sporting fixtures.
5. To find information about selected recent events (local, country-wide or international).
6. To develop your own character and personality, general know-ledge and opinions, by following the course of current affairs and so becoming aware of your own place and your firm's place in the world around you.

WHAT IS IN THE NEWSPAPERS AND WHAT DO THEY OFFER?

A typical list of contents of a general range of daily or weekly newspapers would contain the following:

Home news There will be the continuous news, the kind that goes on from day to day (politics, social and industrial topics, the weather, for example) and the 'one off' occasions that are only significant if reported at once (eg a bank raid, an air or rail accident, a rescue story). These immediate and single incident events, even if they have only a twenty-four hour interest, tell us as much about the times we live in as the daily routine events of longer term interest.

Foreign news   Knowledge of what is going on abroad is vital to any businessman, even if the impact on home affairs is not immediate. In this section will be reported political upheavals in foreign governments, reforms and changes, trade negotiations, news of commodities and supplies (eg oil and gold, which are of particular international importance); delegations and visits to and by national dignatories, human stories, natural disasters, discoveries and inventions, developments and setbacks, the conditions in which people live and work in all parts of the world.

The Arts   News of current developments, recent publications of books and recordings, reviews of exhibitions, concerts, theatres and films. Criticisms, comparisons, trends and influences in all these activities.

City and financial information   Stock Exchange prices, the money market, advice on investments, news of company developments, closures, mergers and new companies; exports and imports; banking and insurance matters, trade figures of all kinds.

Parliamentary news   The reporting of recent debates and speeches, news of election campaigns, political conferences, new legislation.

The leader or editorial   This is the Editor's own article, giving an opinion on questions of immediate importance to readers.

Women's pages   Features and articles on, for instance, cookery, shopping, household matters, children, fashion.

Letters from readers   Selected letters on subjects of topical interest, set out in a Correspondence section.

Sporting events   Reports, scores, forecasts, results, form, betting odds; special reporting of seasonal events, eg Wimbledon, Goodwood, Cowes etc.

Special subjects   Specialised articles, usually according to the day of the week, for instance news about auctions and salerooms on Wednesdays, careers on Thursdays, gardening on Saturdays. Other subjects featured could be the property market, education, holidays and travel.

Court and social column   Some papers set out the events at which Royalty will be present, eg an investiture, state visit, attendance at a charitable function.

Obituaries   Of distinguished personalities.

Town Diary or Gossip columns   This section contains news about well-known personalities in the public eye.

Leisure section   Many papers publish a crossword puzzle, cartoons or comic strips, and horoscopes, for the amusement of readers.

Births, marriages and deaths   Announcements can be placed in these columns on payment of a fee.

Entertainment guide   Announcements of current theatre productions, films and exhibitions.

Television and radio   Programmes for the day.

Weather forecast and reports

Advertisements   Displayed and classified advertisements of all kinds.

A newspaper does not only offer the day's news, it will also help to build up an overall view of all kinds of events in the civil, business and social life of the nation.

Political opinions   The national newspapers differ in their political style, some more strongly than others (see list under section on When do the papers appear?).

Readers usually select a paper which suits their own political point of view, and in consequence there is a danger that assumptions may be made by the reader that the news as reported in any one particular paper is a comprehensive and balanced account of events when it is just possible that a faint bias has crept in. An account of a factory strike, for instance, may be reported in one paper as an unfair move against a management which has done everything possible to pay its workers a fair wage, to the limit of the resources available. Another paper may report the same event as a justified revolt by men who are exploited by being made to work long hours at difficult jobs for which they are underpaid. Both reports may be perfectly true, but the impressions given may be very different in the way they enlist the reader's sympathy.

Keep an open mind when reading any newspaper, and try to see all the implications behind the reporting. In most cases, of course, news is reported in a balanced way, fairly and responsibly, and as fully as space permits.

It is in the leading article, or editorial, written from the Editor's standpoint, that the political trend of a paper shows most clearly. These regular articles are, however, serious and responsible, and usually give a very clear and understanding analysis of events, with well-informed judgements and opinions.

Style and Layout   It is immediately obvious to anyone shopping for a newspaper that there are sharp differences in appearance. The tabloid papers are set out in a way that catches the eye immediately; they have their headlines printed in a dramatic style, often with huge letters, and they frequently make great use of the more sensational types of publicity photographs. The news reporting is more concerned with the home and personal scene and less with problems of international importance. The journalistic style is bright and trendy. The editorial policy is as much to amuse as to inform. There will be plenty of news of pop stars and interviews with showbusiness personalities, with gossip features and competitions for the family.

By contrast the more authoritative newspapers printing a wide range of 'hard' news will rely on their traditional straightforward treatment of material and accuracy of content to attract and keep their reading public. They contain a greater amount of informative reading matter and fewer photographs and illustrations than the tabloids.

WHERE DO YOU FIND THE DIFFERENT TOPICS?

The main news on any topic is generally to be found on the front page. However, as the front page has only a limited amount of available space, the news, apart from that on page 1, is usually grouped into sections. Home news will be printed on its own two or three pages, foreign news all together in the same way and so on. The sports news, the financial pages, etc., will be printed each in their own section.

By reading one particular paper for several days running (you cannot get to know a paper by reading it for one day only and then choosing another one) you will be able to locate the different sections quite rapidly without having to use the summarised index, which is usually to be found on the front page.

Various editions of the same newspaper may differ slightly in content or emphasis. Several editions of each issue will be printed and the earliest editions may print only brief news of an event which can be reported more fully in the later editions. If you are able to buy an early edition of an evening paper and also a late-night edition of the same paper on the same date it should be interesting to compare and contrast the variations in content and emphasis. An item reported only briefly early in the day, which rapidly develops in interest, may be given much more detailed reportage in the latest printing, causing less important items to be dropped to make room for it. National newspapers, printed at the same time but in different parts of the country (London, Manchester, Edinburgh), may also differ in shades of emphasis according to the interests of their local readers.

WHEN DO THE NEWSPAPERS APPEAR?

Daily papers

The Times   Generally reputed to be the most influential United Kingdom national newspaper, of considerable stature in the newspaper world, nationally and internationally. A reliable and quality newspaper of independent political outlook. This paper regularly publishes a useful 'Business Services Guide' page.

The *Daily Telegraph*   Serious news reporting, informative and not sensational, thorough and accurate, with a tradition of soundness and reliability. Has a reputation of being a close second to *The Times*. Independent.

The *Guardian*   Good style of reporting, serious news coverage, informative and responsible. Liberal in outlook.

Financial Times   The businessman's newspaper; specialises in reports and features on all matters affecting finance in the UK and abroad (industry, management, international trade, the Stock Exchange etc). Independent.

Daily Express   Popular family paper, bright attractive style of reporting, makes life out to be dramatic and exciting. Independent Conservative in policy.

Daily Mail   Independent Conservative paper, sound and entertaining, but quieter in style than the *Daily Express*.

Daily Mirror   Left-wing Labour newspaper, directed at the man in the street, personal and home problems being given more priority than international matters. Intended to amuse as well as inform.

The *Sun*   Popular journalism with a leaning towards the trendy lighthearted side of life – showbusiness and sports news, cartoons, studio photographs, etc. Conservative outlook.

The *Daily Star*   Independent Conservative tabloid, very similar to the *Sun*.

Today   Seven days a week. Independent.

Evening paper

The *London Standard*   A family paper, widely read for its classified advertisement content as well as for the latest news reports.

Sunday papers
As these are intended for more leisurely reading than the dailies they contain considerably more material, some having a special review or arts section and also a colour supplement of general interest (eg the *Observer,* the *Sunday Times, Sunday Telegraph* and *Sunday Express*). These supplements have a very high standard of photography and presentation. The papers carry full reportage of the week's events, with background articles, reviews, supplementary material of all kinds, features on leisure occupations, travel, gardening, books and music, sports and entertainment, as well as classified and general advertisements of all kinds.

The *Sunday Times*　　Issued by *The Times* syndicate.
Sunday Telegraph　　Independent.
Sunday Express　　Independent Conservative.
The Observer　　Independent.
News of the World　　Independent; popular and gossipy style.
Mail on Sunday　　*Daily Mail* syndicate.
Sunday People　　Left-wing Labour.
Sunday Mirror　　Popular journalism, left-wing Labour.

Provincial papers　　These are published for the major towns and rural areas, some having a large circulation (over 100,000 copies), others not so widely distributed, with perhaps only half as many in circulation figures. There is a considerable number of daily and weekly provincial papers and these have the same kind of contents list as the national dailies, but with a definite preference for things of purely local interest.

The provincial paper will be the place to look for news from the Town Halls and local Councils, whose affairs will be covered in some detail. Here will be found reports from the local Courts, notices from local sports and social clubs, educational matters concerning schools in the area, reviews of local festivals and entertainments, requests for planning permission on local sites, and advertisements of all kinds concerning the business and social life of the area.

Other papers and journals　　Other publications, such as periodicals and magazines, trade and professional journals, religious papers etc., as well as reporting and news agencies in London, can all be found listed in the current edition of Whitaker's Almanack.

HOW DO THE NEWSPAPERS AFFECT THE BUSINESSMAN?

If a businessman, or his secretary, is not aware of the conditions and influences around him in trade and industry, or if he is aware but does not fully understand them, he will not be likely to prosper or even survive in the business jungle. To be aware of events and understand their significance is to be able to plan and work out a business strategy to the best possible advantage.

Also when a question is asked, even in quite casual conversation in the office, about a matter of current interest, it does not improve anyone's reputation if he does not know the answer. For instance, could you reply to any of the following questions, or could you find the answers quickly?

Who is the Chancellor of the Exchequer?

Is the new play at the Haymarket worth seeing?

What was the result of the most recent by-election? Was there a big majority?

What is the latest price of Pneumatic Trainrails?

What is the latest Test score?

Who won the 3.30 yesterday at Newmarket?

What is the weather like in Venice?

No good secretary need ever say 'I don't know' to anything. The nearest she should ever come to it is 'I'm not sure, but it won't take me a minute to find out' – and then to do so.

Daily study   Before anyone can do justice to a particular newspaper, or decide whether it is worth taking regularly, it should be studied for several consecutive issues. Over a period you will be able to get the feel of any particular type of newspaper, and be able to assess its content. Explore the market before you settle on the most suitable paper for you and your interests.

Select an ongoing subject   As part of the process of selecting a paper for regular reading, choose one particular continuous subject to follow. Perhaps there is an election being fought, an interesting journey being undertaken, an industrial dispute emerging. Pursue the subject carefully from day to day, think of it as a serial story, and you will be surprised how, with a little concentration, the subject increases in interest. Further, you may find yourself able to anticipate what will happen next, and there is much satisfaction in forecasting events and eventually finding yourself proved to be right.

Compare treatment and style   As a separate exercise, select a particular item of news and see how it is reported in several different daily papers. This will give an interesting insight into the varied degrees of priority afforded by different editors to the same subject, the variety in journalistic style and the sensationalism or otherwise of the headlines and general treatment.

Assess the business background   The papers may seem to be full of things very remote from your own world, but you and your firm may be more affected than at first appears. Will the troubled situation abroad alter the prospects of next year's export drive? Will the next budget be likely to affect your firm's profits? What will your company do if the projected strike becomes a reality? Will the recent disaster overseas make any difference to the expected imports deliveries? Will the change in market trends mean that your firm's consumer goods need to be adapted or updated? Read your newspaper from the business angle, as well as from the viewpoint of purely human interest.

As well as following the everyday news it is useful to keep track of the activities of business colleagues, rival firms, and others in peripheral or associated lines of business; customer demands; trade outlets; changes in manufacturing materials; trends in your firm's trade or profession – in fact to pay special attention to anything that affects the background to business. You may be surprised to find how much there is.

It can be seen that intelligent reading of a good newspaper will forearm a businessman to a considerable extent by helping him in planning ahead, and the good executive secretary will also make a point of keeping up with current news and opinions.

A EUROPEAN DAILY NEWSPAPER

The *Wall Street Journal/Europe* is the European edition of the American-based *Wall Street Journal*. This is edited in Brussels by the Dow Jones publishing organisation and is available throughout Europe on the morning of publication. It is a distinctly 'European' paper, although it also carries material from American and Asian journals. It contains hard news, financial facts and figures, commercial information, political analysis and a variety of business and general news, advertisements and features.

FUTURE PUBLICATIONS
At the time of going to press plans are being made to launch several other daily and Sunday papers, as well as a new evening paper. It remains to be seen whether any of these will actually materialise, but in any case it is useful to inspect newsagents' shelves from time to time, to keep up to date with any new productions.

14 RECORD KEEPING AND STORAGE OF INFORMATION

The case for replanning; storage space; retrieval; disposal; method of reorganisation; centralised or departmental records; methods of indexing; card indexing; cross-referencing; 'miscellaneous' file; continuity of control; microfilm, microfiche and comfiche; stocktaking; stock records in the office; checking and overhaul

THE CASE FOR REPLANNING

Modern filing systems range between two extremes. At one end of the scale is the comparatively small personalised system, suitable for the immediate needs of a secretary and her chief, or for a department with a limited number of staff. At the other end are found the enormous installations catering for the records of whole sections of industry, such as the automated-retrieval computer-controlled centralised schemes which cater for licensing departments, insurance, banking, marketing, warehousing, the health services and many other concerns with country-wide records which continually increase in numbers. (See also section on automated filing under Electronic Offices.) It is in the more personal and departmental field of filing that problems are most likely to arise for the executive secretary.

In any busy office concerned with record-keeping it will be found that all systems grow. A familiar and well-tried system may eventually need modernisation and expansion. Alternatively, a secretary in a new post may find that she has inherited an inadequate system from her predecessor. In either case the time taken in replanning and redesigning will be well spent, in order to get the best possible results from reorganisation.

Three basic essentials that any secretary must have in her record-keeping system are:

1. Adequate and suitable storage space, as records must be kept clean, tidy, undamaged and secure. Confidentiality and security must be ensured where required.
2. Easy retrieval, as records must be simple to locate and files must be capable of being taken out and replaced easily and quickly.

3. Orderly disposal. Out of date records should be stored separately, away from the current files, for as long as they may be needed, and finally taken out of the system altogether.

Before taking any action to improve an existing system, a thorough survey of the present state of affairs should be made, and the problems identified and listed. These are likely to include:

> overcrowded or unsuitable types of shelves and cabinets
> over-full folders and boxes
> inaccessible files and folders
> inadequate or out of date indexing and listing systems
> lost or mislaid files.

The answers to the following queries will also influence any replanning:

1. Which section of the system is used most frequently, and by whom?
2. What variety of types and sizes of papers and other articles are to be stored?
3. Will new cabinets be necessary or will rearrangement of the existing ones give enough storage space of the right kind?
4. How much extra space is needed for future short-term or long-term expansion?
5. How much floor or wall space can be spared for storage facilities?

When you have your firm's official permission to go ahead with replanning and redesign, as many catalogues of up-to-date equipment as possible should be consulted and the new requirements listed, with prices, not omitting allowances for trade discount and any available deductions for bulk buying. Information about the latest storage ideas on the market can be found in any of the numerous office equipment journals which are now published regularly, and the Yellow Pages will also list office equipment specialists and suppliers in your district. If you can get to any of the excellent business exhibitions which are held from time to time in various parts of the country, this would be an excellent way of seeing for yourself what is available and what would best suit your particular office needs. Everywhere now there are firms which specialise in good neat co-ordinated storage systems, with streamlined units in cheerful colours, sophisticated and safe, which provide suitable accommodation and quick easy retrieval of every kind of item.

Makes and prices should be carefully compared before a final choice is made, the cheapest articles are not always the most durable; on the other hand, prestige goods are not always necessary.

Your project for modernisation should be submitted to the appropriate responsible authority, with an estimation of costs, and acceptance obtained from the finance department concerned before any goods are ordered. Dealers will advise on availability and delivery periods.

Plan comprehensively and in some detail. Remember that as well as space for basic office paperwork there will certainly be storage required for some or all of the following:

Art work and photographs, plans, diagrams and large working drawings. These may require hanging racks arranged laterally, perhaps with sliding fitments and hanging pockets or clips for suspension. Deep expandable pockets can be obtained, to take bulky as well as sizeable loads. Alternatively, flat shallow drawers may be acceptable.

Catalogues, journals and miscellaneous bulky documents. These may require special shelves and cupboards; legal papers may best be kept in lockable deed boxes. Cabinets can be open-fronted, or with hinged or folding doors or roller-blind fronts, lockable and/or fire-resistant, and with fixed or pull-out shelves. A small set of books or journals could alternatively be kept in a mobile filing trolley.

Tapes, discs and cassettes, rolls of film, cartridges and cards in special jackets or aperture frames. Boxes, racks and drawers of all kinds have been specially designed for all these articles by office equipment firms, with corresponding labels and indexing systems to facilitate rapid location of the items required.

Diskettes. These can be kept in neat pockets and folders in hinged storage binders, on rotary stands, wall stands or desk units.

Microfilm and microfiches. These should be stored in flat pockets and panels, in cases or racks, in cabinets, on rotary stands of pockets, or in card-drawers and trays. (One retailer has claimed that 3,000 microfilmed documents can be stored in a box four inches square by one inch deep.)

Computer printouts. These pose a particularly bulky problem, but can be neatly kept in specially devised binders on suspension racks or in deep drawers.

STORAGE SPACE

Shelves and wall units   Shelves should not be so high up that the shortest members of staff cannot easily reach them, nor uncomfortably close to the floor. Also they should not be arranged too far apart vertically, as this wastes valuable wall-space, but should relate to the height of the articles for which they are intended. Box files, books, magazines and journals should be ranged standing up, side by side, not laid flat on top of each other, even if it is possible to stack more on the shelf in this way.

Apart from the traditional types of cupboards and cabinets, there are also adjustable and mobile wall units of all sizes and types, specially designed for a variety of special needs.

For storage of records in a comparatively small area, a fixed automated retrieval system could be considered, with a rotary arrangement of shelves or racks. The touch of a button brings a stack of shelves, on a continuous vertical belt, moving down to the required position for easy selection. The press of another button, index-coded, will bring the individual file required across to the retrieval point. Another system incorporates shelves or racks in a rigid upright framework, which can be power-assisted to glide, as a whole unit, over rails set in the floor. Two or more frames of shelves can therefore be kept packed closely together when not being used, but still be easily and smoothly moved apart when a file is to be taken out. These innovations make the most of a limited floor space. Another contemporary storage system has a push-button retrieval process, linked with a desk-top visual display unit, which will bring into view on a screen the selected information for reference, without the actual document having to be produced.

Floor space, cabinets   In most smaller offices the system of storing papers in flat folders or binders within a suspended pocket in a drawer or rack is still the most commonly used method, the folders being easily extracted and replaced by hand. The 'vertical' system of cabinets, with deep drawers that have to be pulled out forwards towards the user, occupies the most floor space. The same amount of papers within a 'lateral' system could be kept on about two-thirds of this area, because lateral folder-pockets are suspended with their ends towards the front of the open cabinet, so that drawers are unnecessary and therefore less space has to be allowed in front of the shelves for access.

Confidentiality   Confidential files should be kept in locked cabinets, and only selected responsible members of staff should have keys (a spare key being kept at the bank for emergencies). When confidential files become out of date they should still be treated as confidential, kept in a secure area and only accessible to authorised staff.

RETRIEVAL

If retrieval is to be quick and efficient the following principles should be noted:

1. The record system should be situated near to the users.
2. The storage equipment must be suited to the contents.

3. Members of staff should be requested to return files, etc, immediately they have finished with them.
4. Regular checking and overhaul of the system should be undertaken to see when and where pruning of out of date papers and renewal of folders is necessary, and to avoid cramped and overloaded shelves.
5. Out of date and 'dead' files should be removed from the original system but still be easily located when required.
6. If records are centralised there should be trained staff in attendance and a telephone link with the supervisor.
7. Automatic equipment should be regularly checked and serviced.
8. A clear and regularly updated indexing system is essential.

DISPOSAL

Dead files   Out of date files take up unnecessary space within the system and should be removed to a specially reserved area and listed separately.

Files should either be closed and renewed at set periods (at the beginning of each calendar or fiscal year, for instance) or else a new file should be started when the old one becomes full. In the latter case close the old file, if possible, after a complete section or transaction is finished. Label the finished file with its opening and closing dates, and keep it nearby for a time, until it has ceased to be of use for reference. Then put it away, clearly labelled, in the out of date or dead file area, and add its title and dates to the *Dead File* list, with a note of where it may be found; also, inside the cover of the new replacement file, make a note of where its immediate predecessor has been stored.

Occasionally an important paper needs to be transferred from an old file to the new one for convenient reference, so check carefully before putting old files away to see whether this is the case.

Many firms, legal firms in particular, keep everything indefinitely, but others economise on space by keeping essential papers only. Files may be much reduced in bulk by sensible checking and pruning. A notice of a meeting may be discarded after the meeting has been held and the minutes recorded, and an acknowledgment of a letter is superfluous when the actual reply has been received.

In the long term there are not many office records that need to be kept after a space of six years, although some firms keep them for seven years or more before destroying them.

Methods of final disposal   Paper merchants collect large quantities of waste paper by arrangement and the normal refuse collection services may be used for lesser amounts. Discarded confidential papers should be shredded before being sent out as refuse, or else consigned to an incinerator. A small paper-shredder does not take up much room in an office, and shredding is far more thorough than tearing up papers by hand.

METHOD OF REORGANISATION

When your reorganisation plan has been worked out, submitted and passed and new equipment begins to arrive, you will be in a temporarily disorganised situation while the old system gives place to the new. Take special care not to mislay any files in this transition period.

First of all clear a working area, such as a large desk or table top, for sorting.

Select a batch of folders and put them into a labelled box, or stack them with 'guide cards' between, on your sorting area. If you take a small group of folders at a time you will find the task is not too difficult; you should not try to accomplish too much all at once.

Check the contents of each folder, renew worn covers, and retitle as necessary. Work steadily, step by step; each batch may be worked over separately, as time permits. Make out a temporary list as you go, for eventual indexing purposes.

If any folder needs to be divided to make a subsidiary one, or because it is over-full, do so at once and make out a fresh title accordingly, adding it to your index list. Prune surplus material out of the folders as you go, with caution. Do not actually discard anything yet, wait for the final all-over checking up. Keep spare empty folders by you as a temporary home for 'query' papers.

Take out dead or out of date files and put these on one side, marked with their opening and closing dates, for re-listing and re-storage away from the main filing system.

When one or two batches of folders have been treated and relabelled in this way, put them into their new position and start on the next group. The space released by repositioning can be used as a further temporary storage or sorting area. Work through until all the batches have been dealt with.

After this general resorting and checking throughout, make a thorough final overall inspection, and find suitable places for the odd miscellaneous 'query' papers.

Check through your final indexing list and retype it neatly, and renew and bring up to date all related cards in the card-index racks.

CENTRALISED v. DEPARTMENTAL FILING SYSTEMS

When a departmental filing system grows sufficiently large to become inconveniently space-consuming a choice will have to be made as to whether to reorganise departmentally, with possibly a special centralised filing section for routine papers, or whether to instal a completely centralised system to service all departments from one single focal point.

Advantages   The advantages of a centralised filing system, servicing the needs of a whole business, are:

1. Specially trained staff will be required, with a supervisor who will take responsibility for the whole system, to record, label, index, and generally organise and supervise the storage of all records.
2. Fewer copies of documents will be required, one of each usually being sufficient for one system.
3. All files on one subject may be grouped together.
4. All equipment may be standardised, with economy of purchasing and renewal costs.
5. The special staff will be responsible for a master index of all records, supervise the 'outgoing' file system for borrowed folders, make periodic checks on withdrawals to round up missing files and, when a new file is made up, will allocate a code number and add it into the indexing system.

Disadvantages   The disadvantages of centralising are:

1. The actual supervision may be remote and out of touch with the individual record-keeping needs of different departments.
2. There is greater risk of loss, with more people using one system and therefore more places in which to mislay papers.
3. There will need to be a strict system of rules and regulations to make a centralised filing system work well for everyone using it.
4. There may be delays in the movement of files between those using them.

The major point in favour of centralisation is the saving of time and space within different departments of one large concern, and it is very suitable for storage of a large volume of routine information to which various sections of a business need access.

METHODS OF INDEXING

The alphabetical system   The alphabetical system of filing forms its own index, but addition and expansion may become difficult, as when a sudden influx of extra files under A or B within a four-drawer cabinet necessitates moving down all the others, from C to Z, throughout the other three drawers, in order to accommodate the extra ones in the top section.

The alphabetical system can be broken down into sub-sections. If it should be required to group files within areas geographically, for example, the counties or countries may be arranged alphabetically and the firms within each area may be in sub-groups, as CANADA: Brown & Co., Robinson Ltd., Smith & Sons; FRANCE: Cartier et Cie, Monoprix, Prisunic; NEW ZEALAND: Hamilton Construction Inc., Thompson & Son, Wellington Ltd. Estate agents may group their files alphabetically in this way according to towns and counties; manufacturers may file according to alphabetically listed products, subdivided into numbered categories.

The numerical system   This, by contrast, can be easily extended without disturbance of any kind, simply by adding new files to the end of the sequence, giving each one the next free number; an accompanying alphabetical card index will, however, be required. For example, Mrs Mary Brown's file may be the 3000th in the system. It will be listed under B in the card index, and the card will state the file number, 3000. The file can then easily be located by checking along the racks until the correct number is reached.

The scope of grouping and indexing may be adapted to suit any business or department by using numbers or the alphabet or a combination of both.

Any indexing system needs to be constantly checked and updated, to allow for files being added to or deleted from the records system.

The Dewey decimal system   Designed principally for libraries, this is a system of cataloguing books by dividing their total number into a maximum of ten sections, numbered from 0 to 9 inclusive. Any necessary subdivisions are numbered with three figures to correspond, eg in the first group subdivisions are 000 to 099 inclusive, in the second group 100 to 199. Further subdivisions are possible by using the decimal point, eg within 198 we might find 198.1, 198.2 and so on as required. Libraries have their own allotted categories (for example 800 for Literature, within which 821 may be English Poetry, and 900 for History) but the system could be usefully adapted wherever a large collection of publications needs to be listed so that those on the same subject can be kept together and quickly located.

Card Indexing   Cards for indexing may be set out in various ways, from a simple series of loose cards stacked on edge within a box to sophisticated systems of specially designed drawers, racks, holders and cabinets. Cards may be laid out on special trays, their edges overlapping so that the key name or subject typed at the bottom is seen immediately, and the card may then be turned up to display further details. Cards may be linked on a spool and set out as the spokes of a wheel, which is turned until the required card comes to hand. The limitations of available space and the number of cards required will influence your choice of indexing equipment.

Coloured cards help to distinguish between different groups quickly; a hospital, for instance, might keep pink cards for heart cases, green for maternity, blue for geriatrics, etc. Alternatively all cards may be white but with a coloured tab attached for quick identification, or coloured 'guide cards' may be used to separate one group from another in their racks. These may be linked with the same colour in the folders on the shelves.

Card index systems can provide a mode of fast reference in themselves, saving routine journeys to the files. As well as giving a name and file number they may show an address, telephone number and brief details of, say, policy (for an insurance company), state of account (for hire purchase) or health record (for a hospital service). Cross-references with other files, where appropriate, can also be entered on the index cards.

CROSS REFERENCING OF CORRESPONDENCE

When letters which relate to more than one subject have to be filed, three choices are open:

1. Keep the original letter in File 1, a copy being made for File 2. Each of these will be marked with the location of the other, eg the original letter has 'Copy in File 2' and the copy has 'Original in File 1.'

2. Keep the original letter in File 1. In File 2 put a note (dated to correspond with the letter) saying where the original letter is to be found, giving the source, the date, the heading and a brief note of the contents.

3. Keep the original letter in File 1. File 2 (and possibly others) is given a typed extract of the portion relevant to that file, and a note saying where the full original is to be found. This method is adaptable to as many different files as there are separate subjects in the original letter.

MISCELLANEOUS PAPERS

The Miscellaneous file is not just a pocket for infrequent subjects with no special significance. If a subject runs to more than a few papers it should have a folder of its own. Enquiries that have come to nothing, and consequently been left in Miscellaneous, may be discarded, or grouped together in a folder labelled for this purpose. The same may apply to circulars or advertising matter that is not immediately useful but may be needed in the future. Use caution about discarding papers, but on the other hand do not allow Miscellaneous to become the bulkiest file in your collection.

CONTINUITY OF CONTROL

There is no reason why any paper should be mislaid, even for a short while. A system of 'outcards' will guard against this, a card being put in the place of the file on the shelves, marked with the name of the person who has taken it, his department and the date. When the file is replaced the card is removed. Alternatively an 'outregister' may be employed, wherein are entered the signature, date of withdrawal, and the title of the file by the person who has withdrawn it. When the file is replaced the entry may be crossed through and dated, to cancel it. A file can thus be quickly located, wherever it is, and retrieved when urgently required. If everyone using the system follows this procedure no file should ever be lost. A list of instructions, on this and any other relevant points might be put on or near the filing cabinets.

MICROFILM, MICROFICHE AND COMFICHE

This specialised method of reducing bulky volumes of papers, or large-scale maps or drawings, to a tiny photographic image very much smaller than a postage stamp, performs miracles of space-saving in any record-keeping system.

Microfilm is lightweight and compact, it takes only about 2 per cent of the space required by equivalent paper records. A disadvantage is, of course, that special equipment is needed to read the information, and to make copies of it, and also that it is not easy to update existing microfilmed pages. However, given the right equipment, processing and retrieval are rapid and easy by today's methods, and storage and indexing present no problems.

Microfilm may be produced as a long strip, but a more convenient method for quick reference purposes is to have the tiny images mounted, singly or in groups as a series on A6 'frames', ie pages, which are then known as microfiche. The frames may have a capacity of between 60 to 98 images (microfiche), up to 200 images (superfiche) or between 1000 and 3200 (ultrafiche). Index references or titles may be printed across the top of each frame, or the frame may be mounted in an aperture card which can be identified on the margin for filing and reference purposes.

Information can be retrieved automatically by press-button selection of the strip or fiche filing code number, which brings the required frame into view on the reader screen, so that the information is then read without any handling of the original document. Large maps, plans, engineering drawings etc are especially suitable for microfilming, as are sets of papers making up a continuous record of one particular process or transaction, perhaps more than usually comprehensive and lengthy.

Microfilm and fiches may be sent through the post to any office which has a reader, and this is a safer, less bulky and more economical process than sending the originals.

A further development in microfilming is *Computer Output Microfilm* (COM). This is a process whereby the display is produced directly on film from computer-recorded information, without the intermediate process of a printout on paper, ie direct from storage in a computer. Retrieval is fast, by means of a VDU screen. This useful service can be seen in use in, for instance, banks, booksellers and building societies. Printouts can be made from individual frames of information if required. An indexing list for COM information can also be compiled, set up and read as part of the COM system.

Storage   Rolls of microfilm can be stored in containers in labelled boxes on shelves, microfiches may be arranged in sequence similar to a card index, in a box or drawer or on racks. Short strips of film can be 'jacketed', that is, kept in narrow transparent envelopes within a special cover, and the indexing scheme can be designed either for overall control or for sub-sections of a system.

STOCK-KEEPING

for any really sizeable system of stock-keeping it may well be an economy to enlist the help of a computer. Programmes can be set up to deliver printouts on stocks available on any given day (and their individual stock numbers), items on order, costs and sales figures, and other relevent data. For smaller systems, particularly for such office stationery and supplies as are needed for clerical and secretarial work in a department or division of a company, manual stock-keeping may be all that is required.

STOCK RECORDS IN THE OFFICE

Anyone responsible for buying office stationery is likely to be in a state of continual astonishment at the way in which stocks seem to melt into thin air. It is very important in these days of high costs that office supplies are responsibly used and reliably accounted for. A systematic method of recording stock movement is necessary as, even with a few shelves of varied stationery in a single cupboard, supplies should not be allowed to disappear without trace.

The person responsible for issuing office stationery will need to:

1. Take in a signed requisition form from the person requesting supplies.
2. Enter on a stock card the supplies:
   a) given out to staff and

b) received from the buying department.
3. Keep stock in store neat, tidy, accessible and clearly labelled.
4. Request renewal of stocks in plenty of time from the buying department.
5. Make periodic checks of stock at stated times, eg every six months or annually, and be able to make an analysis of the findings, if required.

Requisitions   Preprinted blank stationery requisition forms, as in Figure i, should be issued to all departments which request stationery from stock, and each of these forms should be completed, dated and authorised before being handed in; stocks may then be issued against them. These completed requisitions will then be numbered (consecutively as received) and signed and dated by the person who has given out the stock. These completed forms will be filed away in numerical order.

```
┌─────────────────────────────────────────────────┐
│                                                  │
│           STATIONERY REQUISITION                 │
│                                                  │
│   From:  Name ..................... Reqsn. No. ...│
│          Department ................              │
│          Date .....................               │
│          Authorised by: ............              │
│                                                  │
│   Please supply:                                 │
│          Quantity      Item      Description      │
│                                                  │
│                                                  │
│                                                  │
│                                                  │
│   Received........................               │
│                                                  │
│   Issued by:........................ Date.........│
│                                                  │
└─────────────────────────────────────────────────┘
```

Figure i

Stock Cards   From the completed requisition forms the stock cards will be updated. Each item of stationery will have its own stock card, as in Figure ii, eg one for headed A4 letter paper, one for plain A4 flimsy, one for B4 manila envelopes, etc.

On each stock card will be specified the minimum level to which stocks may fall and the maximum to which they may rise. Over-stocking is not economical as stores take up valuable space and, if a supply of printed stationery should need to be redesigned, or if it is suddenly no longer needed, then valuable reserves of paper become useless. The most convenient limits of stock level should be worked out for each item, according to how quickly they are likely to be used up and also how long the delivery period is likely to be for replacements. Never run out of stock – by regularly checking the stock cards and ordering before minimum level is reached, adequate supplies should be safely maintained.

After each delivery of stocks into store, direct from the suppliers or by way of the buying department, and also after each withdrawal, the stock card should be updated and balanced so that the actual amount of stock on the shelves can be seen at a glance from the card.

STATIONERY STOCK CARD							
Item............. Minimum stock: ..... Maximum stock:							
	Received			*Issued*			*Balance*
Date	Quantity	Invoice No.	Supplier	Quantity	Reqsn. No.	Department	

Figure ii

Stock cards can be arranged to form a convenient card index system, and tabs or colour signals can be added to show where items are due for re-ordering or where replacements have been ordered and deliveries are awaited.

At stocktaking times all numbered requisition forms will be checked against the stock card entries of supplies issued, and all stock cards against the actual supplies on the shelves. 'Stocks received' entries on the cards should also tally with the invoices sent in by suppliers.

All supplies of goods should be stacked tidily, small articles being kept in boxes, and all shelves, as well as containers and parcels, should be neatly and adequately labelled.

CHECKING AND OVERHAUL

Every system of record keeping, whether for general office purposes, microfilmed information, stock control or any similar function, should have a regular 'overhaul' period. If time cannot be found to do this at set intervals during the year, a special period should be set aside, annually at the same time, when it can be given special priority.

15 RECRUITMENT AND INTERVIEWING

> *The type of work to be done; the best*
> *person for the job; recruitment: where to*
> *look; application forms; preparation for*
> *interviewing; conducting the interview;*
> *closing the interview; final selection; re-*
> *ferences and testimonials; documenta-*
> *tion; induction course; payslips*

Any substantial company will have a trained personnel officer whose duty it is to deal with all aspects of staff recruitment, but in many smaller firms a personal assistant or senior secretary may be asked to find and interview applicants for a job.

As an unsuitable appointment can involve a firm in wasted time and money, to say nothing of considerable inconvenience, the task of engaging new staff should be undertaken with great care and, if possible, in an unhurried manner. The following points should be clarified at the outset:

> the type of work for which the newcomer will be engaged
> the kind of person envisaged for the job
> where such a person can be found
> the documents necessary for the firm's staff records
> when and how applicants will be interviewed.

THE TYPE OF WORK TO BE DONE

The object of the recruiting exercise is to select a suitable person for the job, not vice versa; it will not be the intention to adapt the job to suit the person unless the circumstances are exceptional in some way. Therefore it is vitally important for any interviewer to have a full knowledge of the kind of work required to be done.

Not only should the interviewer understand the firm's requirements, it is also necessary to see the applicant's point of view. Questions about working conditions should be anticipated and may well include the following:

1. What are the hours of work and will overtime be required occasionally, or as a matter of course?
2. Will the employee be working alone, in a small group or with many others?

3. Will there be constant supervision or opportunities for initiative?
4. Is there any provision for further training and are there good promotion prospects?
5. Is the work indoor or outdoor?
6. Are the conditions clean or dirty?
7. Does the work carry any special hazard?
8. Is any kind of protective clothing needed, and if so does the firm provide it?

All these questions and any others relating to working conditions can be answered and discussed at a personal interview, and the interviewer should be well briefed with the correct answers.

THE BEST PERSON FOR THE JOB

Before interviewing, discuss with other members of staff the qualities needed for the job; some qualities may be absolutely necessary, others merely desirable. List them all, keeping the basic essential qualifications to the most reasonable minimum, and ask the opinions of those people who will be affected by or involved in the appointment.

Typical questions to ask them are:

1. Does the job require any special personality traits? (For example great patience, a talent for leadership, or a good social manner).
2. How important is an attractive appearance or a good voice?
3. Will a school or college leaver be adequate or is experience essential?
4. What kind of person is envisaged?

Be prepared to compromise should the ideal applicant not materialise within the time available; it is unlikely that you will find everything you are looking for in one person and a little latitude may have to be allowed.

RECRUITMENT: WHERE TO LOOK

Schools, colleges, polytechnics and universities   If working experience is not necessary, the principal or the careers officer in a school, college, polytechnic or university may know of likely candidates. However, young people completing their formal education are unlikely to be available before the early summer, and many firms contact these establishments earlier in the year, notifying them of vacancies to be filled after the final examinations have taken place.

A very great number of firms regularly send a representative to visit school sixth-forms and training colleges to talk to students about work opportunities in their company, describing career structures, promotion prospects and available training schemes.

Local employment bureaux   Employment exchanges, careers advisory services and youth employment organisations exist to help all types of people to find suitable work. These useful services can be located in the Yellow Pages of the telephone directory.

Agencies   There are numerous government sponsored employ-ment agencies, as well as private employment specialists, whose addresses can be found in the Yellow Pages. Providing the specific needs are made clear to them an agency offers a very useful means of finding staff. They will do some of the preliminary screening, sending for interview only those who are likely to be suitable.

As well as employment agencies dealing with staff on a general basis, there are professional and executive agencies specialising in qualified experienced staff of management calibre.

External advertising   An advertisement in the situations vacant or business opportunities columns of any of the following will make direct contact with people in any chosen field of interest:

> the local press
> national daily newspapers
> national evening newspapers
> professional and trade periodicals of all kinds.

An advertisement should be:

> brief, in the interests of economy, but nevertheless attractive enough to bring in replies
> sufficiently informative to interest the right type of candidate
> clear and concise as to where replies should be sent – the name of the firm need not necessarily be given as some firms prefer to give a telephone or box number only
> accurate, and in no way misleading.

Internal advertising   Vacancies may also be advertised within the firm, on staff notice-boards or in house magazines. These may bring in replies from employees who are looking for a change of depart-ment or better prospects of promotion, or may bring in an outside introduction from an existing member of staff. The advantages of making an internal appointment are:

1. The applicant is already familiar with the firm, the staff and the working structure of the company and is likely to have the self-confidence that comes with this experience.
2. Full personal and business details, with references, will already be in the records of the personnel department.

A disadvantage of an internal appointment is that, if the post is regarded as a promotion, tact may be needed to avoid staff jealousies.

Direct application   Firms are sometimes approached directly by people wishing to work for them. All these applications should be answered, but if no suitable vacancy occurs at that time their names and addresses can be kept in an appropriate 'pending' file, so that they may be contacted when an opportunity arises. This file can provide a very useful reserve list.

APPLICATION FORMS

It has become general practice to ask prospective employees to fill in an application form, even if they have first sent a letter containing full information about themselves.

A formal application form carries special advantages to the firm because all the initial information required will be asked for and will be set out in the most convenient order. Any future analysis or comparison of staff recruitment is thus made easier, as this kind of work would be complicated and very time-consuming if miscellaneous letters of application had to be sorted through.

The keeping of personnel records will be made easier if more than one type of preprinted application form is stocked, catering for different types and grades of employment; a form for college leavers, for instance, will differ from one sent to experienced staff. Two examples are given. The actual layout may vary (see section on Form Design) but the name of the applicant should be at the top, for quick reference and filing. The following items will be required:

For School, College or University leavers
 1. Surname in block capitals, other name, sex
 2. Address and telephone number
 3. Age, date of birth
 4. Nationality
 5. Education: schools and colleges, with dates
 6. Examinations passed, specifying grades (BEC, CSE, O-levels, A-levels and others)
 7. Further Education and university courses, with dates, giving main courses of study, degrees, diplomas or certificates obtained.
 8. Place of education at present attending
 9. Any other courses of training undertaken
10. Hobbies and leisure interests
11. Two referees, one being the principal of the present or last place of education, the other personal, with address and telephone number of each.

For experienced staff   As above as far as 7 inclusive. For 8 omit 'School or college at present attending' and substitute 'Work Experience' as follows:

Names and addresses of past and present employers, with dates
Status and responsibilities
Present salary (NB: not all firms ask for this)
For 11, three referees, one being the last employer. The other two may be more personal, but it is helpful if they come from a friend or acquaintance with some responsible and official status, eg a justice of the peace, member of Parliament, magistrate, vicar or doctor.

Space is often allocated on application forms for 'additional qualifications' such as first-aid certificates, driving licence, special knowledge of a foreign language, any special courses of training taken and voluntary work. This kind of information can give a very useful indication of the type of person who is applying.

Each of the foregoing application forms will end with a line for the applicant's signature and the date.

A space is sometimes left at the foot for the firm's use, to be filled in with:

date of interview
date appointed
department
position
starting salary
signature of Interviewer.

PREPARATION FOR INTERVIEWING

After the completed application forms have come in they should be sorted into two groups, those from unsuitable applicants and those from candidates to be short-listed for interviewing. A polite note will be sent to each of the former, thanking them for their application and saying that the vacancy is now filled. It is not necessary to give a reason or go into details. The others will be sent a letter asking them to attend for an interview, giving the time, date and place.

Scheduling of appointments   Liaise with other members of staff who may wish to see any of the applicants, so that the most convenient time is chosen for everyone who wishes to attend. It is important that the person for whom the applicant will work is given the opportunity to be present.

Plenty of time should be allowed for interviewing; it is unforgivable to ask someone to make a journey to see you and then appear to be short of time. Work out the list of appointments with this in mind; it is better to allow too much time than not enough. It is considerate to ask those with the longest journeys to attend mid-way through the schedule. Those with short journeys can be seen earliest and latest.

Contacting applicants   When sending out letters asking candidates to call:
>   set out the time and date clearly, and the address
>   give brief directions, such as the nearest tube station or the number of any bus that passes close by
>   give the name of the person who should be asked for at the reception desk
>   ask the applicants to write or telephone promptly if they are unable to keep the appointment, so that an alternative time may be arranged.

When the schedule of appointments is finalised and agreed, the reception office should have a copy of the list of names, with the time when each is expected, so that the candidates may be met on arrival and brought to the interviewing room.

Interview room   The atmosphere for both interviewer and interviewee should be quiet, relaxed and businesslike.

Seating   Chairs set face to face or slightly at an angle are usually the most satisfactory. They should be comfortable and at a matching level; it is intimidating for an applicant to find himself sitting in a low chair with his interviewer towering above him. He should not be placed opposite a mirror or window, nor with a bright light shining into his face.

Noise   No interview can be properly conducted against a background of disturbance. Ask the switchboard operator to divert telephone calls during the interviewing session to someone responsible who can deal with them, and arrange that you will not be interrupted by other visitors.

Waiting area   Candidates should be welcomed on arrival and made to feel that they are expected. The waiting room should be quiet and comfortable, with papers and magazines available. The offer of a cup of tea or coffee may be very acceptable, and while waiting an interviewee ought never to be allowed to feel forgotten or in any way neglected.

CONDUCTING THE INTERVIEW

When called into the interview room the applicant should be introduced to those present and offered a seat.

Putting the candidate at ease   The purpose of the interview is:
>   to acquire information not already on the application form
>   to explore the candidate's personality
>   to assess his usefulness to the company.

To do this successfully it is necessary to dispel any tension and help him to relax and this is especially important in the case of inexperienced applicants, such as college leavers and other young people looking for their first job. However, interviewees of any age are liable to feel nervous and at a disadvantage.

Talk quite informally at the start. It is not advisable to plunge in straight away with direct and purposeful questioning; in that way it is possible to terrify people and thereby lose an excellent candidate because he was too nervous to do anything but appear tongue-tied or half-witted.

Make sure you have the right application form before you for each interviewee. Call the candidate by his name, making sure you have it correctly, and have ready a casual opening comment or question. 'Come in, Mr Smith, perhaps you would sit here. Did you have difficulty finding us?' 'Good morning, Miss Robinson, I think that chair is comfortable.' If you can discover a matter of common interest on the application form, make the most of it. 'I see you went to my old college, did you enjoy your time there?' 'I know your home town well, have you lived there long?' This kind of informal chitchat may not last more than a minute or two and is not to be seen as a waste of time – it is a very necessary way of settling down a nervous candidate and easing the way to the more formal and purposeful conversation to follow.

Tests   If the candidate is to have a test, notification should have been given earlier, in the letter he received setting out the time of his interview. Some firms may ask for a skill demonstration or even a medical test if the proper facilities and staff are available.

Arrangements for the necessary test equipment to be available should be made well before the interview; testing may be undertaken in an area near to the interview room, with a supervisor who will conduct the test and bring the candidate back to the interviewer afterwards.

Discussion and questioning   After the opening pleasantries keep to the purpose of the interview. Lead into the subjects on your list and keep the atmosphere businesslike but friendly; it is not a social occasion and should not resemble one.

Talk as little as possible yourself, it is by drawing out your candidate that you can assess his disposition and personality, and his motivation for applying to your firm. The application form should of course have been studied earlier and if there is more than one interviewer settle beforehand the range and type of questions each will ask.

Techniques of interviewing   Direct questions, requiring a 'Yes' or 'No' reply should be avoided, or at least kept to the minimum. Instead of asking 'Can you do – ?' which only requires an answer of a single word, spread your question over a wider area. Ask what varieties of duties he is able to carry out, ask about the depth of experience he has had in these duties. Enquire whether he found them easy or difficult and which he preferred to do and why this was so. He might also be asked whether there were any duties he could do or would like to try doing, but for which he had not yet had an opportunity. Ask about his ambitions and whether he has any special goal for the future.

Try to overcome the candidate's nervousness, prompt him if necessary, help him to talk freely. Ask for opinions and follow up the reasons for them, but never let an argument develop if you disagree with anything that is said. 'Really, that is very interesting' should be sufficient to keep any controversial subject under control.

Have your own list of subjects to explore, but do not appear to be using it as a check-list. Refer to it occasionally as a reminder, and perhaps make an occasional brief note on it, particularly if a good point is made, but do not give the impression that the candidate is undergoing an oral examination and that you are writing down the answers. If you wish to make notes to any great extent, do this after he has gone.

If there are unexplained gaps in the dates on the application form, during education or previous employment, find out the reason for these. Frequent changes of employment may indicate instability.

Never bully or try to trick a candidate. It will be remembered and rightly resented.

Personality   Personality and character are as important, in fitting someone into the structure of a firm, as the ability to perform the specified duties. Try to find evidence of real interest in the work, qualities of application and perseverance, or of special initiative.

Hobbies and leisure pursuits may give useful clues to the type of person you are dealing with, from the quiet retiring character who just prefers to relax with a book to the cheerful extrovert who is the life and soul of a sports club or dramatic society.

Prejudices   Some interviewers do have unconscious prejudices, and would be astonished and unbelieving if it were pointed out to them.

The sole purpose of this kind of interview is to engage the best person to fill the vacancy, and the best person to choose is the one who will do the work best. Be sure therefore that there is no possibility of a good candidate's being turned down because of anyone's dislike of, say, red hair or colour of skin or a regional accent, or any other superficial quality that will in no way affect the person's ability to do the job well.

Guard also against rejecting a candidate because he seems to be deficient in one quality that can be cultivated on the job, if this is his only disadvantage. With time and training he should become more suitable and may even develop into the ideal person for the work.

Assessment sheets   A grading assessment sheet may be useful on which may be entered a rating for those qualities that can only be discovered during a conversation. The kind of qualities assessed on the form will differ according to the type of worker under review.

The actual layout may vary and all or any of the following items are suitable for inclusion. Against each a grading will be allowed, eg A, B, C, D, etc, with a 'key' giving the assessment, such as Outstanding, Good, Fair, Unsatisfactory. The name of the interviewee will be at the top of the page, with the date.

Appearance, dress sense, grooming
Speech, ability to express him/herself, voice and vocabulary
Personality and manner
Health record, physical defects or disabilities
Educational level, BEC, CSE, O-level and A-level passes
General work experience
Any special experience
Professional education, diplomas and degrees gained
Special aptitudes or abilities (manual, mechanical, musical, artistic, linguistic, mathematical, organisational and leadership qualities)
General intelligence (displayed at interview and/or by special IQ test administered)
Special interests, sports, private studies, social activities
Interest and enthusiasm displayed
Character and disposition (whether the candidate appears reliable, steady, nervous, excitable, diffident, introvert, extrovert, mature, possessing initiative, having a warmth of personality, etc)
Motivation (interest, ambition, determination)
Domestic/family circumstances
Driving licence, possession of a car
Additional remarks
Recommendation made by assessor, signed and dated.

Grading assessment sheets are not only useful for the assessment of a new employee, but also for existing members of staff who are being interviewed with promotion or re-grading in mind, or a transfer to a different duty or department.

For a receptionist or switchboard operator there should be a special grading assessment for voice, manner and vocabulary, and a comment as to whether the applicant is a fluent speaker or inclined to be hesitant or terse.

For a receptionist or secretary or any other post involving direct external liaison, entries for grooming and clothes sense would be appropriate, as well as for general appearance and manner, poise and confidence.

For any job involving responsibility, a grading for intelligence and ability to use initiative is important.

At the foot of the assessment form add your own personal impression and any particular relevant points that have occurred to you. This is a good place for such comments as 'Consider for training scheme next year', 'Salary review in six months' or 'Not suitable for this vacancy but keep in 'staff pending' file for consideration later'.

The candidate's point of view   When you have sufficient information about the candidate, and he appears to be suitable, it is his turn to take the initiative. Encourage him to ask questions. It is in both your interests to iron out any small snags at this early stage in case they become major problems after he is employed. It may be that he is likely to have problems in keeping to the firm's working hours or regarding transport, due to personal or domestic circumstances, and perhaps your firm may be able to suggest something to help him.

Make sure that he understands fully the duties to be undertaken, salary and bonuses, terms and conditions of work, courses of training available, holidays, and pension schemes. Many firms have their own printed booklet giving details of all aspects of employment within their organisation, produced especially for issue to new staff.

Date of commencement   Anyone accepting an appointment to replace an outgoing member of staff would probably appreciate a short overlapping period of engagement if it can be arranged, before that person leaves. The newcomer will then be able to see at first hand how the job was previously carried out.

If it is necessary to wait for a newly appointed member of staff to work out his notice with his present firm, or if it is agreed to honour holiday arrangements which are imminent, it may be possible to bridge the gap with a temporary appointment.

Withdrawal of application   School or college leavers, looking for work for the first time, are not always clear in their minds about the full implications of the duties described, and may need to have these explained to them very carefully at the interview. Occasionally a young applicant discovers during the conversation that the job is not what he had expected, and he then changes his mind about wanting it. If this is the case he should of course be given the opportunity to withdraw and there need be no reason for him to feel absurd or inadequate because he was mistaken in applying.

A good young candidate should always be encouraged as far as possible. He should be thanked for his interest in the firm and asked whether he would like to leave his name and address with the personnel department in case suitable work should be available in the future. The personnel officer will thus be able to make a useful addition to his reserve or pending staff lists.

CLOSING THE INTERVIEW

When the interview is over it is the interviewer who should make a move to indicate that the applicant is free to go, and he can bring the session to a conclusion quite pleasantly by putting his papers together, standing up and holding out his hand for a handshake, and saying 'I think that's everything, thank you very much for coming. We'll be letting you know within a day or two' or 'Perhaps you would like to wait in the waiting room' or a similar closing remark according to the particular circumstances. The interviewer may then move over to the door and open it for the applicant, who will find himself moving outside with the minimum of awkwardness and fuss, and the interviewer's secretary should see him to the waiting room or out of the building.

After the short period necessary to complete the assessment form the next candidate may be called in.

FINAL SELECTION

When a suitable applicant is found but there are other people still to be seen before a final choice is possible, tell him when he may expect a decision. He may wish to wait, if the decision can be made in a reasonably short period, or he may have to return home to wait for a letter.

Make the decision as promptly as possible. It is unfair to keep people waiting for the result of an interview, as it may affect their chances of applying elsewhere. Unsuccessful applicants should always be thanked for coming to an interview and informed politely that the vacancy is now filled. The successful applicant will be sent a formal letter of appointment as soon as possible.

REFERENCES AND TESTIMONIALS

Some firms like to follow up references before compiling a short-list, others make a conditional appointment after interviewing, subject to satisfactory references, which are then taken up for the successful candidate only. Two examples of a request for a reference follow.

Personal, for school and college leavers

Dear Sir
(*Applicant's name and address*)

The above named person has applied to us for a post as (state capacity) and has given us your name as a referee.

We should be glad if you would kindly let us know how long you have known him/her and whether in your opinion he/she is of good character and will prove suitable in this position. Your reply will be treated in the strictest confidence.

We thank you for your assistance and enclose a stamped addressed envelope for your reply.

Yours faithfully,

Business, for experienced staff   Letters of this kind sent to a firm should be addressed to one responsible person and marked 'Confidential'. The salutation and heading will be as above.

The above named person has applied to us for a post as (state capacity) and has given us your name as a referee, stating that he/she was employed by you as (state position) from (give date) to (give date).

We should be glad if you would kindly let us know whether during this time you found him/her to be a satisfactory employee, reliable and of good character, and whether you consider he/she is capable of undertaking the duties of the position we are offering. Your reply will be treated in the strictest confidence.

Final paragraph and complimentary close as above.

In each case the stamped addressed envelope for a reply should be marked 'Confidential'.

If a referee has any criticism or warning to give to a prospective employer he may do this more readily over the telephone than in a letter. However, even if an applicant cannot be said to have been very satisfactory in the past with another firm, it does not necessarily mean that he will not work well with your company. People work best when they are happy and fulfilled, and it may be that in his previous job he was neither. Common sense and your impression at the interview should be your guidelines in a case of this kind, as a past record may not always be a true indication of future potential, and a fresh start may prove to be entirely salutary.

A testimonial from a private or business source, which the applicant may bring with him to the interview and which is usually addressed 'To whom it may concern', is a useful but impersonal document which may need to be followed up by a letter or telephone call to its originator. A direct reference addressed to your firm, given after a provisional appointment is made, is likely to be more up-to-date and reliable.

DOCUMENTATION

When the vacancy is filled the new member of staff should be sent a letter of appointment and a formal contract, setting out all the terms and conditions of the engagement. At the same time the new employee may be sent any literature published by the company, if he has not already been given this at interview, with full details of the firm and the conditions of work.

A new file will be opened in the personnel records section, under the newcomer's name, containing:

his letter of application and/or application form

the assessment form

his references

a copy of his contract and letter of appointment

a copy of his job description (see Figure i)

his record card for use during his period of employment (see Figure ii)

any special comments in writing that the personnel officer wishes to place on record.

This new file, being part of the personnel records, should be marked 'Confidential'.

INDUCTION COURSE

The business of recruiting new staff does not end when the letter of appointment or contract is sent out.

The first day in a new job can be a traumatic experience for a new recruit, whatever his age. With unfamiliar colleagues in strange surroundings, in a busy and bewildering atmosphere which is not yet fully understood, a new member of staff may feel lost and be at an unfair disadvantage.

Many firms arrange induction courses for new employees, which can be for one person only or for a group, may last for only half a day or for several days, or one day a week for several weeks, or continuously. Any kind of programme can be worked out to suit the circumstances and the number of new employees.

Subjects to be covered   These may include all or any of the following:

1. A talk describing the background and history of the firm. If the

JOB DESCRIPTION

Title	Senior Secretary
Promoted From	Secretary
Promotion Prospects	Executive Secretary
Department	Personnel
Hours of Work	0930 hrs – 1730 hrs Monday to Friday
Responsible to	Personnel Manager
Authority over	Junior Secretaries
Job Function	To perform secretarial and associated duties for the Personnel Manager by providing efficient service for the handling of correspondence, telephone calls and personal contacts and to supervise the work of Junior Secretaries in the Department.

DUTIES/RESPONSIBILITIES

1. To receive and entertain visitors to the Personnel Department.
2. To schedule business and personal appointments for the Personnel Manager and keep the office diary up-to-date.
3. To prepare itineraries and organise travel arrangements either direct or through the Travel Department.
4. To receive, open and distribute incoming mail; collect and despatch outgoing mail.
5. To take and transcribe dictation including highly confidential matter and to maintain general and confidential files and records.
6. To receive incoming telephone calls, answer general enquiries and to take messages during the absence of the Personnel Manager.
7. To arrange and attend Departmental meetings, prepare and distribute documents, take notes and compose minutes.
8. To supervise and check the work of Junior Secretaries within the Department.

Figure i

STAFF RECORD CARD

Name   **Date of Birth**
Address   **Sex**
                                  Nationality
                                  Marital Status
Telephone No.   **Staff Employment No.**

Type of Education

    Examinations Passed (Give grades)

Further Training

Other Qualifications, Degrees etc.

Date appointed	*Status*	*Department*	*Salary*	*Remarks*
a.				
b.				
c.				
d.				

Special training undertaken or experience gained:

Further relevant information

Date of leaving
Reason for leaving

Signature of Personnel Manager   Date

Figure ii

firm has other UK or overseas branches a film showing the work that is done there will help to give an overall view of the company and its activities.

2. A survey of the premises from a geographical point of view, with the issue of floor plans and sketch maps, and including a conducted tour of the area, office blocks, factory and workshop premises, laboratories, etc.

3. A talk by a member of the management staff on the firm's policies, past, present and future, and the progress and expansion achieved.

4. A talk on staff structure, with charts or diagrams of the departments and inter-relating responsibilities of each.

5. An explanation of the formalities for new employees regarding insurance and pension details, the necessary deductions from salary or wages, working hours and holidays, social opportunities, welfare arrangements, fire drills and other safety precautions.

Newcomers should be encouraged to ask any questions they wish about the firm, and at an induction course time should be allocated for them to do this.

Learning 'on the job'   If only one person is to be given an induction course the procedure of formal talks and lectures may be reduced to one member of the established staff being detailed to explain the various points, take the newcomer round the firm, accompany him at his first lunch break, show him where the various offices and amenities can be found, and generally help him through the first few days. If someone can be spared from their usual work to do this it is of great help to the new recruit.

If it is not possible to deploy a member of staff for induction duties of this kind, the newcomer will be dependent on his supervisor, or a colleague working nearby, to help him, answer his questions and show him where to go to find the canteen, mailroom, cloakrooms, etc. Such a person should be specifically available and unquestionably willing to do this, and should not appear too busy or impatient to deal with the natural questions and problems of a newcomer. He may be required to make a report to the personnel officer on the way the new recruit settles in.

A new employee in a workshop may need to have his job actually demonstrated to him before he is clear about it, and in an office a new junior secretary will have to be shown the house style for layout of letters and memos, the number of copies required, where they are to be sent, the kind of filing system employed, the mailroom procedures, when and how often to expect internal messenger delivery and collection, and where to go to replenish a stock of stationery when it is running low.

Advantages   However modest in scale, the advantages of induction for new staff can be listed as follows:

1. The new employee is helped to understand what is going on around him and can thereby see his work in the context of the working environment, not in isolation but as part of a whole process.

2. He will not feel that his working colleagues are complete strangers, as he will have met some of them and will know something about the others. Consequently he is unlikely to feel shy or diffident in talking to them.

3. He will know his way around the firm without having to waste time in finding someone who can direct him.

4. The self-confidence the induction course will have given him will make him more relaxed in his new surroundings and thus quicker in assimilating his work. This will in turn save the time of the firm and their money, as he will be working more efficiently and confidently from the beginning, making fewer mistakes and needing less attention and help from others around him.

5. The impression received by employees that the company cares for the needs of its staff and looks after them from the very beginning makes a valuable contribution to good staff relations.

PAYSLIPS

Finally to this section, the following notes may be of assistance to a P.A. faced with explaining a first payslip to a newcomer.

All firms have their own preferred arrangement for payslips and the variations are infinite, although all payslips have a common basis of essential information. On each slip an employee's gross (total) pay is shown, deductions are set out, and the net pay, to be actually received for a given period, is given as a final total.

If the employee is paid monthly the salary will usually be paid direct into his or her bank account, and the slip will therefore just be a notification of the amount credited.

If the employee is paid weekly there will be actual cash accompanying the payslip, which should be checked against the net figure shown. Any discrepancy between the amount received and the figure given on the slip should be investigated at once with the cashier's department.

Depending on the type of firm and the kind of work done, the following are typical details to be found on an employee's payslip:

Employee's name and department or works number

Tax code number

National Insurance number

Bank account number (for monthly salary credits)

Date of payment

Week number (of the tax year). In most cases the tax year runs
from 5 April, to coincide with the income tax period. Weeks
1, 2, 3 etc are calculated from this date, not from 1 January.

If the employee is paid at an hourly rate:

the number of hours worked

the basic rate for each hour

other hours, paid at a higher rate (eg for overtime or weekend
working)

the total gross amount earned as a result.

If the employee is paid on a weekly or monthly basis:

the gross figure due for that period.

Deductions may be made for the following:

Income Tax

National Insurance

Pensions fund

Superannuation

Union or Club subscriptions

Loan repayments, etc

These will be totalled, and deducted from the figure of Gross Pay.

Also shown on the payslip may be:

Contributions made by the employers, for National Insurance
and Superannuation, and

The *total* figure of these contributions (for National Insurance
and Superannuation), made by both the employee and the
employers, added together.

A typical payslip will show not only the different sums periodically deducted, but also how these sums have accumulated through
the financial year, increasing through the week numbers 1 to 52.
Such cumulative sums may be for:

Pension contributions deducted so far, to date

National Insurance contributions

(a) deducted to date from the employee's gross pay

(b) paid by the employers

(c) as a total of (a) and (b)

The total taxable pay to date. This is not the same as the total
gross pay, as everybody has a certain proportion of their
income free of tax

Total tax deducted from pay to date, for the present tax year.

A payslip should therefore show you:

1. Your earned pay for the actual week or month

   The deductions made from it, and therefore

   The net amount due to you for that period.

2. Your *total* earned pay from the beginning of the tax period

up to the present tax week

The *total* deductions made so far for that tax period to date

Therefore the *total* net amount that you have received, up to the present time, within the tax year.

Payslips should be kept carefully, as they can form a useful check for income tax purposes, when an income tax return is made out after the end of the financial year.

The sum total of all the individual staff payslips is the *Payroll*, which is thus a detailed record of all wage or salary payments for a given period (weekly or monthly). Payroll and payslip operations are now largely done by computer. Programmes can be set up to calculate, with speed and accuracy, the figures for gross pay, tax adjustments, National Insurance, pensions and income tax deductions, and the eventual net pay figure for each employee, and can even be programmed to give a note and coin analysis for the making up of wage packets.

Bibliography

John S. Gough: *Interviewing in Twenty-six Steps* (BACIE Handbook, 1981).

Janis Grummitt: *A guide to interviewing skills* (The Industrial Society, 1980).

Clive Goodworth: *Effective Interviewing for Employment Selection* (Business Books, 1983).

Smith & Robertson: *The Theory & Practice of Systematic Staff Selection* (Macmillan, 1985).

16 SAFETY AND SECURITY

> *Office maintenance; electrical equipment; telephone conversations; correspondence; visitors; individual personal responsibilities; prevention of fraud; suspicious circumstances; safety in workshops; security agencies; leakage of information; organised spying; kidnapping; bomb threats; fire precautions and prevention; insurance; costs and priorities of safety measures*

Accidents happen because somebody, somewhere, is not thinking. Accidents can be embarrassing, inconvenient, expensive and, at worst, fatal. Even the most self-possessed and calm secretary can, under pressure, be in danger of being just a little careless, letting her concentration slip, or not getting her priorities quite right. It is far better to avoid an accident than to have to cope with the consequences. It is necessary to consider where the hazards may lurk, and the many different identifiable areas of risk.

OFFICE MAINTENANCE

In your office block are there dark corners, badly lighted stairwells, where the replacement of a dim or faulty light bulb might make all the difference to a safe footing? You may know every uneven stairtread like the back of your hand, but remember that a visitor may stumble where you instinctively go safely. Clear, well-maintained, well-lit, level passage-ways will help everyone to move around with confidence and safety. Is there an uneven floor tile or woodblock, a loose piece of carpet or a frayed edge where a heel may catch and someone fall headlong? Loose flexes leading to a heater or typewriter are dangerous to the unwary. Where do you put down your briefcase? Out of the way or somewhere where a passer-by might fall over it? This is all a matter of good housekeeping.

Equally, it is not sensible for people to carry too much at a time. The clerk staggering under an enormous pile of books and files, who cannot see where he is going because of the bulk of material clutched to his chest, could easily collide with his colleague, doing the same thing and coming from the opposite direction. The girl who carries a tray of coffee-cups into the boardroom and has to fumble with the door-knob to enter, or the cleaner with mop and bucket as well as vacuum cleaner, are both taking foolhardy risks if they do not enlist help, or convey their burdens in more than one journey. The girl with the coffee tray may trip at the top of the stairs, fall to the bottom, sprain her ankle, scald herself with hot coffee, cut herself with broken china, and be rushed to hospital. Small hazards tend to escalate.

There may be situations where living dangerously is exciting and attractive, but business life is not one of them, and a word of caution or advice to business colleagues will not necessarily be taken as interference and might well prevent a nasty accident.

ELECTRICAL EQUIPMENT

Electric plugs can become faulty through overloading, and old or worn wiring may lead to a serious fire. Regular maintenance checks should be undertaken on all electrical equipment – it is irresponsible to neglect this sort of thing. Not only is it bad for the article itself, it is false economy to allow equipment to deteriorate and become potentially dangerous. Never leave a typewriter switched on, even if you are only going for a quick lunch break. Never leave electric heaters or desk lights on when not in use.

TELEPHONE CONVERSATIONS

Be careful what you say on the telephone, as people can hover nearby, overhearing 'accidentally'. If a call comes that you think is likely to be confidential, and there are people about, there are several things you can do.

1. Have the call switched through to somewhere where you can talk in privacy.
2. Ask your caller to ring back later, saying that it is difficult for you to speak to him at the present time.
3. Ask the caller if you may ring back later, not forgetting, of course, to make sure you know where you will be able to contact him.

CORRESPONDENCE

Confidential letters should always have the words 'Confidential', 'Personal' or 'Private' typed at the head of the letter itself, as well as on the envelope. Copies of confidential mail must be kept in special folders, locked away quite separately from those in the general filing system.

Registered post and the recorded delivery services offer protection against loss in transit when important papers are despatched. It is unwise to take chances on safety. The consequences can be disastrous if confidential information is allowed to reach the wrong destination.

Information can also be leaked by way of carelessness with papers and equipment. In offices where security is of the highest priority, typewriter ribbons are locked away at night as they can be read. Carbon papers can also be read, and tapes can be rewound and replayed; even when wiped clean they can be retrieved electronically. Wastepaper baskets are an obvious danger; when you discard papers use a shredding machine or an incinerator.

Typewriters with memory banks are a particular risk, as not only may the typewriter be stolen, but also the banked information that goes with it. The same applies to computers, and this danger is not always realised. Computer-stored information can be tapped, and data can be read by any unauthorised person who knows how to retrieve it. Computer rooms should always be regarded as a vulnerable area in any security plan.

VISITORS

All visitors should be supervised. In ninety-nine cases out of a hundred they will be genuine and above suspicion, but there is always the hundredth chance that somewhere, some time, someone is not what he or she appears to be, is in an unauthorised area, and up to no good at all.

Is your receptionist watchful and efficient? A well run reception area is invaluable. Is anyone able to walk in from outside, and wander round the building, perhaps looking like a delivery man with a parcel, a salesman with a case of samples, a man in an overall who has come to clean the windows, or even someone as confident and smartly dressed as one of your directors? All callers should be checked by a doorman or commissionaire, receptionist, or the secretary concerned, who can identify them and see that they are taken to their destination. People waiting for appointments should be under someone's discreet eye.

When a visitor's appointment is over, he or she should be seen off the premises and not left to walk away unsupervised; common sense is the over-riding factor here. An obsessive suspicion of all callers is not required, but rather a wariness of strangers and a watchfulness while they are under your roof.

The general system of all staff having passes for daily entry is a good one, provided it is used properly. If the senior executives do not bother to show their passes, subordinates will notice and will not bother either; the system will then become slack and it will be a simple matter for unauthorised persons to pass through the checkgate. General staff will follow managerial practice, so the management *must* show an example. Senior staff especially should agree to, and be seen to agree to, being searched on occasion. If senior staff agree, lower level staff will also co-operate and resentment will be reduced to the minimum. If a pass is lost or stolen it should be reported immediately to the security officer.

Visitors may be issued with temporary named and dated lapel stickers by which anyone can see that they are authorised visitors for that day, the badge being handed in when they leave the premises.

As supermarket and departmental store managers know only too well, walk-in thefts are rapidly increasing, and are common in offices as well as shops and storerooms. Various precautionary devices are now available on the market. Closed-circuit television cameras may be installed to watch over large floor areas. There is also a system whereby a tiny alarm valve is attached to an article, and this sets up a warning signal if it is carried out through the monitoring control at the exit. When the goods are correctly paid for at the desk the alarm tag is removed, otherwise the alarm will go off and the store detective will move in.

New anti-theft devices frequently appear on the market, and it is worth investigating the possibilities if your firm is losing goods, and therefore money, in this way. Firms listed under 'security services' in Yellow Pages will be able to advise.

INDIVIDUAL PERSONAL RESPONSIBILITIES

It is not fair to put temptation in other people's way, so keep your handbag in a locked drawer.

Personal or confidential papers should never be left lying around, and anything valuable should be in the safe, or sent to the bank for safe keeping. (This is a recognised bank service).

See that all drawers are closed, the confidential ones locked, and the keys not left in an obvious place when you leave the office. The first place a thief will look is under the typewriter pad below your machine.

Make a list of the trade numbers of all machines in your office. Each typewriter, duplicator, etc. will have its own manufacturers' release number to be found somewhere on the framework. Alternatively, have a special identifying mark put on each machine. The reason for this is that, in the case of theft and eventual retrieval by the police, you may not claim your property unless it can be positively identified as belonging to you, and in some cases identification may be very difficult.

In case of loss of keys, a set of duplicates should be kept safely by a responsible member of staff, for use in an emergency.

Before you leave the cloakroom see that the taps are all firmly turned off. Water from an overflowing basin can seep through to the room below and drip onto desk or carpet.

Lock windows when you leave the office; you do not want an unexpected rainstorm to blow in and make a mess, nor do you want to invite burglars.

PREVENTION OF FRAUD

Stories regularly appear in the press of an employee who has falsified the firm's books and made a bolt to foreign lands with a large suitcase full of illgotten banknotes. The underlying principle here is that no single person should ever have sole responsibility for dealing with money in the office.

All money transactions should be regularly and thoroughly checked by a second and even a third person. This applies to the petty cash just as much as to larger amounts. No cashier should keep account books without frequent on-the-spot checks by someone else. This is an elementary and universally accepted precaution, and therefore no-one should object.

Money should be banked as soon as possible after its receipt. More than one person should be in attendance, and it is wise to vary the route to the bank, and the day and time of day when the journey is made.

SUSPICIOUS CIRCUMSTANCES

If, in your capacity as secretary or personal assistant, you find yourself suspicious of a particular individual, or conscious of circumstances that do not seem quite right to you, what should you do?

Really, you have no choice at all, you *must* report it at once to your employer. There is no other course open to you. Ask if you can have a quiet word, mention your suspicions privately and confidentially and say why you are concerned. Very possibly no further steps will be necessary, but you will have passed the responsibility on to a higher authority and, if action needs to be taken, your conversation will be well justified. If not, there is no harm done.

The worst thing you can do is to keep silent, perhaps through a mistaken sense of loyalty or a feeling that it may not matter. It does. If you keep this sort of problem to yourself the situation could deteriorate and become really serious.

SAFETY IN WORKSHOPS (WAREHOUSE AND FACTORY AREAS)

This is a specialised subject, as workshops and production areas vary so enormously, some equipment carrying very dangerous hazards and others capable of being used with comparative safety. The responsibilities of management are vitally important whatever the kind of work being carried on.

The British Safety Council publishes a comprehensive range of helpful pamphlets on all aspects of industrial safety and the safety codes to be observed in different situations. As well as general safety precautions in office, laboratory and factory conditions, they cover particular areas such as the main causes of accidents, special safety affecting transport, the lifting of heavy loads, protective clothing and the use of guards round machinery, and the special duties of supervisory staff. This organisation, whose address is the National Safety Centre, 62–64 Chancellor's Road, London W6 9RS, gives advice and help on every aspect of industrial safety.

SECURITY AGENCIES

There are outside agencies which specialise in security matters. First and foremost there is a Crime Prevention Officer to be found at every police station, who is waiting to be called in to advise on security in your firm. From his point of view, as well as yours, prevention is much better than waiting until damage has been done. Nothing is too small or too large, any aspect of security may be covered, and his services are absolutely free. He will probably be able to identify hazards that have not yet occurred to you. The advice of the professional is well worth taking in working out the most suitable precautions against any sort of crime in your own particular business situation. To be aware of the extent of any problem is a good step towards dealing with it in the most effective way and with the most efficient assistance.

There are also enquiry agents, detectives and confidential service agencies, who will deal with suspicious circumstances for you and make absolutely confidential enquiries quietly and unobtrusively. Contracts can be made over a time basis or overall for special work.

Securicor, or similar organisations, will guard your cash on its way to and from the bank, or the transport of valuables from place to place.

There are guard dogs to deter evildoers during the daytime or at night. Night patrols and night staff can be a deterrent to anyone contemplating a break-in. Further advice obtainable from local security firms or from the Security Officer at your local police station.

LEAKAGE OF INFORMATION

It is very easy to be guilty of leaking information without having had any idea that it has happened. Certainly your dinner companion of last night, who turned the conversation, after a delicious little meal and a bottle of wine, to how busy you must be in the office, is unlikely

Safety and Security

to tell you just why he is interested. You could have said that things were a little slack at the moment, as Mr Smith went off to Brussels yesterday and is calling at Antwerp and Amsterdam before he comes back again. To you it is a small item of unimportant chitchat. To him it may be the missing piece in a jigsaw that his employer has been painstakingly putting together. Never to discuss any aspect of your firm's business at all, with anyone, is the only really safe maxim.

ORGANISED SPYING

People have been found, even outside the pages of espionage fiction, to have been planted in a firm for months, even years, solely in order to make friends with top level executives and their staff. Confidential secretaries and personal assistants, in an unguarded moment, could disclose valuable information to an industrial thief, and any agent from a rival concern knows this well. It should never be forgotten that one cannot be too careful, even when well away from business premises.

What is it that other business organisations would like to know about your firm? It depends on the circumstances. In the fields of research, for example, a company could save large sums of money by knowing what its rivals are up to. Why go to great lengths to set up a research scheme, if someone else is also doing it and a copy of their report can be obtained? Even if their project is not a success, considerable expense will have been saved by knowing that they were pursuing a particular line of enquiry and it turned out to have been a waste of time and money in the end. It is very useful to be able to find out what other people are doing.

Sales promotion ideas are valuable – someone may have thought out a good scheme and the firm that gets in with it first will reap the benefits. Information about possible mergers has Stock Exchange implications, and someone with advance information could use it for unfair personal advantage.

Government departments, and other organisations where security is of vital importance, usually have a security officer who will discuss this aspect with all newly engaged staff. Newcomers will probably be employed on a probationary basis, and before being taken on permanently will have exhaustive enquiries made into their backgrounds and previous records, both of a business and personal kind. Any firm engaging in especially confidential business might do well to consider this principle when taking on new employees.

Equipment used in espionage   Because of the very nature of the work, the methods of a competent agent are quiet, painstaking and subtle. His strength lies in the fact that he will not be noticed.

Industrial spying is an insidious and increasing evil. Over half the directors questioned in an investigation said, when asked, that however much they disliked it, it was accepted and even found to be necessary. There are consequently plenty of people whose job it is to ferret out secrets, and behind this there lies a flourishing industry. Espionage leads to counter-espionage, the work of spying out the spies and preventing them from doing their work.

There are all sorts of little devices on the market. Tiny microphones, bugging attachments, and a variety of other small contraptions are commonly and frequently used, far more than is generally realised. There is, of course, little publicity. The reasons for this are clear enough when it is realised that a firm engaged in industrial spying will have to be absolutely silent on the subject. Similarly a firm suspecting that it is being spied upon will be equally silent, not wishing to give the impression that its security arrangements are inadequate.

If this were not a very serious subject, the gadgets available might sound amusing:

> microphones, transmitters and recorders, small enough to fit neatly into fountain pens (conveniently worn in the top pocket) and wrist watches; also into cigarette packets, books, cigar cases or desk diaries
>
> short-wave receivers and recorders, made to fit into a briefcase or a hat or book
>
> suction microphones, suitable for attaching almost invisibly to walls, window panes or furniture
>
> transmitters which, when fixed to a telephone, are capable of relaying conversations to a house or van several streets away
>
> a flexible video apparatus, which has been devised for looking around corners
>
> cameras – readable typescript can be photographed from 100 yards (91 metres) away, as well as close up.

Wherever there are political or industrial rivalries, spying is a possibility. That it is often an actuality is now one of the unavoidable facts of business life. Some firms engage security agencies to check their boardrooms for bugging devices before an important meeting is held. There are several reputable firms in this country who will attend to this for you.

KIDNAPPING

We assume that you do not want to lose your employer – he is a nice man and he pays your salary. Think how much more important he is to his family, and to his firm he is also a very valuable person. It may even be that he is also internationally significant in some way. In fact, he may have sufficient importance to be a possible potential kidnap victim, and may be worth a substantial ransom. Have either of you thought about this? As an intelligent person you read the news-papers. You must realise that kidnapping is a real possibility for any kind of VIP, and this should not be dismissed lightly as something that only happens to other people.

If your chief is at all likely to be a kidnap victim, there are things he should consider. He may dismiss the idea lightly, but nevertheless ask him to read this chapter. He may have cause to thank you, although of course we hope the occasion will never arise.

New Scotland Yard, Section A7 (3), have compiled a list of commonsense precautions for those who might, in their words, be used as 'bargaining power to extract political or monetary conces-sions'. Briefly, the points they cover are as follows:

The executive's place of business

1. The place of business and grounds, and/or surrounding areas and overlooking vantage points should be the subject of a security report.
2. Access to executive suite areas, offices of top executives and their staff, should be controlled. (Special 'access control' schemes are available).
3. Action to be taken, subsequent to the use of alarm systems and bandit attack buttons, should be laid down.
4. Training should be given to all proven responsible staff connected with VIPs as to the course of action in case of attack, and procedures set out for staff to follow in the event of any violent intrusion.
5. Care is necessary to restrict prior information on an executive's movements, including appointments in desk diaries, travel tickets, information in publicity or press material. These should always be concealed.

Place of residence   This site is particularly vulnerable. Area checks as above, including access roads and neighbouring property, should be made. Advice on alarm systems and precautions against unauthorised entry is available. Precautions relating to non-business engagements and social visits should be taken.

Travel   Consideration should be given to the following points:

1. In trains.   Advisability of choosing different seats when making regular journeys, and avoidance of easily recognisable hall-marks, eg a buttonhole, distinctive briefcase, etc.

2. In cars.   Variations in starting times, the advantage of an inconspicuous car and a plain-clothes chauffeur, and of using the general staff parking space with a different position each day, rather than an individually reserved special VIP bay. A radio or

telephone link should be installed on the executive's car, and regular checks made to base during journeys.

3. In aeroplanes. Booking in another name and changing to the correct one at the last moment; using plain inconspicuous luggage.

4. Abroad. Security arrangements may be needed at the point of destination; these should be discreetly organised and confirmed before the journey is begun.

5. The chauffeur. Should be trained in defensive driving techniques and should know the full capabilities of his car. He should check that the car is absolutely roadworthy, has sufficient petrol, is lockable, and that any identifying stickers or badges are removed. He should be watchful of following cars, and unexpectedly blocked roads or diversions, as he may need to take a quick decision to make a detour. In unfamiliar country detailed forward planning of journeys is very important, noting possible alternative routes and local police stations.

6. Prior arrangements. The best procedures to be followed in an attack on the car, and the course of action in an emergency, should be decided upon beforehand as far as is possible.

Just before leaving, a responsible person at the destination should be telephoned, to inform him of the time of departure and the expected time of arrival.

A code word should be established, to be used as confirmation that any messages given later by the executive are genuine, this word should be known by the chauffeur and the executive's family.

Preliminary plans should clearly lay down the company's policy on whether or not any ransom demanded should be paid.

7. Insurance. Any insurance policy taken out to cover such eventualities must be kept secret.

Scotland Yard are very specific on one point. In their pamphlet *Advice to persons considered vulnerable to kidnap* they say:

> 'It is understood that many small companies, in countries where this type of crime is prevalent, pay small ransoms and do not inform the police. IT IS VITAL THAT POLICE BE CALLED AND ASSUME RESPONSIBILITY IMMEDIATELY ON EVERY OCCASION, FOR ONCE A RANSOM HAS BEEN PAID ANOTHER DEMAND MAY BE MADE SOON AFTER'. (The capital letters are theirs.)

On receipt of a call from the kidnapper There are two kinds of information you need to obtain, and you must not lose your nerve.

Keep calm and keep talking. You want to know if the hostage is well, and you want to find out as much as you can about the kidnapper. The conversation may not be easy or even remotely informative, but there are a few things that you should have in mind, if you can keep your head. The police will question you later, so try to write everything down. Make notes on as many of the following points as possible:

> the date and time of the call
>
> ask for as much information about the hostage, and his condition, as possible
>
> ask if you may speak to him. Get the pre-arranged code word from the hostage if you can
>
> ask who is calling and where the caller is
>
> ask for any special physical characteristics of the hostage which can be confirmed by his family or relatives
>
> ask what is wanted, and how the money should be delivered, when they want it, and whether this time or date can be met
>
> ask how the person collecting the money can be identified
>
> if the money is delivered, when will the hostage be released, and where?
>
> get the caller to repeat instructions, tell him the telephone line is bad and you cannot hear him properly
>
> try to judge whether this is a genuine threat or a hoax
>
> listen to the voice, trying to ascertain nationality, age, male or female, whether there is a stutter or other distinctive feature
>
> listen for background noises, if any.

Kidnapping, as has been said earlier, is a matter for the police. Any organisation in the United Kingdom which has this particular security hazard in mind should apply to the Crime Prevention Section of New Scotland Yard, for their comprehensive help and advice or, in any other country, to their corresponding top security organisation.

BOMB THREATS

It is a regrettable sign of present-day violence that this subject cannot be ignored in a chapter on business safety and security. Safety measures against bomb threats are also very definitely a matter for the police, and fully detailed help and advice may be obtained on planning precautions, and action to be taken in such emergencies from the Crime Prevention officer. The following can be therefore only a very general guide as to what may be expected and what should be done to minimise the dangers.

A bomb warning usually comes first in the form of a telephone call; to the switchboard operator, a selected member of staff or the safety officer, and the person receiving the call should do his best to get as much information as possible. The caller should be asked:

where the bomb is, what it looks like and when it is timed
to go off

the reason for the attack

where the caller is.

The member of staff should try to keep talking, listen for
background noises, try to assess an accent if any, and write down as
much as possible. If the safety officer did not receive the call himself,
he should be informed at once. Two things must then be done
promptly:

call the police

decide whether the building is to be evacuated and, if so, do so
quickly and with due precautions.

If security staff have had preparation for such eventualities, and
the general personnel are used to fire drills, subsequent procedures
should be carried out with the minimum of delay and confusion.

The safety officer will:

arrange for someone to meet the police when they arrive

organise his search crew, and start looking

inform whoever is responsible for evacuating the building to set
this procedure in motion

see that the scheduled place of shelter is searched before
personnel are allowed in.

The best way of warning staff depends on the type and size of the
building. If there is a public address system the person using it should
be calm and give instructions in a clear voice. If the fire alarm system
is used, there should ideally be two separately identified methods of
signal, one for fire and one for bombs. The reason is that in the case of
a bomb threat some escape routes may be dangerously impractical
and in consequence the number of exits will be restricted.

Where there is danger of explosion, staff should not remain near
plate glass windows or glass partitions. In some cases it may actually
be safer for personnel to remain in the building, lying on the floor of a
strongly walled corridor, than to go outside and remain near large
windows. Preliminary planning is of vital importance, and an
architect's advice on which walls may withstand blast may be
invaluable. It should go without saying that if there is warning of a
car bomb, staff should not be allowed to file out into the car park.

Car bombs   A sensible precaution is to keep a car fully locked,
and the windows closed, whenever it is left in a street or place to which
the public has easy access. An internal bonnet lock should be fitted
and used.

Visual checks should be made under the car, under the wheel
arches, along the exhaust pipe and under the engine. Look for wires
or packages or wooden switches. If you see anything suspicious,
inform the police.

Postal bombs   These are designed so that the action of opening causes an explosion. If you are suspicious, look for the following:

possibly excessive weight for the size

protruding wires

a tiny hole, like a pin hole, in wrapping or envelope

grease marks

a smell of almonds or marzipan

an unsolicited book

in a letter, something stiff or hard, weight about 2 oz (60 grammes) or more, thickness about 0.2 in (0.5 cm)

an inner envelope with any of the above features or tightly taped or tied with string, inside an outer normal envelope

look for the point of origin, postmark, or name of sender if given. If in doubt, check with sender.

If you find something suspicious   Place the letter or packet on the nearest horizontal surface, not in a corner or on the floor.

Handle it very carefully, it will have to be examined from all angles when the police arrive.

Do not try to open it, or allow anyone else to touch it.

Do not put it in sand, water, or any container.

Leave the room, lock the door, make sure the key is available when the police come.

Keep the corridor outside clear.

In conclusion, it cannot be over-emphasised that liaison with Scotland Yard's Crime Prevention Section is of vital importance in forward contingency planning in this particular field of security.

FIRE PRECAUTIONS AND PREVENTION

Perhaps the most dangerous and terrifying accident is one that leads to fire, fire on a large scale and out of control. All possible steps should be taken to prevent this ever happening, and there is plenty that can be done, with foresight and planning.

In a small office it is a fairly uncomplicated matter to work out a set procedure; the most important thing is that everyone, even the newest member of staff, should know exactly what to do in any emergency. In a business of any size with, for instance, storerooms, workshops and factory premises spread over a large area, a more detailed strategy needs to be worked out. This is virtually a battle campaign, estimating the possible size of the enemy, where he may appear, and what may be done to overcome him in the shortest possible time before he can do much damage.

General Planning   Most firms appoint their own Fire Officer, either a full-time employee or someone who can combine these duties with others, a trained man with overall responsibility for fire-precautions, fire drills and fire control. The man who has this position should have a trained deputy or deputies, so that someone will be able to take over should there be an emergency when the official fire officer is away from the premises. This ensures that there is always someone qualified, at night or during the day, who can deal effectively with an outbreak, with fully accepted status and over-riding authority.

The management has two main responsibilities here – for the safety of their staff and for the continuation of their business. The interruption of work caused by a fire can be crippling to an industry, especially if it occurs in a key area on which other departments or branches or sub-contractors are dependent. The Fire Protection Association, in their leaflet MRI, Fire Safety data, on *Management responsibility for fire prevention*, sum up the situation very clearly when they say:

'A building or operation which is so planned that the risks from fire are understood, where the chances of a fire occurring have been reduced to the minimum acceptable, and where steps have been taken to ensure that any fire that does occur will be controlled to its area of origin, will be a satisfactory building or operation both from the viewpoint of people's safety and the prosperity of the business.'

Your Fire Precaution Planning Scheme should be structured on a firm basis and the chart in Figure i is issued as a guide by the Fire Protection Association.

Most likely hazards	These fall into the following groups:
Electricity	Neglect or misuse of wiring and equipment.
Rubbish	Waste should be stored in metal bins, and bonfires supervised and kept well away from buildings.
Smoking	Carelessly discarded matches and cigarette ends.
Portable heaters	These should be firmly based, placed safely away from draughts and not in contact with or near combustible articles.
Dangerous goods	Some articles, such as paint, chemicals, aerosols, gas cylinders, etc, need special storage conditions.
Arson	Guard against mischievous children or an adult with a grudge. Doors and windows should be safely shut at night.

Everyone has a constant responsibility, without being specially

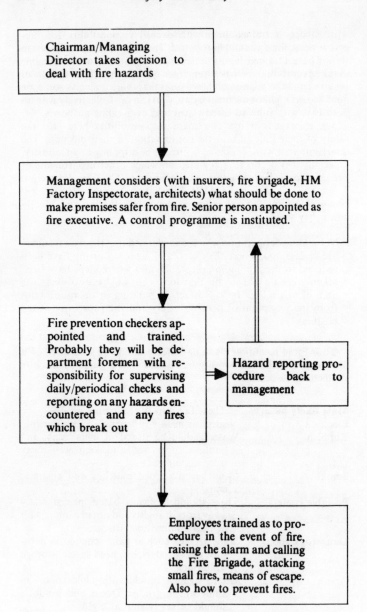

Figure i: Fire Protection Association Action Chart

instructed, to guard against these possibilities, and it may be helpful to put up posters to remind staff that such care is always necessary.

Action required   When a fire officer has been appointed he should be able to identify the main fire risks in your particular area and the kind of work that is carried on there, and will be able to work out a plan that will be based on the following lines:

1. There should be a set procedure for raising the alarm, calling the Fire Brigade, evacuating personnel and attacking the fire. The order in which these are done depends on the circumstances.
2. The fire warning system must be clearly heard and recognisable by all staff throughout the premises.
3. All personnel should know clearly what action to take when they hear the alarm, whether they have special fire duties to carry out or have only to follow the nearest escape route.
4. Fire-fighting equipment should be constantly checked and maintained. Escape routes should be clearly signposted and escape doors easily opened. Lifts should not be used in an emergency.
5. Regular safety checks should be made, especially when staff are leaving the premises, to see that plugs are pulled out, switches off, doors and windows closed, and that nothing is left hot or smouldering.

Outside help and training schemes   Two organisations that can be of great help are the Fire Brigade, through your local branch, and the Fire Protection Association. They will advise you on planning your scheme of protection, identifying the main hazards in your particular business, recommending suitable equipment and giving information on the available training schemes for fire-safety personnel. Details of training schemes are issued on request, and a variety of very helpful leaflets and brochures, film strips and posters, are also obtainable. Training schemes in fire protection are principally available from the FPA, and those in the use of fire fighting equipment from the fire brigades.

If you are not satisfied that the place where you work is covered by as good a safety system as can possibly be devised, perhaps you may be able to initiate a revised and up-to-date protection scheme. It is no exaggeration to see this as a matter of life and death.

INSURANCE

All insurance policy renewal dates, personal policies as well as business, must regularly be entered in your desk diary. See that the value of the policies are regularly adjusted to keep up with the rising costs of repairs and replacements in the event of a claim for compensation. New policies may need to be taken out from time to time, to cover new or changed conditions. It is false economy to neglect insurance cover.

Burglar and fire alarms should be regarded as a form of insurance and should be checked regularly to make sure they are in perfect working order. If this does not fall within your scope of responsibilities, enquire tactfully to ensure that someone is doing it. A non-operational alarm system or lapsed insurance policy could prove to be a major calamity.

It is worth remembering that some insurance companies insist on certain security measures being taken or installed before they will undertake to cover fire and safety risks.

COSTS AND PRIORITIES

When the possible financial loss caused by a serious fire or other accident is considered, the expense of setting up efficient preventive measures appears as money well spent. Tax allowances may be given on the cost of fire defence systems, and regional development grants may be payable towards approved schemes. Some insurance companies also give premium reductions to companies who instal recommended fire protection equipment.

'It is better to be safe than sorry' has always been a sound precept, but it is a fact that good security measures are often a low management priority. The idea that accidents always happen to someone else is still very prevalent, and it is true that good security systems are expensive to set up and maintain. It is unfortunate that money spent on safety is the one thing that cannot be proved to be justified in terms of results, and a board of directors, conscious of possible criticism from their shareholders, may sometimes hesitate before authorising such large sums of money. How can anyone be sure that an expensive system has proved its worth several times over by preventing outbreaks of fire? An efficient security system may save millions of pounds in fraudulent operations that did not take place, but who can say that fire or fraud is inevitable? They may never happen.

Many companies, particularly large industrial concerns, will take advantage of an insurance consultative service, whereby a Risk Assessor is engaged to advise on the firm's individual needs. He would investigate all aspects of the company thoroughly, assess all possible fire and safety hazards, advise on methods of reducing these risks as much as possible, and then report and advise on the insurance needs that still remain. In other words, he would balance a risk-reduction scheme against an insurance plan. This would have obvious cost-productive advantages for the client that engages him. The profession of Risk Management is a growing one, and most established insurance companies are able to give advice in this capacity.

It can be seen that managements have a heavy responsibility to keep everything and everybody as safe and secure as possible, even if some security measures are still not required by law.

Bibliography

British Safety Council publications, list obtainable from the BSC, National Safety Centre, Chancellor's Road, London W6 9RS.

Fire Protection Association publications, list obtainable from the FPA Publications Centre, Aldermary House, Queen Street, London EC4N 1TJ.

Royal Society for the Prevention of Accidents (RoSPA) publications on all aspects of Safety, available from the Industrial Safety Training Centre, 22 Summer Road, Acocks Green, Birmingham B27 7UT.

William Handley (Ed.): *Industrial Safety Handbook* (McGraw Hill Ltd., 1977).

In the office; executive suite or dining room; restaurants, hotels, assembly rooms, banqueting halls etc.; budgeting; guest list; invitations; reservations; transport; excursions; the PA as helper and firm's representative; the PA as guest

The provision of food and drink, amusements, accommodation and transport all come under the heading of 'Entertainment' and the good Secretary/PA will be able to rise to any occasion and make whatever arrangements are necessary, smoothly and with self-confidence. Some secretaries, in the course of their own professional career or that of their chief, become regularly involved in many varied social duties, others may meet this side of business life less often. As social and business entertainment can be casual or formal, completely impromptu or the result of long-term planning, for one or two business colleagues or very many at a time, it can be a very interesting and enjoyable, although sometimes very hard-working, side of business life.

For the organiser there are three locations for business entertaining:

in the office

in the firm's executive suite or dining room

in outside restaurants, conference or assembly rooms, banqueting halls and hotel accommodation.

The Secretary/PA will probably be concerned with the following aspects of business entertaining:

budgeting

guest lists, invitations, acceptances and refusals

reservation of various types of accommodation

the organisation of transport and booking of excursions

her own personal role as helper and firm's representative

her own personal role as guest, when the occasion arises.

IN THE OFFICE

Coffee and Tea   Compliment your chief's visitors by serving tea or coffee in a good-looking matching set of china, serve biscuits separately for people to help themselves, and have saccharine available for those who are weight-watching.

The working or snack lunch   This will mean making a request to the firm's canteen or kitchen staff to send up a tray of something light, such as soup and sandwiches or a salad, but if these facilities are not available within your firm there are outside concerns who will help. Your local Yellow Pages will doubtless reveal names such as 'Dial-a-Meal' or 'Dial-a-Sandwich' or you may already know of a caterer in your locality who will give a prompt and efficient delivery service. However, it is not wise to order from a new and unknown source when visitors are involved.

If your firm has its own catering facilities, make friends with the supervisor or manager. Attractive china and cutlery, clean and polished glasses, table napkins, a jug of ice-cold water, all go towards making a trolley or lunch-tray look appetising. Establish a good rapport with the catering staff, and express warm thanks and appreciation when the service is good, and your chief will never have to hesitate about sharing a working-lunch session with a colleague or visitor.

EXECUTIVE SUITE OR DINING ROOM

Drinks   Your chief will doubtless have his own preferences regarding the contents of his drinks cabinet. As for any other form of stock-checking it is important to re-order before supplies run out, so make an occasional inspection and re-order when necessary. This also applies to cigars and cigarettes kept for visitors.

Lunch or dinner   The catering staff should be given as much notice as possible when visitors are to be entertained to lunch, and your chief may wish you to liaise with the catering manager on the subject of the menu. If you are not sure what to order, the following guidelines may help you:

    Cold – hot – cold: ie a cold starter followed by a hot main dish and then a cold sweet

    Hot – cold – hot: ie a hot starter, cold main course and hot sweet

    Avoid more than one dish with the same theme, eg steak and kidney pie with pastry to follow

    Avoid a repetition of flavours, eg a cheese flan followed by cheese and biscuits.

If there is a last minute change in the numbers expected, notify the catering manager at once, in time for extra settings to be laid or removed before the guests arrive at the table.

Dinner on the firm's premises is only possible if the kitchen staff are available after office hours, or a firm of caterers can be called in to use the kitchens and serve dinner and clear away afterwards. It will probably be more convenient to book an outside restaurant for an evening meal. However, if the firm does wish to engage caterers and give a dinner in its own rooms there will be various preliminary duties:

1. Catering firms should be contacted as early as possible and asked to send specimen menus and wine lists, with details of any extra services such as waiter or waitress service or a bartender with portable bar for pre-dinner drinks, with full details of all charges. It is wise to compare several different brochures before deciding.

2. When the catering firm is chosen and the menu selected you or your chief will wish to select wines from the wine list. Telephone the catering firm with your decisions and make an appointment for their representative to come to your premises and discuss exactly what will be required. They should have every co-operation and help. After the visit, confirm all arrangements to them in writing.

3. Warn the caretaker that there will be a late evening, and see that he or someone else responsible will check the premises and lock up when the guests have all gone.

4. Order flowers, and when they arrive arrange them in suitable vases; you may have to beg or borrow these but at all costs do not find yourself at the last minute unexpectedly dependent on makeshift containers.

5. Check the heating and ventilation of the room; some rooms become unbearably stuffy during dinner.

6. Appoint someone to direct visitors to the cloakrooms and see that there is somewhere for them to leave their coats. If there is to be a large party there should be someone on continuous cloakroom duty during the evening.

7. On the day of the dinner-party you will have plenty of last-minute checking to do, not forgetting to see to the wines. Do not, of course, attempt to do the catering manager's job for him, but it may be useful to know that red wine should be put out in time for it to adjust to room temperature, and white wine should be suitably chilled.

Informal drinks party   The firm's executive suite will probably have good accommodation for a party of this kind, or a suitable room may be hired at a local hotel. The size of the room should relate to the number of guests, being neither too large, nor so small that it will become overcrowded. It is important to:

clear chairs away, as there should not be enough of them to allow
everyone to sit down at once; people should circulate
cigarettes and ashtrays should be available
have enough useful surfaces where people can put down their
glasses
have flowers, but not in places where they may easily be knocked
over.

Most wine merchants will supply drinks on a sale or return basis,
and will also supply glasses without charge except for replacement of
breakages. Your chief may wish to hire a portable bar and
professional bartender.

Your catering manager will advise on food, but anything very
substantial would be out of place. However, there should be a variety
of little savouries, such as small sausages on sticks, olives, tiny
asparagus rolls, smoked salmon, etc, placed on side tables or around
the room where guests can help themselves.

The times on the invitations should be precise, for instance '6.30 to
8.00' so that guests will be able to plan their evening and will not
outstay their welcome.

The Secretary/PA should be ready to help with hostess duties for
her firm if she is asked, and do her best to look after guests, circulate
with a tray of refreshments, make introductions and be generally
useful. She should also be prepared to stay behind at the end to see
that the tidying up arrangements are taken care of, and that other
members of staff who have helped are thanked for their efforts.

RESTAURANTS, HOTELS, ASSEMBLY ROOMS, BANQUETING HALLS, ETC

For a small or medium sized lunch or dinner party your chief may
have a favourite hotel or restaurant; if not, ask what kind of place
he has in mind for his guests, and consult your *Hotel Guide* or *Good
Food Guide*. If he is taking his guests out to dinner he may feel they
would like a cabaret or dancing afterwards, or an early meal and a
concert or theatre to follow. Out of town or overseas guests may
appreciate dinner combined with some kind of entertainment to
follow, and others may simply prefer a good country hotel with a
reputation for homecooked food, log fires and oak beams.

An important point to consider when arranging entertainment for
business colleagues is that visitors of other races are often subject to
strict dietary restrictions. Jewish and Islamic visitors are particular
examples, and care should be taken that dishes unacceptable to them
are not on the menu chosen.

When your chief has decided on the hotel or restaurant, telephone
to book the table. Ask for the manager and tell him how many will be
in the party and at what time they wish to have their meal. Your chief

may also wish you to ask whether there is a bar or lounge where his party can have drinks beforehand.

It is as well to confirm an advance booking in writing. It is up to you to do this; the hotel will not unless specially requested. On the morning of the date chosen, telephone once more to make a last-minute check that the party is expected and that everything is in order. For a telephone booking at very short notice, of course, written confirmation may not be possible.

A specimen confirmatory letter may be something on the lines of the following example:

(Date)

The Manager
The White Lion Hotel
Riverside Walk
Silvercombe

Dear Sir

We confirm the reservation made with your hotel on the telephone this morning, as follows:

We wish to book a table for eight people for dinner at 8.00 pm on Friday, April 20th, and are glad to hear that you are able to let us have the table in the bay window overlooking the river.

With thanks
Yours faithfully

Publicity Manager

By previous arrangement with the manager, or if your firm is already known to the restaurant, the host can sign the bill and the account can be settled later when sent in direct to the firm's accounts department. For a casual occasion, when the host pays the bill on the spot, the receipt should be carefully preserved and brought back to the office, as business entertaining is allowable for tax purposes and the receipts provide evidence of the expenditure. It is very important that all hotel and restaurant receipts are kept for the accounting records.

If dinner with a cabaret or floor show is chosen, ask for a table with a good view when you telephone; guests should not find themselves seated behind a pillar or too far away to see properly. If there is a band or an orchestra ask that the table is not too near to it, otherwise conversation may be impossible.

If a theatre party is to be arranged, or an evening at the ballet or a concert, dinner will have to be early in order that the guests may finish their meal and get to their seats before the curtain rises. Check the time of the performance before deciding when the meal should be booked; do not choose a restaurant too far from the theatre. There are a number of theatres where the restaurant service on the spot is very good, and bookings for dinner and the performance may be made at the same time. The Shakespeare Theatre at Stratford-upon-Avon is only one example of many.

Find out from your chief what sort of show he wishes to take his guests to, perhaps he knows that they would like to see the latest musical, or the cliff-hanging thriller they have read about in the papers. In any case you should know about current productions from the reviews in the newspapers, and should be able to advise if you are asked. (See chapter 13, Reading the Newspapers.)

Telephone the theatre or use an agency – the latter will probably be quicker. An agency will obtain tickets and send them to your office for a small extra charge. Keep these in a safe place until they are needed and do not forget where you have put them, nor omit to check that your chief goes off on the evening in question with them safely in his pocket.

If the dinner party is arranged for a visiting colleague and his wife it is likely that your chief's wife will be one of the party as well. In this case, first ascertain that she will be free on the date chosen. Make sure tactfully that your boss knows that she has no other commitments that evening; if he does not know, telephone her and ask.

Ask him also if he wishes you to arrange for a car to take the party to dinner or on to the theatre, and/or pick them up afterwards and take them home or to their hotel. If a car hire or taxi firm is used, see that the driver knows beforehand who is going to pay his charges.

For a large-scale dinner or banquet a catering firm will be indispensable and you will be required to liaise with them from time to time as arrangements take shape. At the outset you should go to inspect the room offered by the restaurant, hotel or banqueting hall and check:

    whether there are any problems of size, with regard to the number of guests and the arrangement of tables

    that heating and ventilation facilities are adequate

    that the sound and amplifying equipment, if there are to be speeches, are adequate and in working order

    that the distance from the kitchens does not mean that meals will be less than hot on arrival

    that cloakroom accommodation and car-parking space are satisfactory that fire exits are clearly signposted.

Further points for consideration are:

If there is to be music or dancing, what sort of band or orchestra will be most suitable? Will the tables be cleared away for dancing, in which case will there be a room for the guests while this is done? Will dancing be in a separate room, and if so is it suitable and large enough?

Special occasions   Dinners and receptions may be arranged predominantly for business purposes, for instance to celebrate the launching of a new product or the completion of a successful trade mission. (See also section on Conference Planning.) It will then be necessary to have suitable publicity, and a photographer should be booked and press representatives invited to attend. A demonstration model may be on show or a special exhibition set up in adjoining rooms for the guests to see. When this is the case, and the guests are invited specifically to represent their firm, the acceptance or refusal of the invitation may have to follow a particular style (see under Invitations for an example).

Banquets and formal dinners   Additional points which may concern the Secretary/PA on very formal occasions are:

1. Seating arrangements. The guest of honour, principal guests and any others who are to speak should be placed at the top table, and a copy of the plan of place names should be given to the banqueting or catering firm before the dinner takes place.

2. Toastmaster. The telephone directory will help you in finding a professional toastmaster if his services are required, and there are a number of Toastmasters' Associations which can assist and advise.

3. Speeches. Select your speakers, and any guests who will be proposing a toast, in plenty of time for them to prepare their after-dinner speeches.

4. Microphones. Amplifying equipment should be installed and should be finally re-checked on the day to make sure that the speeches will be heard all over the room and not only by those sitting at the top table.

5. Cloakroom facilities. Very special guests should have their own separate cloakroom accommodation. A separate room in which to welcome them before dinner may also be required.

6. Presentations. If a presentation is to be made, make quite certain that the order for the gift is put in early enough for it to be ready by the due date, especially if further work has to be done after the

article is purchased; for instance a silver cup or bowl may have to be engraved before presentation. The ordering time should be sufficient to allow for unexpected delays in delivery.

BUDGETING

Most firms have a regular annual sum set aside for business entertaining but for any large unusual occasion special funds will have to be made available. On this amount of money depends the size of the entertainment, the number of guests, or both. The first thing to ascertain before planning any entertaining is the amount of money you may spend. The next step is to allocate it as sensibly as possible. It is not good management to make extravagant bookings and then be informed by the accounts department that the money is not there to cover them.

If rooms are to be hired, time your programme as precisely as possible; hire charges are sometimes based on the time spent on the premises, including cloakrooms, lounge-bars and so on, and an extra hour's occupation may make a very big difference to the size of the bill.

GUEST LIST

When a function is to have a particular theme, the guest list will come from those directly concerned with that theme, and perhaps also from associated peripheral groups. You will have to consider whether guests should be invited from outside the 'core' list. Perhaps the press should also be asked, and perhaps representatives from firms similar to your own. Your chief will have his own suggestions for the guest list, and you may be able to augment them.

If you do wish for publicity, issue invitations to the press and/or have a press release ready to send out. The press should not be neglected as regards refreshments, and should be catered for separately if they are not included in the guest-list category.

Make a list of acceptances and refusals as they come in.

Your chief may wish to have admission tickets printed, to be sent out to those who have accepted. If these tickets are numbered, and each one handed back on arrival is checked against the guest list, they will provide a useful confirmation of those actually attending. These tickets need not give full details, all that is needed is the title of the function, the date and time, and 'Admit One'.

Keep a copy of the menu in your Entertaining file, with the guest list. If the same people are invited on another occasion you will then be able to guard against providing a similar menu.

INVITATIONS

Invitations for a small party may be sent out neatly typed, but formal invitation cards can be obtained pre-printed from any stationer, to be filled in with typed or handwritten details. For special occasions a firm will have its own cards printed, with a blank space left for the name to be written in, or it may be printed with room for the name to be added at the top left-hand corner. Any good stationer will show you sample layouts from which to make a choice.

Invitations are set out in the third person; two examples of style and layout are given below:

THE SOUTH RIDING YOUNG FARMERS' ASSOCIATION

request the pleasure of the company of

....

at their
HARVEST DINNER
on Wednesday, 15th October 198- at 7.30 for 8.00 pm
at the
Corn Exchange Buildings, Main Street, Thruxton Magna

RSVP to the Secretary

A more personal invitation would be as follows:

MR and MRS PETER BLACK

request the pleasure of the company of

....

on the occasion of the Wedding
of their daughter Valerie to Mr Benjamin Brown
at St Stephen's Church, High Street, Bicklestone
at 11.30 am on Tuesday, 15th June 198-
and afterwards at The Manor House, Bicklestone

The Manor House
Bicklestone   RSVP

Each invitation sets out clearly the details of the occasion, where it is to be held and at what time. RSVP (*répondez, s'il vous plaît*) should be taken seriously; it is a courtesy to reply at once, as the secretary or hostess must know in plenty of time how many guests to expect.

If you are asked to accept or decline it must be done in the same style as the invitation. We will assume that your chief, in this instance Mr John Perkins, is unable to go to the dinner but he and Mrs Perkins are happy to accept their personal invitation to the wedding. The two replies will then be set out on the following lines:

(Mr Perkins's address)

Mr John Perkins thanks the South Riding Young Farmers' Association for their kind invitation to their Harvest Dinner on Wednesday, 15th October 198- at 7.30 for 8.00 pm at the Corn Exchange Buildings, Thruxton Magna, but much regrets that he is unable to accept owing to a prior engagement.

(Date)

The date is always placed at the foot on the left. The sending address is not given, and there is no need for a signature.

The reason for a refusal should always be given, even if (as above) it is not precise. It might be necessary to decline 'owing to his being on holiday on that date' or 'owing to his being abroad on business at that time'.

The form of acceptance may be as follows:

(Mr Perkins's address)

Mr and Mrs John Perkins thank Mr and Mrs Peter Black for their kind invitation to the Wedding of their daughter Valerie to Mr Benjamin Brown at St Stephen's Church, High Street, Bicklestone at 11.30 am on Tuesday, 15th June 198-, and afterwards at the Manor House, Bicklestone, which they are delighted to accept.

(Date)

It will be seen that in each case the wording is faithfully reproduced. This may seem unnecessarily pedantic, but the Young Farmers and also Mr and Mrs Black may be sending out several sets of invitations for different occasions on different dates and it should always be made clear exactly which one is being answered. In most cases there is no possible likelihood of a mistake, but it is a useful custom and should be followed.

When replying to an invitation sent from a married couple the reply envelope should be addressed to the hostess only, it being assumed that she is the one making the arrangements.

Replies may normally be neatly typed, but it is an extra courtesy in the case of an invitation from a very eminent person to send a hand-written reply.

A variation in wording may be necessary in some cases in response to a business invitation. If, for instance, the editor of a magazine has been invited to a function by virtue of his office, and wishes to have his publication represented although he cannot be there himself, he may pass the invitation on to a colleague of similar status. In this case no-one will mind if he sends a substitute and then the acceptance of the invitation, which was addressed to, say, 'The Editor of the *Weekly News*', will follow the usual 'thanking' formula, adding –

> . . . regrets that he is unable to accept owing to a prior engagement, but his deputy, Mr James Robinson, Financial Correspondent of the *Weekly News*, has pleasure in accepting in his place.

If there should be the slightest doubt about the substitution being acceptable to the host, the secretary should first telephone to enquire and explain. The name of the person deputising should always be given.

RESERVATIONS

If your chief is expecting business guests to stay overnight or longer and you are not sure what grade of hotel is required, ask him for suggestions, ie five-star or something more modest. The *AA* and *RAC Members' Handbook*, good hotel guides of all kinds and local Yellow Pages will all give possible addresses for accommodating the visitors. Probably your firm has a list of suitable hotels already, or you may have had a recent recommendation of a good hotel.

Telephone the manager to state the date of the visit and the duration, the kind of accommodation required and the number of people involved. When the booking has been made it is up to you to confirm it in writing. Address the letter to 'The Manager' and make it clear whether the bill is to come to your firm or not. Put all the details you gave over the telephone into the confirming letter. If your firm is paying the bill it is only necessary to give the guest's name and his accommodation requirements. If he is to settle his own account set out his address as well. The following is a specimen letter of confirmation:

(Date)

The Manager
Fern Court Hotel
Kings Road
Manston
Kent

Dear Sir

We confirm our telephone conversation with you this morning, and should be glad if you would kindly reserve the following accommodation for Mr Peter Fraser:

Single room with private bath, from Friday August 4th to Tuesday August 8th inclusive. Bed and breakfast only, but dinner is required on the evening of August 4th.

Please let us have your account in due course.

Yours faithfully
PERKINS, PERKINS & CO LTD

JOHN PERKINS
Managing Director

An alternative style of letter, for a guest who will settle his own bill, is as follows:

(Date)

The Manager
Winchester House Hotel
Beverley Street
London W38 4RK

Dear Sir

Following our telephone booking this morning, we confirm that we should like you to reserve a double room with breakfast and dinner for Mr and Mrs K Richardson, of 15 Priory Road, Sandwich, Kent, between the 17th July and the 2nd August.

Mr and Mrs Richardson will be arriving in the afternoon of the 17th July and leaving during the morning of 2nd August. They will settle their own account.

Yours faithfully
PERKINS, PERKINS & CO LTD

JOHN PERKINS
Managing Director

TRANSPORT

Visitors travelling from a distance, but not in their own cars, should be met at the airport or station. You should check the time of arrival and arrange for them to be collected, using the firm's own car facilities or a car-hire firm, and allowing plenty of time for the car to arrive before they do, in case of traffic delays. It is better to have time to spare than to keep people waiting. A car may also be needed to take guests from place to place during their visit, and to the airport or station when they leave.

In these days of fast long-distance travel it should be remembered that a guest who arrives from, say, Los Angeles one afternoon is not likely to be interested in a full-scale reception and dinner an hour or so after he touches down. Time is required to adjust to the new time scale and recover from the jet-lag period. If a tight schedule is unavoidable, arrange the lightest appointments first and the more important ones, requiring the most concentration, towards the end of his visit. This may not be entirely possible, but every effort should be made to allow a period of recovery. A free afternoon or morning to 'sleep it off' will be very much appreciated. The very least you can do for your transcontinental visitor is to make sure that his first evening is a quiet one.

EXCURSIONS

Perhaps your business guests would like to be taken to see a special place of interest or be present at some special function. Overseas visitors in particular may wish to go sightseeing or, according to the season, might appreciate tickets for Wimbledon, or a visit to Cowes for sailing or Ascot for fashion and the races. There may be interesting historical buildings or stately homes not too far from your office; perhaps they would like to see them. You should have suggestions ready to make for the visitors' leisure hours.

Sometimes, in the case of a visiting married couple, one will be occupied with business appointments, leaving the other free to go sightseeing or shopping. If you can discover beforehand what they would like to do you will be able to make arrangements in advance. Arrange for a car for transport, get tickets for the theatre, an exhibition or a fashion show or excursion, book a meal at a pleasant hotel or restaurant, look ahead as much as possible to ensure that your visitor or visitors will have an enjoyable day. You may have to re-arrange your own timetable in order to accompany them, or else see that they have a congenial member of staff to go with them and act as guide and companion.

THE PA AS HELPER AND FIRM'S REPRESENTATIVE

Social functions with a business background often take the form of a little reception, an informal gathering with drinks or a small party, with guests invited from outside the firm. On these occasions the Secretary/PA should not forget that she has duties to perform, helpfully and unobtrusively, as she is a representative of her firm and is therefore there to assist.

Generally speaking you can be of enormous help on these occasions, but should never appear conspicuous or 'managing' while doing all you can to make guests feel that they are welcome. Wear something quietly suitable, not too obvious or extreme, and try to look happy and unflappable.

If you are helping to welcome visitors to a gathering of this kind, do so by name. Be prepared to make introductions and keep guests circulating and happy. Study the guest list beforehand so that you remember names perfectly. Be ready to ask people 'Is there anyone you would like to meet?' and then be able to introduce them.

Introductions   Introduce male to female; if both people are of the same sex introduce the younger to the older. To put this differently, speak first to the lady or to the older or more important of the two. 'Mrs Brown, this is Harry Robinson. Mr Robinson, this is Mrs Brown – ' and then add something that they can both talk about to help them in starting a conversation. Or 'Sir Charles, may I introduce my friend Peter Brooks? Peter, this is Sir Charles Cornwall, who would like to hear about your trip to Hamburg'.

Help to keep people circulating, which does not mean breaking up a conversation which is going well but watching out for anyone who appears bored or neglected. It is a good plan to ask certain other members of staff, when you make your arrangements for this sort of occasion, to be responsible for selected guests and see that they are looked after and able to meet the people they wish to talk to, and ensure that no-one is ignored or left out of things.

THE PA AS GUEST

You may at some time find yourself at a social function representing your firm purely as a guest and not in a working capacity, and even if you do not know many of the other guests you can still be relaxed, poised and self-confident. For a very informal gathering there will be no problems, but if there is even a hint of formality it is as well to remember a few basic guidelines.

When you are formally introduced to someone 'How do you do' is the acceptable and safe response, from both parties. There are variations of course, such as the American 'Glad to know you' or something on the lines of 'How nice to meet you at last', although 'Pleased to meet you' should be avoided.

When offered a drink or something to eat, accept or refuse definitely, never say 'I don't mind' which is guaranteed to make the questioner confused. A truthful 'Yes please' or 'No thank you, not just now' will be clearly understood and appreciated. Incidentally, be sure you know your drinking capacity; a glass of milk or a thick slice of bread and butter is a good thing before a party if you feel unsure of yourself, although there is no need to drink alcohol at all if you prefer not to, there are sure to be non-alcoholic drinks available.

If you find yourself with a group of people, help the conversation along on general lines, so that no-one feels out of it or unable to contribute. Safe subjects to which everyone can relate are, for instance, travel, holidays, children, leisure activities. Subjects to avoid are politics, race and religion, which can lead to heated arguments or hurt feelings.

Enjoy the occasion (but do not be the last to leave) and remember (of course) to thank your host or hostess when you say goodbye, and your evening should be a complete success.

18 SOURCES OF INFORMATION AND SERVICES

> *Routine office information; basic reference books; daily and evening press; office files; specialist knowledge within the firm; local public libraries; specialist libraries; extracting facts; books of reference; consultancy and agency services*

An efficient and resourceful secretary will not only be familiar with standard works of reference but will know how and where to obtain accurate information on almost any topic. Nobody can be expected to know everything, but practically any fact can be traced; it is just a question of knowing what sources of information exist and where to start searching for any material that is needed.

ROUTINE OFFICE INFORMATION

Most secretaries anticipate daily queries by keeping carefully updated files and cards for telephone numbers, names and addresses of customers, agencies, sources of supply, names of suitable hotels and restaurants for social and business occasions and any relevant press cuttings. In the event of an unexpected breakdown of a typewriter, duplicator or office copier, a burst pipe in the cloakroom or an electricity failure, it is a simple matter to refer to one's own emergency services list and ring for a mechanic.

BASIC REFERENCE BOOKS

Your own standard reference books will, naturally, vary according to the type of job but few would argue against any basic set of office reference books including a good English dictionary, a book on correct English usage and forms of address, the current Post Office Guide, telex directory, phone books and Yellow Pages, an atlas with a gazetteer, a ready reckoner and a year book relevant to the firm's activities. (All industries and professions have their own reference works.)

DAILY AND EVENING PRESS

Newspapers provide up-to-the-minute news on current affairs at home and abroad, marketing and City news, Stock Exchange prices, the arts, theatres and exhibitions. See section on Reading the Newspapers.

OFFICE FILES

Office files containing a record of the departmental office correspondence and communications will be carefully and methodically stored and indexed so that instant recall of information is always possible. It is probable that certain files kept in other departments of the firm will contain related material to which the secretary needs to refer from time to time. See section on Record Keeping and Storage of Information.

SPECIALIST KNOWLEDGE WITHIN THE FIRM

Some firms have their own library containing books relevant to their type of business. They may also run an information centre or department whose staff will collect and store press cuttings about the organisation and its policies. Specialist members of the firm such as an accountant, lawyer, press officer or public relations officer would be able to answer specific queries or suggest where more detailed information could be obtained.

LOCAL PUBLIC LIBRARIES

Libraries arrange and classify their non-fiction books according to subjects. In order to find a particular book, the subject card index or the author's card index should be consulted. Library staff are usually most willing to help to locate books. If the local library does not have a copy of any book which is needed, the librarian will generally manage to obtain a copy fairly quickly from another library by telephoning or telexing.

SPECIALIST LIBRARIES

ASLIB – Association of Special Libraries and Information Bureaux – deals with specialised published information. The ASLIB directory, published in two volumes, gives information sources for science, technology and commerce in volume I and medicine, social sciences and humanities in volume II.

LASER – London and South Eastern Region – holds a directory of all its member libraries which includes several polytechnics, the BBC, the British Council, the House of Commons, City of London Lending Library, Guildhall Reference Library and City Business Library. Each library holds a catalogue of every other LASER's holdings on microfilm and each member library specialises by collecting all books relating to a special subject area. For example, Croydon Public Library's special subject is Economics and Enfield's is Languages.

The British Library is one of the most comprehensive national libraries in the world. Its very rapid development was made possible by the existence of the British Museum Library, the National Lending Library for Science and Technology, the National Central Library and the British National Bibliography, as the services of all these libraries complement each other to a remarkable extent. The chart below illustrates the structure of the British Library's resources.

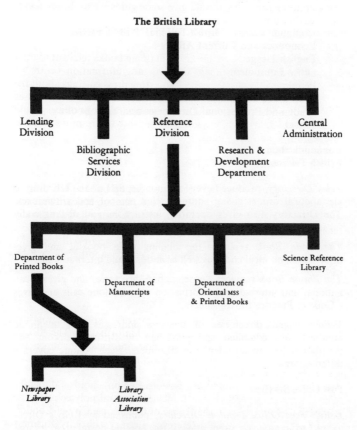

The British Library

Lending Division

Bibliographic Services Division

Reference Division

Research & Development Department

Central Administration

Department of Printed Books

Department of Manuscripts

Department of Oriental MSS & Printed Books

Science Reference Library

Newspaper Library

Library Association Library

The British Library

EXTRACTING FACTS

Before extracting facts from any reference book check that the work is of recent publication. Note any special arrangement of the contents page and the indexing method used. Try an alternative subject if there is no exact entry under the heading you have in mind. Check any cross-references and note whether a bibliography is given for sources of further research.

BOOKS OF REFERENCE

It is quite impossible to give a complete list of all available reference books but the following should give some guidance to those seeking information on:

     Communications – British Telecom, Post Office Services
     Economics and Current Affairs
     English Usage
     Office Equipment
     People
     Press and Publishing
     Trade and Professional Directories and Year Books
     Travel

Communications:
British Telecom

Telex Directory, produced every six months, lists all the UK users in alphabetical order, giving address, telex number and answerback. The Directory also gives operating instructions and dialling codes for international calls.

The Code Book replaces the dialling code booklet and gives information on local codes as well as national and international.

The Phone Book replaces the telephone directories and gives local, national and international information on telephone calls and gives a Code of Practice for consumers.

Yellow Pages, directories of business addresses and telephone numbers, are compiled and published by British Telecom and distributed free to all telephone customers. Each volume covers a different area.

Post Office Services

Kelly's Post Office London Directory, published by Kelly's Directories Ltd, contains a street atlas of the London postal area, a large map of the London underground system and an index of buildings and streets. It is the official directory of Royal Households, Government Ministers, MPs of Greater London and adjoining constituencies. It also gives Commonwealth High Commissioners, Foreign Ambassadors and Consuls in London and Her Majesty's Representatives abroad.

Postal Addresses and Index to Postcode Directories This contains the correct postal addresses of place names in the UK (excluding London) and the Irish Republic.

Postal Directories giving full postcodes are held at all main Post Offices.

Post Office Guide is published annually with supplements issued from time to time throughout the year. It gives complete information on all departments of the Post Office including principal inland and overseas services, postal conditions, National Girobank postal orders, savings schemes, remittance and all related services.

Economics and current affairs

Annual Abstract of Statistics is published by HMSO and contains statistical surveys of the social and economic life of Britain in all its aspects. It is supplemented by publications of *Monthly Digest of Statistics* and *Financial Statistics*.

Britain: An Official Handbook is prepared by the Reference Division of the Central Office of Information for HMSO and it is revised each year. It describes the machinery of governemnt and other institutions, together with the physical and social background of the UK and shows the part played by government in the life of Britain.

British Business, published each week by the Department of Trade and Industry, provides statistics of wholesale prices.

Employment Gazette is an official journal of the Department of Employment which gives statistics on manpower, wages, hours of work and an index of retail prices.

Hansard, published by HMSO, gives daily and weekly verbatim reports of the proceedings in the House of Commons and the House of Lords.

Keesing's Contemporary Archives News sheets are issued weekly by the Longman Group Ltd, Journals Division and bound into annual volumes. This is an international news reference service abstracted from the world's press and news information services.

Lloyd's List and Shipping Gazette presents daily records of detailed movements of shipping throughout the world.

Pears Cyclopaedia, published by Pelham Books Ltd, provides a considerable amount of background information and reference material for everyday use. Among the many topics are: public affairs, economics, money matters, The English Novel, music, and the Environment.

Whitaker's Almanack is published annually in three editions with world-wide information about public affairs, government, industry, finance, commerce and the arts. It also contains a considerable amount of detailed information in regard to modes of address.

English usage

There are many excellent dictionaries such as *Chambers Twentieth Century Dictionary*, the *Oxford English Dictionary* and the *Heritage Illustrated Dictionary of the English Language*. There are also many specialist and technical dictionaries such as *Chambers Dictionary of Science and Technology* and *Black's Medical Dictionary*.

Bartlett's Familiar Quotations by John Bartlett (Macmillan Press Ltd) has a wide collection of passages, phrases and proverbs traced to their sources in ancient and modern literature. It was much used and recommended by Sir Winston Churchill.

Fowler's Modern English Usage, revised by Sir Ernest Gowers and published by OUP, is learned and witty on points of grammar, style and accepted English usage.

Pitman English and Shorthand Dictionary (Pitman and Sons Ltd) gives the meaning of words together with their shorthand outlines.

Roget's Thesaurus of English Words and Phrases This 'Treasury' of English words and phrases was first published in 1852. Classified and arranged in word groups of similar meanings, it is designed to assist writers to express their ideas in the clearest possible way. The first full revision for 20 years was published in 1982.

The Complete Plain Words This book, first written in 1954 by Sir Ernest Gowers, has been revised by Sir Bruce Fraser and reprinted by HMSO. It was originally written to make a positive contribution to the improvement of 'official' English and is intended primarily for 'those who use words as tools of their trade in administration or business'.

Titles and Forms of Address, a Guide to Their Correct Use Published by A. & C. Black, this sets out the correct method of address in writing and speech and includes a guide to the pronunciation of unusual surnames. A full list of the order of priority for decorations is also given.

Webster's New Dictionary of Synonyms, published in the UK by G. Bell and Sons Ltd, is a dictionary of synonyms and antonyms, analagous and contrasted words. The introduction gives an informative survey of the history of synonomy.

Office equipment

Business Education Today incorporating *Office Skills*. This monthly magazine of Pitman Publishing Ltd is written mainly for business studies teachers and lecturers.

Business Equipment Digest, published monthly by BED Business Journals, is intended for management executives responsible for the purchase of business equipment.

Business Equipment Guide, published annually by BED Business Books Ltd, is a product specification manual which covers all business equipment and gives full information on individual firms' products.

Business Systems and Equipment, published monthly by Maclean-Hunter Ltd, gives up-to-date and comprehensive news about business equipment together with practical advice on its application in working systems.

Mind Your Own Business, published monthly by Cairnmark Ltd, aims to assist in the management of business by astute application of equipment and techniques.

Office Equipment Index, published monthly by Maclaren Publishers Ltd, gives details of new equipment.

Office Equipment News, published monthly by Business Publications Ltd, is intended for executives and administrators in the UK who, in the course of their duties, are required to specify or buy office equipment or services.

Office Pride is a bi-monthly journal published by the Office Machines and Equipment Federation.

Office Trade News, published monthly by Patey Doyle (Publishing) Ltd, is the only publication dedicated to the dealer rather than the user.

People

Air Force List, published bi-annually in the spring and autumn by HMSO, lists details of officers and certain senior NCOs serving in the Ministry of Defence, Command Headquarters and in the RAF generally in the UK and overseas. A section is included on Princess Mary's RAF Nursing Service.

Army List, published annually by HMSO, is in two parts; the first gives details of Army Commands and lists senior officers on the active list and Royal Marine officers. It also lists all regiments, corps and military establishments. The second part lists officers in receipt of retired pay.

Burke's Genealogical and Heraldic History of the Landed Gentry, published by Burke's Peerage Ltd in conjunction with Shaw Publishing Co Ltd. The people recorded here are those who, although not peers, nevertheless are, or whose ancestors have been, proprietors of considerable territorial possessions. Some of the families recorded here can trace their descent and ownership of their lands even further back than some of the oldest families in the peerage. As high-ranking commoners their contributions to local and central government have often been of great importance in UK affairs.

Burke's Genealogical and Heraldic History of the Peerage, published by Burke's Peerage Ltd in conjunction with Shaw Publishing Co Ltd. Entries are restricted to those people, barons, baronesses, and those of higher rank, who, as hereditary or life peers, are entitled to sit in the House of Lords. Authoritative articles on such subjects as precedence, the constitution and correct modes of address are included.

Chambers Biographical Dictionary published by W. & R. Chambers Ltd. This, unlike the Dictionary of National Biography, also includes important people still living. The entries are concise; eg for the poet William Wordsworth there is one single page against the fifteen pages about him in the Dictionary of National Biography.

Crockford's Clerical Directory, published by OUP, is a reference book of the clergy of the provinces of Canterbury and York and of other Anglican provinces and dioceses.

Debrett's Correct Form, gives information regarding protocol and forms of address.

Debrett's Handbook, the successor to *Kelly's Handbook*, is a comprehensive biographical work which covers a wide range of leaders in every field.

Debrett's Peerage and Baronetage, jointly published by Debrett's Peerage Ltd and Macmillan London Ltd (the Knightage and Companionage sections appear in *Debrett's Handbook*). The contents include life peers, a guide to the wearing of orders, table of precedence, forms of addressing persons of title and orders of knighthood and chivalry.

Dentists Register, published under the direction of the General Dental Council, lists the names and addresses of dental practitioners registered with the General Dental Council.

Dictionary of National Biography contains biographical details of all noteworthy inhabitants of the British Isles and the colonies from very early days to the present, excluding people still living.

Diplomatic Service List Part I contains lists of Ministers, senior officers and Home Departments in the Foreign and Commonwealth Office. Part II lists British representatives in the Commonwealth, foreign countries and the Republic of Ireland with addresses of missions and consulates. Part III gives a chronological list of Secretaries and Ministers of State, Permanent Under Secretaries, Ambassadors and High Commissioners. Part IV gives biographical notes and lists of staff. Representatives of Commonwealth countries and foreign States, serving in London are shown in a separate publication, the *London Diplomatic List* published by HMSO every three months.

Medical Register, published by the General Medical Council, comprises the register of medical practitioners in alphabetical order.

Navy List, published by HMSO, contains lists of ships, establishments and officers of the Fleet and is published annually each spring. The appendix gives rates of pay, conditions of retirement, entry regulations, etc, and there is a separate retired list.

Solicitors' and Barristers' Directory and Diary incorporates the Law Society List of Practising Solicitors and the Senate of the Inns of Court and the Bar List of Members

The Times Guide to the House of Commons, published by Times Books Ltd, contains biographies of present Members and unsuccessful candidates together with photographs of all Members, texts of Party manifestos and a statistical analysis of the last general election.

Who's Who, published by A. and C. Black Ltd, contains short biographies of prominent people in all walks of life and gives information regarding their careers, recreations, addresses, clubs etc. There are many specialised *Who's Who* editions such as the *Business Who's Who*, which is a biographical dictionary of chairmen, chief executives and managing directors of British registered companies together with the board of directors of the top two hundred companies; *Who's Who in the World*; *Who's Who in the Theatre*; *Who's Who in the Motor Industry* etc. *Who Was Who* gives information on prominent people who have died.

Press and publishing

Authors and Writers Who's Who, published by Burke's Peerage Ltd, gives biographies of living authors with lists of their works and where applicable their pseudonyms. It also gives a list of literary agents.

Benn's Press Directory is published in two volumes, UK and International. The UK volume contains a master A-Z index to all listed UK publications, a county/regional index to newspapers and a classified index to periodicals, agencies and services for the communications industry and media organisations. There are also many Benn directories, year books and business magazines.

British Books in Print, in four volumes, is published by J. Whitaker & Sons Ltd, is produced annually and gives details of all books published and still in print in the UK.

British Education Index/British Humanities Index/Current Technology Index are all useful sources for tracing articles which have appeared in magazines and newspapers.

British National Bibliography The objects of the BNB are to list every new work published in the British Isles and to describe each work in detail. It excludes periodicals, music, maps and certain government publications.

Cassell and the Publishers Association Directory of Publishing in Great Britain, the Commonwealth, Ireland, South Africa and Pakistan. Part I – The publishing and promotion of books, including book societies, book clubs, literary foundations etc. Part II – Representatives and services, including picture and photographic agencies, television and radio organisations, translators, etc.

Current British Directories published by CBD Research Ltd.

Directory of British Official Publications A guide to sources. First published in 1984 by Mansell Publishing Ltd.

Ulrich's International Periodicals Directory, published by R. R. Bowker Company, is a classified guide to current periodicals, both foreign and domestic.

Willing's Press Guide, published by Thomas Skinner Directories, is a yearly guide to the press of the UK and to the principal publications of Europe, Australasia, Gulf States, and the USA. It also contains a list of trade journals for particular trades and professions.

Writers' and Artists' Year Book, published by A. and C. Black Ltd, is a directory for writers, artists, playwrights, writers for film, radio and television, photographers and composers.

Writers' Directory Published biennially by St James' Press, this book gives brief information on over 18,000 living writers in English from many parts of the world. It also contains a 'yellow page' section listing authors under their various writing categories.

Trade and Professional Directories and year books

1. Directories

Directory of British Associations and Associations in Ireland, published by CBD Research Ltd, gives interests, activities and publications of trade associations, scientific and technical societies, professional institutes, learned societies, research organisations, chambers of trade and commerce, agricultural societies, trades unions, cultural, sports and welfare organisations.

Directory of Directors, published by Thomas Skinner Directories lists, in alphabetical order, the directors of the principal public and private companies in the UK with the names of the concerns with which they are associated.

Kelly's Manufacturers and Merchants Directory, published by Kelly's Directories Ltd., gives an alphabetical and classified list of manufacturers, wholesalers and firms offering a service to industry, together with their trade descriptions, addresses, telephone numbers, telegraphic addresses and telex numbers. The directory also lists British importers under the goods they import and international exporters and services sub-divided by countries.

Ryland's Directory, published by Fuel & Metallurgical Journals Ltd, is a standard work of reference for the British Engineering Industry. It gives names and addresses of firms and particulars of products manufactured and merchanted. It also provides a comprehensive index to Brand Names and Trade Marks.

UK Kompass, which is produced by Kompass Publishers Ltd in association with the Confederation of British Industry, is a register of British industry and commerce. Volume I gives products and services and volume II gives company information alphabetically and geographically. *Kompass* also provides European volumes devoted to Belgium-Luxembourg, Denmark, France, Holland, Italy, Norway, Spain, Sweden, Switzerland-Liechtenstein and the Federal Republic of Germany.

2. Year Books

Bankers' Almanac and Year Book published by Thomas Skinner Directories, is the standard international banking work of reference and gives full particulars of principal banks world-wide.

British Standards Catalogue contains a digest of Standards and revised numbering.

Civil Service Year Book summarises the functions of government departments and lists Ministers and civil servants down to Assistant Secretary level.

Hospitals and Health Services Year Book, and Directory of Hospital

Suppliers, published by the Institute of Health Service Administrators, provides an annual record of the hospitals and health services in Great Britain and Northern Ireland.

Kemp's International Film and Television Yearbook gives full details of technical specialists in all aspects of TV and film production. It lists addresses of broadcasting organisations and companies providing specialist services in 60 countries (including the UK).

Municipal Year Book and Public Services Directory, published by *Municipal Publications Ltd*, gives information on public services, government departments and agencies and local government authorities.

Personnel and Training Databook, published by Kogan Page Ltd, supersedes the *Personnel and Training Management Year Book and Directory*.

Statesman's Year Book, published by Macmillan Press Ltd, has two sections, one containing current information on each country of the world and one covering international organisations such as NATO, FAO, WHO and UNESCO.

Statistical Year Book, produced by the United Nations Department of Economic and Social Affairs Statistical Office and published by HMSO, gives a summary of currently available international statistics. It is part of a co-ordinated and inter-related set of publications issued periodically by the United Nations and its specialised agencies.

Stock Exchange Official Year Book published by Macmillan Press Ltd, includes details of all officially listed securities, a classification of listed companies and a list of registrars together with the companies for which they act, and it includes a general information section on various aspects of the stock market.

Text Retrieval A directory of software published by Gower Publishing Co Ltd.

Who Owns Whom: UK and Republic of Ireland, is published annually in May by Dun & Bradstreet. Parent companies are listed with full names, addresses and trade classification. Each parent entry shows the structure of its subsidiary and associate company and the index has an alphabetical list of subsidiaries and associates indicating their parent companies.

Travel

ABC Hotel Guide is published twice yearly as a free supplement to the **ABC** World Airways Guide. Worldwide hotels are listed alphabetically under countries and towns.

Good Food Guide is published annually in spring by the Consumers' Association and Hodder & Stoughton Ltd and includes establishments all over the United Kingdom and Ireland, with a special section for London. Half-way through each year a free news supplement is sent to buyers of the Guide.

Hints to Exporters These booklets are produced by the British and Overseas Trade Board and cover many countries. They give advice on travel, customs, entry regulations and hotels, etc, for each country.

Hotels and Restaurants in Great Britain, published annually by the British Tourist Authority, contains details of hotels and restaurants in England, Scotland and Wales and has a gazetteer of many touring areas with interesting additional notes.

Times Atlas of the World (New edition 1985), published by Times Books Ltd in collaboration with John Bartholomew & Sons Ltd, gives a truly comprehensive collection of maps of all parts of the world with a glossary/index/gazetteer.

Travel Trade Directory, published by Morgan-Grampian Book Publishing Co Ltd, provides, in one volume, a wealth of useful and up-to-date information regarding travel by air, rail, sea, car and coach. It lists travel agents and national travel agency organisations; gives details of British Rail and foreign railways, principal airlines and airports, shipping companies and hovercraft operators. It also contains a large section of travel trade information with addresses of visa and passport offices, travel consultants and PR services, travel trade clubs, insurance, finance and a Prestel directory.

World Holiday and Time Guide, published annually by the Morgan Guaranty Trust Company. This is a good reference booklet to consult in order to avoid sending someone on a swift business trip to a foreign country only to discover that the entire population is enjoying a public holiday. Holidays and time zones are listed by country.

1. Travel by Air
ABC Air Asia This is a new guide designed with the needs in mind of the frequent traveller in Asia and the Pacific.

ABC Air/Rail Europe, published monthly, provides a quick reference guide for the businessman to air and inter-city rail timetables throughout Europe and the Middle East, plus details of direct flights to North Africa, New York and Washington.

ABC Air Travel Atlas, issued twice a year, shows scheduled air routes throughout the world. Trunk routes are given for each continent followed by regional routes for specific areas.

ABC Guide to International Travel, published quarterly, gives information about passports, visas, health requirements, climatic conditions, journey times between major cities, details about baggage allowances and has a large section of country by country information.

ABC World Airways Guide, published monthly, contains complete timetables for regular air services throughout the world. Details are given of fares, international travel requirements, passports, visas and health regulations as well as sections on Car Hire and Advance Airline Schedules.

Executive Travel A magazine published monthly, intended for frequent business travellers. It is on sale at newsagents and carried aboard many international airlines.

2. Travel by Rail
ABC Air/Rail Europe (See Travel by Air)

ABC Rail Guide is published every month and gives full services, timetables and fares from all London main-line termini. It includes a provincial inter-city section and all rail services for London and Southern England.

Business Executive Handbook, published by the British Railways Board, gives complete information about Inter-city trains, travel by Motorail and Rail Drive.

Cook's Continental Timetable, published monthly, is a guide to the principal rail services of Europe.

Cook's Overseas Timetable, published bi-monthly, covers the principal rail services for the rest of the world.

Passenger Time Table, GB is published yearly and gives Inter-city, local and suburban services. It also gives Irish, Channel Islands and coastal services.

Passenger Time Table, International provides information for travellers on the continent of Europe.

3. Travel by Road
AA and RAC Handbooks provide detailed information about road travel in the UK and on the continent together with maps and plans of many important cities and towns and a considerable hotel gazetteer. Full details are included of all services offered to members – breakdown service, legal and technical advice etc.

ABC Coach and Bus Guide has full information on coach and bus routes and services available throughout the UK.

ABC London Atlas	All contain sectional street maps, under-
London A-Z	ground railway map and guides to
London Street by Street	places of interest and theatres.
London Street Finder	

National Express Guide This guide to express coach services includes services of the Scottish Bus Group.

Ordnance Survey Maps A free catalogue can be obtained which lists
all the maps published by the Ordnance Survey. Address is Romsey
Road, Maybush, Southampton SO9 4DH.

4. Travel by Sea
ABC Shipping Guide, published each month, gives a worldwide guide
to passenger shipping services and cruises. The main section contains
schedules and fares for transocean lines, shipping services and car
ferries within each continent, and cargo/passenger lines. It also
contains an index to operators with details of head office, branches,
main agents and all services operated.

CONSULTANCY AND AGENCY SERVICES

Sometimes a reference book is not sufficient and help of a more
practical nature from outside sources is required. It is a good idea to
compile a personal list of names, addresses and telephone numbers
most frequently used, adding a comment as to whether they have
been satisfactory and, if not, why not.

Some suggestions are listed below in alphabetical order. Most of
these services can be located through the Yellow Pages or advertisements in the daily papers:

Accommodation agencies Centralised information is available
on vacancies at different grades of hotels. Most main line terminal
railway stations will have agencies. They will advise on suitable
vacancies and will make bookings.

Accountants and income tax consultants These will make up or
audit accounts, make out income tax returns, provide stock-taking
services, make out stock records, and deal with all relevant financial
matters.

Advertising and publicity agencies Publicity of all kinds can be
arranged, by way of magazines, newspapers, posters (eg on railway
stations) and also by films (commercials in the cinema and on
television). Agencies will arrange for 'stills' from their photographic
studios to be reprinted in trade magazines. They will despatch

circulars and can advise on the most suitable methods of advertising products. See also section on Community and Public Relations.

British Institute of Management Foundation The BIM Foundation is the national clearing house for information on management and allied subjects in the UK, and its Management Information Centre contains one of the largest management libraries in the world. An Individual Subscriber Service is available to anyone interested in management but not qualified for corporate membership of the BIM. Individual subscribers receive copies of the monthly journal *Management Today*, a monthly copy of *Management News*, and can purchase, at a discount, management survey reports, checklists, information sheets, and a series of *Guidelines* specially developed to help the owners and managers of smaller businesses.

British and Overseas Trade Board and **Central Office of Information** These provide export intelligence services on such matters as publicity for exports; exhibiting effectively abroad; tariffs and non-tariff barriers; and they supply advance notice of trade fairs, exhibitions, seminars and symposia.

British Standards Institution This is the recognised body in the UK for the preparation and promulgation of national standards in all fields.

The Technical Help to Exporters service at Hemel Hempstead provides technical information and assistance to all sectors of industry engaged in exporting. These services cover the identification of overseas specifications and assistance in meeting their requirements. A range of publications covering various matters of interest to exporters is continuously being expanded. Detailed information on regulations and approval systems is disseminated through enquiry, advisory and consultancy services and special projects undertaken to meet the individual needs of industry. The Technical Help to Exporters service can also help manufacturers with the translation of specifications and regulations and can assist in the actual export of products to particular markets, eg in obtaining test certificates and in arranging for testing and factory investigation in the UK, if this is acceptable to the overseas organisation concerned.

The library at British Standards House contains a full set of British standards, international standards publications and the standards issued by the national standards bodies of other countries, together with their catalogues and journals.

Catering services Anything from a sandwich to a full banquet can be arranged but it is advisable to check the charges before making a definite booking and it is sensible to compare different estimates before contracting. Most catering companies will provide leaflets of menus and services available, with scales of charges. See also section on Social and Business Entertaining.

Chauffeurs, couriers and guides   See local Yellow Pages.

Cleaning and maintenance services   Many firms specialise in total cleaning or in sectional work; for example they may arrange for window cleaning once a week and walls once a fortnight. Some firms will take out double-glazed windows and put them back again after cleaning. Staff can be engaged to vacuum daily and generally clean up before and after office hours. Weekly telephone sterilising and clean towel services can be arranged.

Conference agencies   These will book halls or rehearsal rooms, provide wedding and other social reception services, etc. They will also provide recording equipment, fix microphones and arrange catering services and flower decoration. British Telecom provides a special audio-visual conference facility (Confravision) which operates in the UK and international videoconferencing link-up between a number of countries.

Contractors' plant and machinery   For infrequent or seasonal work it is often more economical to hire machinery than to buy it. For instance, scaffolding and cleaning equipment might be required for a special building renovation job.

Daily Telegraph Information Bureau   This Bureau provides a telephone service and will answer all sorts of queries on current affairs and general matters such as etiquette, history, geography, etc, but it does not deal with anything legal, medical or highly technical.

Debt collecting agencies   These will undertake the embarrassing task of collecting debts from customers who have fallen behind with payments.

Duplicating and copying services   These can be very useful in assisting with a sudden rush of extra, urgent, clerical work.

Educational services   Educational agencies will advise and help with all queries on schools, colleges and universities, training, special courses, fees, etc.

Employment bureaux   These are a source of supply for temporary or permanent staff of all kinds.

Entertainment/theatre ticket agencies   Advice and information can be obtained about current shows and exhibitions, and bookings made.

Exporters and importers   These agencies will be able to advise on the various restrictions and regulations concerning trade with foreign countries, and on sending goods out or bringing them into the UK. They will find markets for your goods and make contact with buyers and sellers abroad. They will buy and sell goods on your behalf and will advise on customs formalities and suitable packing methods. Some will themselves arrange for packing or will put your firm in touch with a shipping and forwarding company which will do the packing for you in the best way for your particular product. They will advise on the necessary forms and give a full and specialised consultation and information service. (See also British and Overseas Trade Board, British Standards Institution and London Chamber of Commerce and Industry.)

Government bookshops   HMSO publications, including both Parliamentary and non-Parliamentary publications and catalogues, can be obtained from government bookshops and through principal booksellers in London and other large cities.

Government departments   These will help with queries within their own areas of responsibility. Addresses are given in *Whitaker's Almanack*, the *London Telephone Directory* and in the *Diplomatic Service List*.

Industrial Society   This Society is a leading UK advisory and training body in management and industrial relations. Its practical services include in-company advice and training, courses and conferences, information, visual training programmes and a bi-monthly magazine.

Legal services   Any firm of solicitors will give advice and recommend or provide help with legal problems.

Location of Offices Bureau   This will advise on all matters regarding the re-location of offices – rents, staff availability, access and communications, facilities, housing, government grants, etc.

London Chamber of Commerce and Industry   The Research and Information Department of the London Chamber of Commerce and Industry is responsible for providing factual information on all aspects of domestic and overseas trade and industry, both to members of the Chamber and to the staff of the various departments and associations within the Chamber. *Chambers of Commerce Worldwide – a Selected List,* published by the LCCI, lists over 700 Chambers of Commerce throughout the world and covers 190 countries and territories.

Maintenance of machines   Many office machines can be regularly maintained under contract from their suppliers or manufacturers.

News and press-cutting agencies   These will undertake to collect news coverage of any particular event and will supply cuttings from reviews, features and news reports in the press and magazines.

Security/detective agencies   Confidential services are available for all security problems in a firm. Security services such as Securicor vans may be provided. These agencies can deal with a comprehensive and varied range of problems, from the personal to all aspects of the commercial world. They will give advice on how to make the office a safer place, safeguarding against fraud etc. Your local police station can also provide help and advice. See also section on Safety and Security.

Stockbrokers   These will advise on investments and arrange the buying and selling of stocks and shares.

Taxi and car-hire services   Keep a note of the nearest taxi and car-hire service telephone numbers. There are also van-hire services for transporting goods and it is possible to hire lorries for road transport of bulky commodities, or coaches for a party of people.

Travel agents   They will provide foreign currency and give information on exchange rates, timetables, passport and visas, obtain tickets for bus, coach, rail and air travel and advise on all travel problems. (See also Travel Arrangements Chapter 20.)

19 STAFF RELATIONS

*Signs and symptoms of unrest; finding the
cause of discontent; pay; conditions of
work; personality problems; feelings of
neglect; lack of effective communication;
Flexitime; constructive criticism*

When the management has built up a team of reliable, trained people
it is worth taking the trouble to keep them; when employees are not
happy they leave. To obtain long service and good results from its
workforce a company should never allow job satisfaction and
personal contentment with working conditions to be left to chance.

Personal problems are officially the prerogative of the personnel
department, but as an executive secretary rarely works in isolation
you should be aware of the likely causes of discontent and also be able
to 'tune in' to the working atmosphere of the company. A little tact
and elementary psychology often works wonders, and you can be of
great assistance in keeping staff relationships pleasant and smooth-
running.

If staff are happy, production increases and there is an un-
mistakable atmosphere of well-being. It is equally noticeable, to
anyone at all sensitive, when staff are discontented. The reason *why*
there is discontent is not necessarily always so clear, and without
knowing the reason it will be difficult to find the remedy.

SIGNS AND SYMPTOMS OF UNREST

The most common signs of growing dissatisfaction are:
> gossiping and murmuring in little groups that break up on
> approach
> deteriorating standards of work
> irritability and impatience in individuals
> lack of co-operation and even deliberate obstruction of work
> unpunctuality, 'clock-watching' and absenteeism
> high turnover of staff

FINDING THE CAUSE OF DISCONTENT

An alert Secretary/PA or Personnel Officer may be able to identify
minor problems and prevent them from growing into major ones, but

she will have to be prepared to use the utmost tact, to assist communications between the managers and the managed, and to help with advice and suggestions on ways to solve the difficulties. Below are suggested ways of starting enquiries:

1. Interviewing those concerned, separately and in confidence, in order to persuade them to talk freely about their problems, asking others if they know about the difficulties and whether they can suggest any solution.

2. Interviewing selected members of staff all together, by calling a meeting to try to identify the problem and work out a feasible solution.

3. Issuing a questionnaire to staff asking for suggestions for improving their working conditions. If staff prefer, the replies could be anonymous.

4. Interviewing those who give in their notice. This will usually be done as a matter of course, but in any time of unrest there may be other reasons for leaving than the one given officially. If this is the case, discuss the matter sympathetically and ask for suggestions for resolving the difficulty.

When the cause of dissatisfaction has been identified, and a good method of dealing with it has been worked out, see that the remedial measures are taken promptly and that the staff concerned know, as soon as possible, that this is being done.

Common causes of dissatisfaction in office life relate to:
   pay
   conditions of work
   personality problems
   feelings of neglect
   lack of effective communication.

PAY

If the salary is correct for the job and a formal pay rise is not possible, the money may be augmented justifiably by various means. Many firms offer perks such as:
   luncheon vouchers
   subsidised canteen meals
   subsidised holiday arrangements
   reduced rates for the firm's goods or services
   use of a company car
   cheap mortgages
   non-contributory pension schemes
   special bonus schemes or profit sharing

special recognition in individual cases for good work or a special assignment successfully completed

special training, leading to a worker's promotion or to a higher paid post

health schemes (membership of BUPA, PPP, etc.)

CONDITIONS OF WORK

Under this heading there are several reasons why a worker may have an understandable cause for dissatisfaction.

Routine work   All firms have jobs that become boring at times and they have to be done by someone. The burden may be lighter if:

1. The work is explained in context, in the setting of the firm's overall operations, that is as an indispensable part of a larger scheme. A talk with a supervisor or personnel officer may be of assistance here.
2. The employee knows that, when the opportunity occurs, there will be a good chance of promotion.
3. Arrangements are made to transfer the employee to another department, or to give him different work to do.
4. The employee is offered a training course to enable him to do different work, or the same work but at a more advanced level.

Company-sponsored training schemes provide mutual benefit; the firm gains a more efficient worker and the employee has satisfaction in acquiring higher qualifications. Good use may be made by the firm of training schemes (day-release or sandwich courses) offered by training colleges, or such schemes may be set up within the company. Courses for specified trades and professions, as well as general supervisory and management courses, may help to keep staff up-to-date and enthusiastic. A successfully completed training scheme should lead the employee to higher grade work and pay within the firm, otherwise he may leave to take a better post elsewhere, using his new qualifications to earn a higher salary.

Overwork   If possible some of the workload should be diverted elsewhere, or an assistant may be found to shoulder some of the burden.

Alteration in the job   Since the worker first took on the job it may have changed and he may feel he is no longer the right person to do it. A re-training scheme may help, or the provision of an assistant may be the answer. The provision of better facilities or more up-to-date equipment may also make all the difference to his feeling of confidence and job satisfaction.

Change in methods   A change in work method (eg by the installation of computers) should be introduced gradually and tactfully. This is a case for prior consultation between management and the workers affected, and it may be that considerable persuasion will be required when pointing out the benefits of the proposed changes. There must be genuine assurances that there will be no redundancy and that, if there has to be a reduction in one variety of work, alternative and comparable jobs will be offered instead.

Equipment and materials become obsolete in time and have to be replaced or updated. The firm should make innovations gradually giving plenty of warning so as to avoid any sharp shocks to employees, such as the installation of new machines without notice and virtually overnight. Even a sudden changeover from standard typewriters to the very latest sophisticated models, without an interim period for familiarisation, could bring about rebellion in the typing pool. Whatever kind of plant or machinery is involved, it may be necessary at times to supply special tuition or training courses, when old equipment is replaced by the very newest and most up-to-date models. (See also section on Electronic Offices.)

Lack of social clubs and sports facilities   Friendships are made after working hours and opportunities for fraternising are something to look forward to after a busy day, especially for people who are lonely at home. It is also a great help to business relationships if people can meet their fellow workers in a relaxed and friendly atmosphere, away from the pressures of work. Why not start a club? Make enquiries to find out what people would like. Perhaps someone will volunteer to assist you in setting up a special social group. The 'suggestions box' or a questionnaire may bring in some good ideas.

PERSONALITY PROBLEMS

Sometimes these clashes are immediately apparent, sometimes they are well hidden and only come to the surface as a result of tactful questioning. When this type of friction occurs it may help if you talk to each of the protagonists separately at first. Assume that the problem is based on a misunderstanding – which may well be true. Try to find out each one's point of view, there may be some common ground on which to build some agreement between them.

A supervisor, for instance, may sometimes unintentionally appear to be overbearing and 'bossy', not realising the effect on junior staff; or an employee may be made uneasy because he has gained the impression that someone else is after his job or is undermining a friendship. A tactful enquiry on your part may provide grounds for reassurance, and so may ease the situation. It may be helpful, in some circumstances, to transfer an employee by mutual consent to another section or department.

After talking in confidence to each individual it may be possible to bring them together to clear the air, pointing out the value of mutual understanding and co-operation, at the same time acting as an arbitrator. However this is best not attempted if it is likely to be seen as interfering.

Never take sides; but you may find that a quiet friendly discussion with you, as a sympathetic outsider, may be all that an employee needs to resolve his particular difficulty.

FEELINGS OF NEGLECT

There is no more deadening feeling for an employee than to work hard and conscientiously, perhaps over a period of considerable time, and to feel that no-one cares or even notices.

Need for appreciation   Any good employer realises the value of appreciation and goes out of his way to see that it is given whenever and wherever it is due. A word of praise for work well done, appreciation for the performance of a difficult job, recognition of loyal service or even just of cheerfulness when working conditions are difficult, make an incalculable difference to the attitude of any employee.

It is well known that people who feel they are appreciated will work even better and harder just because of this feeling of being valued. When in doubt as to whether to say 'Thank you' or 'Well done', say it – it is better to do this than to lose an opportunity to show appreciation.

Need for complete utilisation   A frequent cause of feelings of neglect arises when a worker with special skills or qualifications finds that they are not being used to the full. This means that there is a great waste of talent from the firm's point of view, and it is very frustrating for the worker who, if scope is not found for his special abilities, will be quite justified in leaving.

Need for job clarification   A different kind of neglect may occur if there is any confusion as to how duties are distributed between members of staff. Employees do not like to feel that their designated jobs are being done by someone else, especially by someone who does not seem to realise where the work boundaries lie. Each worker should know exactly what his duties are and how far they extend. This should be made quite clear by the personnel officer when engaging new staff, and may have to be reassessed when promotions are made. (See also section on Recruitment and Interviewing.)

If duties and responsibilities are clearly understood there should be no danger of people assuming an authority that is not theirs.

LACK OF EFFECTIVE COMMUNICATION

There is no reason for staff to be kept in ignorance of events; memos, noticeboards, house magazines, telephones are all good channels for disseminating information and unless a subject is confidential employees should continually be kept informed of policy and management decisions.

Joint consultation meetings   These can be an excellent way of exchanging ideas, solving problems and making future plans, at the same time clearing up misunderstandings. Unfortunately, however, there is often a feeling of 'us and them' which generates unnecessary antagonism. When those present are reasonably in accord, with a willingness to co-operate and a common interest in the matters on the agenda, the meeting will be constructive and communication will be good.

Should the opposite prove to be the case – some of those attending the meeting having made up their minds beforehand and being unwilling even to listen to the other side of the question – the meeting then becomes a confrontation, an embarrassing deadlock, and there is mutual dislike and opposition among those present. If people do not *want* to understand each other, meetings are better postponed until the difficulties have been tackled, at least to some extent, by more informal means.

Informal meetings   These can be of great value. A little gathering of a few people, perhaps with a drink and a sandwich in a pub, may be able to make more progress in their relaxed and informal setting than would be possible in the office. Many a deal has been very satisfactorily worked out in a pub, a restaurant or on a golf course, where busy people can get away from the tensions of work and where relationships are relaxed and friendly. The necessary formalities can be covered in the office at a later time.

Suggestions schemes   A 'suggestions box' may be placed at a strategic point in the building, into which any member of staff may post' ideas for consideration by a Suggestions Committee. Suggestions relating to improvements in working methods and conditions may thus be put forward in confidence and should be welcomed. The firm might make a financial award for any good ideas that can be put into effect with consequent advantages to the firm and its employees.

Rumours   Rumours do arise from time to time and may be difficult to correct. One of the most likely subjects of an unsettling rumour in a business would be about a possible loss of jobs. There might be talk of a proposed merger or a takeover bid, closure of a department, resignation of a key figure, cessation of a particular manufacturing process or the prospect of the company being moved to a different area. Any of these rumours would cause employees to worry about possible redundancies and the effect of having to move from one place to another on their families and their finances.

If you suspect that rumours of any kind are circulating, two steps need to be taken immediately. First, flatly to deny any false reports and, secondly, to clarify the real state of affairs, at the same time stressing that there is no cause for concern and pointing out the advantages of the true situation; in fact to give prompt reassurance, allay anxieties, and set out the authentic position.

When employees are in need of this kind of reassurance it should be given fully and explicitly, using all possible routes (house magazine, noticeboards, memos etc) as well as via managers and supervisors who can pass on information within their own departments. Emergency departmental meetings may be held, or an executive may address the whole staff at a meeting or over a public address system. Timing is very important, there should be as little delay as possible.

If the personnel department runs well there should never be any outbreak of rumour but if, in spite of this, there should be an occasion, steps must be taken to stop it firmly, decisively and at once.

FLEXITIME

This system is used in government offices as well as in industry and is becoming increasingly popular; it is a scheme of flexible working hours by which each employee contracts to work a set number of hours within a week.

Each day 'core' times are worked by all staff, eg between 10.00 and 12.00 and 2.00 to 4.00. Before and after these hours periods may be arranged to suit the individual, provided the agreed weekly total of hours is eventually covered. The lunch hour may be taken at any time between 12.00 and 2.00 and there will thus be a period when all employees are working together and periods before and after the core times when numbers vary.

Advantages   These are numerous. Parents who have children to take to or fetch from school, may contract their hours to allow for this. Some grades of workers may contract for fewer hours than others. Those who prefer to start early and leave early, or start late and finish late, may do so. Rush hours may thus be avoided, when transport is crowded and the roads are busy. Hours worked above the weekly contracted total may be carried forward as credit towards a longer weekend or holiday break. There are also great advantages in terms of work satisfaction; employees feel that they are being individually considered and bad timekeeping virtually disappears.

Disadvantages   The calculating of differing wage packets is complex and may be time-consuming unless electronic calculating equipment is used. Supervisors are not always in charge of the same people throughout the working day; also some of the staff may never see each other. However, these problems can be largely overcome with sensible planning.

A Flexitime system needs to be carefully worked out for each company, according to its type and structure, and therefore no two schemes are likely to be the same.

CONSTRUCTIVE CRITICISM

There will come a time when, in your capacity as senior secretary or PA, you will have to reprimand an employee. This is something that most people avoid if they possibly can, but there are occasions when slipshod work, bad timekeeping or some other fault cannot be left any longer and something really has to be done.

What you should *not* do, and we assume it would not even occur to you, is to get cross with the culprit, and shout. What is required is 'constructive' criticism, and this cannot be given in anger.

The best way to reprimand is to use the 'sandwich' technique, that is, to open the conversation as pleasantly as possible with a few appreciative comments. Follow this with the reprimand, put sympathetically but firmly, and end with more appreciation and the comment that of course the fault will not happen again. You will vary this as you wish, when the time comes, but the underlying principle will be according to this formula.

To take a possible typical example, let us suppose you have a clumsy and forgetful junior typist. Make an opportunity to see her privately, tell her how much her work matters, how important it is that the mail goes out correctly, checked and sealed and stamped. Tell her that the office cannot properly function without its juniors, and express appreciation of the work she has done properly – there is sure to be at least something you can praise, eg willingness, neatness or punctuality.

Then refer to the matter in hand. 'By the way', you say, 'Whatever happened yesterday? Mrs Smith tells me that all your letters were dated without the year being typed in, and that she has to watch to see that you remember to put the enclosures in the envelope. She's a very busy person, you know, you should really be remembering things for yourself by now'. Keep the subject going in this way, so that she realises you are concerned about her faults but at the same time are not angry.

Ask if she has any special personal problem; you may find she has an invalid parent to care for or is having boy-friend difficulties, either of which may well affect her concentration. Finally, assure her that you appreciate her work in the typing pool, you feel this is just a temporary lapse, and you know she will be much more careful in the future.

In this kind of situation always show a positive optimistic attitude. Do not say to yourself 'She'll never learn, she's hopeless'. This is hardly ever true. The old adage still holds good, that people learn by their mistakes. Some people only learn in this way, by doing something badly and then being shown how to do it better. If you are approachable and can correct without causing resentment, and can give praise where it is due, you should see an improvement in standards and the employee will almost certainly gain in efficiency and self-confidence.

There are of course instances which require firm discipline, and this may best come officially from your chief or the personnel officer.

Common reasons for mistakes and misdemeanours are:

    carelessness
    non co-operation
    laziness, lack of effort
    dishonesty
    lack of initiative/intelligence
    lateness
    poor communications.

Before deciding to reprimand, check the person's record, and try to find out why the mistake was made. Was it caused by –

    inexperience
    lack of training
    a bad example
    misunderstanding
    circumstances outside the person's control?

Any reprimand should be directly related to the offence, and it is important to follow up the case afterwards to make sure that the objective is being achieved.

Criticism is occasionally necessary, but can do considerable harm if given in the wrong way. Never criticise publicly, and do not tell another person about someone's weaknesses unless they can give you assistance in correcting them. Do not criticise too harshly, as it destroys confidence. Do not expect perfection, remember that a job adequately done is often satisfactory, and it is not wise to set impossibly high standards.

Bibliography

Michael Armstrong: *Handbook of Personnel Management Practice* (Kogan Page Ltd, 1977).

Maurice W. Cuming: *The Theory and Practice of Personnel Management* (Heinemann).

Harry Miller (ed.): *Management and the Working Environment* (Hutchinson Benham).

B. H. Walley: *Handbook of Office Management* (Business Books Ltd).

20 TRAVEL ARRANGEMENTS

> *Travel departments; Institute of Travel Managers; travel agents; planning a journey; making reservations; booking hotel accommodation; obtaining papers and documents; arranging contacts and meetings; preparing the itinerary; air, rail, road and sea travel; useful information; handling work during employer's absence; travelling with employer*

TRAVEL DEPARTMENTS

Not every firm or organisation needs to employ a specialist in business travel, but international travelling is fast becoming a specialised occupation where the most advantageous terms can only be obtained by constant study of the changing market. Some firms have their own travel manager or travel department or employ agents to arrange their business journeys, thus relieving executives and their secretaries of the need to work out their individual national and international travel itineraries. A travel manager can effect considerable economies for his firm by applying up-to-date knowledge of the enormous range of air fares, hotel charges and car hire discounts. This could make a significant contribution in time and money to the company's operational efficiency.

INSTITUTE OF TRAVEL MANAGERS

In March 1956 the Institute of Travel Managers in Industry and Commerce (ITM) was formed because of the need for closer and official contact between people working in the specialised field of business travel. Today its members and associate members represent more than 300 companies throughout the UK. The major airlines, hotel groups and car hire companies are associated with the ITM through a special class of Corporate Membership and seven other European countries now have associations committed to the same basic aims. International communication has been further strengthened by the establishment of formal links with the National Passenger Traffic Association of the USA and Canada.

The ITM organises a programme of educational events and

training courses for its members, produces a monthly *Business Travel Newsletter* and maintains various specialist committees which meet regularly with airlines and other bodies concerned with travel.

TRAVEL AGENTS

The *Travel Trade Directory*, published annually, lists all travel agents and tour operators in the UK alphabetically under town names and indicates those which are members of Trade Organisations such as WATA (World Association of Travel Agents) and ABTA (Association of British Travel Agents).

ASSOCIATION OF BRITISH TRAVEL AGENTS

This Association, founded in 1950, is recognised by Government, statutory authorities, international organisations, the press and the public as the official body representing travel agents and tour operators in the UK.

ABTA has introduced specific measures to ensure satisfactory service to the public, to settle disputes and provide protection in the event of financial failure of a member company.

The ABTA Conciliation and Arbitration scheme came into effect in April 1975 following agreement with the Director General of Fair Trading and the Institute of Arbitrators.

PLANNING A JOURNEY

Any secretary working in a firm which does not have a travel department may find herself involved in the planning of business journeys for her employer either in the UK or overseas. She should start by discussing with him the objectives of his visit, the schedule of meetings and/or conferences he wishes to cover, the method of travel and the route he would prefer to take; then prepare a folder for the visit, list the jobs to be done and keep a running check on all the items, ticking each task when it has been completed so that nothing is overlooked.

The numerous preparations to be made for any journey will probably involve:

    making reservations on aircraft, trains and ships
    booking suitable hotel accommodation
    obtaining all necessary papers and documents
    arranging contacts and meetings
    preparing a detailed itinerary.

MAKING RESERVATIONS

Ascertain the class of travel your employer generally uses; previous files will almost certainly show this. If a traveller is expected to be both mentally and physically alert on reaching his destination, it cannot really be considered a luxury to travel first-class. Some airlines have been experimenting with 'executive class' cabins where business-men can work without being disturbed by children or in-flight films; some even provide special compartments with business reference books.

Contact your travel agent for reservations on planes, trains, ships, car ferries or motorail services. Book as far in advance as possible, especially if the journey is to be made during school and college vacation periods when there is very heavy travel booking.

Any timetables which are consulted must be completely up-to-date and notice must be taken of any special footnotes. If necessary a check can always be made by a telephone call to the airport, railway terminal or shipping line.

BOOKING HOTEL ACCOMMODATION

Files from previous journeys will probably indicate your employer's preference as to category of hotel and whether he likes to have a room with bath or shower. If he is going to a very hot climate he will appreciate being booked into a hotel with air-conditioned rooms. If he is attending a conference he will most likely wish to stay at the hotel where the conference is being held and he may require licensed premises if he is going to use the hotel to entertain his business friends.

Write, telephone or telex for hotel accommodation in good time and confirm a telephone booking by letter. Many major hotel chains have central booking agencies in London and other cities which will make reservations for you. For example, the Holiday Inns have a fast international confirmation system, and accommodation almost anywhere in the world can be booked by contacting the nearest of their hotels. Utell, one of the largest hotel booking companies, representing 1500 hotels, tries to have three classes of hotel available in every major city of the world.

If your employer is travelling by car, check that the hotel has garage space and reserve either a parking space or a lock-up garage.

OBTAINING PAPERS AND DOCUMENTS

Passport   This must be valid and contain spare pages for any necessary visas. A 10-year passport is obtainable from passport offices, the RAC and AA and through some banks. Passport photographs (of approved size) have to be full face; extra copies can be kept for attaching to visa application forms. A record of the passport number must be kept separately for reference in case of loss or theft.

Visas These are usually obtainable from the RAC, AA, travel agent or relevant embassy but a few consulates insist on personal attendance. UK passport holders require visas for journeys to most Eastern European countries.

Health certificate and medical treatment A UK smallpox vaccination certificate is valid for a period of three years. Any country can demand to see a current certificate of vaccination from an incoming traveller, particularly if there is a case of smallpox in the country from which the traveller has come.

If journeying outside European countries, check whether yellow fever, cholera and TAB inoculations are compulsory. It is advisable to have all inoculations well in advance of a journey. However, in an emergency, it is possible for travellers on long-haul flights to obtain inoculations at the Victoria Air Terminal and those on short-haul flights at the West London Terminal.

The National Health Service provides health care only in Britain but the UK has special health agreements with EEC and some other countries. Under these agreements treatment needed urgently can be obtained free or at reduced cost. Arrangements vary considerably from country to country. Full details are given in the Department of Health and Social Security's leaflet SA30 *Medical costs abroad*. In some cases an application form (CM1) has to be filled in, quoting personal National Insurance number, and a Certificate of Entitlement obtained from the DHSS before departure date.

Most family doctors, if asked, will supply a letter advising doctors overseas of treatment being undergone by their patients. It is wise for travellers to take with them small medicinal items such as aspirin, stomach pills, etc, and salt tablets and anti-malaria pills if going to the Middle or Far East.

Travellers' cheques, currency and credit cards Current regulations should be checked as to how much cash may be taken abroad. Credit cards may be used in many countries and, by using a Eurocheque Encashment card for personal identification, cheques up to £50 can be cashed in many selected banks.

A fund of small change and banknotes for use on immediate arrival is probably desirable and it is essential to keep a separate note of travellers' cheques serial numbers so that, if necessary, a claim may be made in case of loss or theft.

Insurance   Most UK companies insure their employees when they are travelling but additional insurances might be desired, such as personal accident, loss of baggage or for driving a car overseas.

Personal documents   Make sure that all personal documents which are likely to be needed during the journey are kept together in a folder or wallet which can be easily produced.

ARRANGING CONTACTS AND MEETINGS

Write as early as possible to clients, customers and the firm's personnel in other branches whom your employer wishes to contact. They will need time to reply and confirm.

Briefing notes   Your employer may be meeting a number of people with whom he is not familiar and it might be helpful to type a few briefing notes so that immediately he meets colleagues or customers he will feel confident that he has sufficient background knowledge about them. This might include information on status, work done, business interests and, if possible, a note on leisure pursuits, travel, etc.

Street maps   If your employer does not know the area very well, try to procure a good street map of the city or alternatively make a sketch map showing the position of his hotel, and mark any meeting places which have been arranged.

Speeches   If it is necessary for him to make a speech at one or more of the functions or meetings, he may require a fully typed speech or brief guiding notes. See section on Public Speaking.

Appointment cards   In addition to a full itinerary it is often helpful to type small daily reminder cards of a convenient size for slipping into a pocket, setting out appointments in chronological order, with times, names and addresses.

Visiting cards   See that your employer has an adequate supply of printed visiting cards. These should be attractive and clearly set out, giving his name and status and the firm's name and address, telex and telephone numbers. Some people like to have their firm's particulars on one side of the card and personal information on the reverse side. Consult him as to style and layout and see that the cards are ordered in plenty of time.

Sales literature   Sales literature and brochures should preferably have been prepared in the language of the country to which he is going. Provided these have been carefully translated and checked they indicate a thoughtful attitude which creates a very good first impression.

Samples and display material   It may be possible for samples of the firm's products to be displayed or demonstrated but a point to remember regarding electrical equipment is that plugs and voltage vary considerably from country to country, and even within one country. It might be advisable for an adaptor to be carried or at least a check made beforehand as to the type of electrical fittings most likely to be encountered in the area.

PREPARING THE ITINERARY

Type the itinerary on paper or card of suitable size for easy handling and make several copies (executive, self, file, spares).

Do not make too tight a schedule. Allow sufficient time for relaxation between flights and meetings. On a long trip it is advisable to leave half-days clear for catching up on correspondence and reports, telephone calls and unexpected changes in programme.

Take weather conditions into consideration and leave plenty of time for any journey to and from airports and railway stations. Remember that journeys take longer during rush hour periods and on roads which carry very heavy traffic.

Check the *World Holiday and Time Guide* (see section on Sources of Information) to make sure that the meeting arrangements do not clash with the country's public holidays and ascertain whether there is a time lag (ie the number of hours in advance or in arrears of Greenwich Mean Time); see appendix on page 252.

State departure and arrival times of planes and trains and add as many relevant details as possible eg checking-in time at airports or car ferries, reservation details of berths on ships and trains etc.

Use the 24-hour clock to avoid any misunderstanding of time schedules.

A sample itinerary is given on p. 226

AIR TRAVEL

Check that connecting flights do connect. Allow sufficient time between the landing of one aircraft and the departure of another; there can be a delay in transporting baggage between the international and domestic flight areas of a large airport. Very long journeys by air can be broken but, if so, check whether overnight stops include meals and accommodation.

Check on the maximum weight of baggage allowed and excess charges; also how much luggage can be taken into the cabin. See that

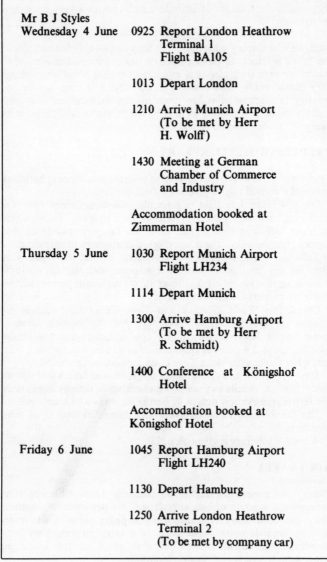

Mr B J Styles
Wednesday 4 June — 0925 Report London Heathrow
Terminal 1
Flight BA105

1013 Depart London

1210 Arrive Munich Airport
(To be met by Herr
H. Wolff)

1430 Meeting at German
Chamber of Commerce
and Industry

Accommodation booked at
Zimmerman Hotel

Thursday 5 June — 1030 Report Munich Airport
Flight LH234

1114 Depart Munich

1300 Arrive Hamburg Airport
(To be met by Herr
R. Schmidt)

1400 Conference at Königshof
Hotel

Accommodation booked at
Königshof Hotel

Friday 6 June — 1045 Report Hamburg Airport
Flight LH240

1130 Depart Hamburg

1250 Arrive London Heathrow
Terminal 2
(To be met by company car)

Figure i: Itinerary

all personal documents are readily available and not packed in luggage which is going into the hold.

If your employer is recognised by airports as a VIP and wishes to use the VIP lounge, notify the airport of this at the time of the reservation of tickets.

If the company's own plane is being used, remember to notify the pilot well in advance so that he can make all arrangements for landing, refuelling, etc.

If arrangements are to be made for a hired car to take the traveller to his hotel, make sure that full particulars have been given regarding flight number, name of airline, and estimated time of arrival.

Anyone travelling on British Airways would be well advised to obtain and study their current brochures including:

British Airways Business Travel, which gives details of individual business packages in the UK, Europe, North America, Africa, Australia and the Middle and Far East. It also quotes inclusive packages for individuals or small groups attending international trade fairs and exhibitions.

Fly-Drive Service For those who hold an internationally recognised driving licence, British Airways offer a Fly-Drive Service with the guarantee of a self-drive car waiting at the airport (minimum rental seven days).

British Airways Universal Air Travel Plan, which is an international scheme offering worldwide credit for air travel and affiliated services. Over 190 airlines participate, including all the major international carriers.

Worldwide Business Centres This international organisation offers a communication centre service to all British Airways business travellers. Mail, telephone calls and telex messages can all be sent to a central location before the traveller's arrival or during his stay in a number of major cities such as Paris, Milan, Rome and Zurich. Rental of fully furnished offices can also be arranged.

Phonecards To make telephone communication easier, British Telecom have installed phonecard phoneboxes at almost all bus, train and inner-city tube stations and at airports, seaports, motorway service areas, shopping centres and hospitals. Phonecards provide full international direct dialling without irritating interruptions being caused to the caller by the frequent insertion of coins. British Telecom phonecards can be obtained in units of 20, 40, 100 or 200. Inside the phonebox will be a notice giving the address of a nearby shop where these cards can be purchased.

The map on p. 232 shows the position of the principal airports in the British Isles.

RAIL TRAVEL

Ascertain your employer's preferences regarding rail travel. Does he like a window seat? Does he prefer to travel at the front, in the middle or at the end of the train? Is he a smoker or non-smoker? For a long journey he may wish you to book him a sleeper. Check whether the train has a restaurant car or a buffet.

Many large cities have more than one main railway station. If your employer has to break his journey to visit clients or attend meetings, make sure which station he needs when continuing his journey.

Inter-City Service   British Rail Inter-City and high-speed trains have fast and frequent services from city centre to city centre. These trains are very comfortable, having air-conditioning, double-glazed windows and reclining seats in first-class compartments.

The diagram on p. 233 shows the main Inter-City network of trains from the appropriate London terminus for each main route (correct when going to press).

Inter-City Sleepers   The diagram on p. 234 shows the Inter-City night sleeper trains which leave from Euston, King's Cross and Paddington. Full details of the sleeper services are given in a leaflet which is obtainable at railway stations or from travel agents.

Motorail Services   The diagram on p. 235 shows the Motorail routes in the UK. This day and night car-carrying service offers reserved seats or sleeper accommodation for driver and passengers. There is no restriction on vehicle length but there is a maximum height restriction (either 1.98 m or 2.15 m, including roof rack) according to which route is taken. Motorail services are also available in Belgium, France, Germany, The Netherlands, Poland and Spain.

Rail Account Orders   These offer credit for many BR facilities such as train tickets in Great Britain and Ireland, Inter-City Sleepers, Motorail, Rail Drive, meals on trains, passenger and car ferries to Europe, etc.

Rail-Drive Service   Arrangements can be made for a self-drive car to be waiting at the end of a rail journey. Advance booking can be made at more than 70 Inter-City Rail-Drive stations or by telephoning a car hire firm (see list on page 247). Even if no prior booking has been made, a car can be delivered to the station on telephoning from a Rail-Drive kiosk.

ROAD TRAVEL

Is the car roadworthy? Make sure that the vehicle has been serviced recently, that it has a valid MOT certificate and has been checked for tyre pressures; also that there is a serviceable spare wheel, a spare-parts kit, that the tank has been filled with petrol and the oil checked. Some car manufacturers supply a comprehensive list of garages throughout Europe which service their particular makes of car.

Is the car displaying a GB plate? Failure to carry a nationality sign can result in an on-the-spot fine, especially in Italy or Switzerland. Special petrol concessions to visitors are available for some countries and a list of these can be supplied by the automobile associations.

Check the current driving regulations in force in the countries to be visited, particularly in matters such as speed limits, compulsory seat belts, and advance warning triangles in case of an accident. Check that headlamps and foglamps can be adjusted for driving on the right-hand side of the road. Obtain adequate road maps, route plans and handbooks.

It is always prudent to carry a first-aid kit but it is obligatory if visiting Austria or the German Democratic Republic. Check on items in the first-aid box and renew any supplies which are inadequate.

Make sure that your employer carries his vehicle registration form and driving licence and that the insurance documents are all up-to-date. To secure the fullest cover it is necessary to hold an international motor insurance certificate (green card), obtainable through the driver's insurance company.

Before starting out, the driver should check that he has a spare car key and also, if he belongs to the AA or RAC, a key to emergency telephone boxes. During the winter months, if there are likely to be snow drifts, it is as well to carry in the car a flask of hot tea or coffee, some food, a spare blanket and a shovel.

Make a note of the mileage at the start of any journey to justify petrol consumption travel claims.

See also:
Car Ferries, p. 230
Phonecards, p. 227
Fly-Drive Service, p. 227
Motorail Services, p. 228
Rail-Drive Service, p. 228.

Sealink, Seaspeed, Sally Line and Townsend Thoresen all offer a choice of routes to the Continent on drive-on/drive-off craft.

SEA TRAVEL

It is not often necessary to book a cabin for a short ferry trip. For longer journeys passengers usually have a choice of a variety of classes of cabin, some with a private shower or bath. Anyone wishing for a cabin reservation should apply as early as possible, especially for travel in peak periods.

Car Ferries   Cars can be carried on ferries to Belgium, the Channel Islands, the Clyde and the Western Isles, Denmark, the Faroe Islands, France, Iceland, the Irish Republic, the Isle of Man, the Isle of Wight, The Netherlands, Northern Ireland, Norway, Orkney and Shetland, Spain, Sweden and West Germany.

USEFUL INFORMATION TO KEEP FOR QUICK REFERENCE

British Telecom's pre-recorded Traveline service   This gives regularly updated information on travel in Britain and on the Continent, including details of weather conditions, strikes or other problems likely to affect travellers:

Rail: 01 246 8030   Road (including coach services): 01 246 8031

Sea: 01 246 8032   Air: 01 246 8033

For regional codes, see front of dialling code booklets.

Books of reference   See section on Sources of Information and Services under Travel.

Current rates of exchange   For countries likely to be visited; these are constantly fluctuating and daily rates are given in the *Financial Times* and other daily newspapers.

Up-to-date timetables   For regularly used airlines, shipping lines and trains.

Telephone numbers   Of airports, shipping lines and railway stations.

Addresses, telephone and telex numbers   For agents and acceptable hotels in various cities.

Permitted amount of duty free goods   Amounts which may be taken out of and into the UK and other frequently visited countries.

Notes on procedure   For contacting your employer whilst he is travelling.

HANDLING WORK DURING EMPLOYER'S ABSENCE

Correspondence   Make brief daily notes of action taken regarding incoming mail. Retain file copies of all outgoing letters.

Technical matters   Seek advice if necessary from responsible technical staff.

Visitors and telephone calls   Deal with routine matters as far as possible. Explain that your employer is away on business and say when you expect him back. Consult colleagues where necessary.

Tape Recordings   Type any work which your employer records and despatches back to the office, following through any special instructions he may give you.

Outline of events   For his information, keep clear notes of business events which have occurred during his absence.   Why not catch up on all the jobs you have been putting off or have not yet had time to do?

TRAVELLING WITH YOUR EMPLOYER

The travelling secretary is a difficult role to play as your on-duty time can be long and tiring, with meetings, conferences, the taking of correspondence, the typing of reports and maybe hostess duties.

If you are fluent in the language of the country to which you are travelling your help will be most valuable, especially if your employer's knowledge of the language is not very good. Remember to take a portable UK typewriter with you if you are not familiar with foreign keyboards.

Take appropriate clothing if there are likely to be formal social occasions and consider well in advance what you will need. Take as many drip-dry garments as possible for easy laundering.

On a personal note, before you leave do remember to stop deliveries of milk and newspapers; turn off gas and electricity at the mains and secure all doors and windows.

Principal Airports in the British Isles

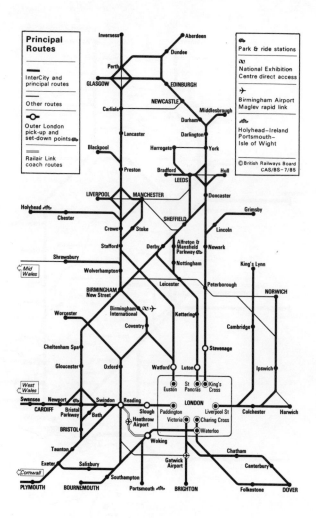

Inter-City and principal routes

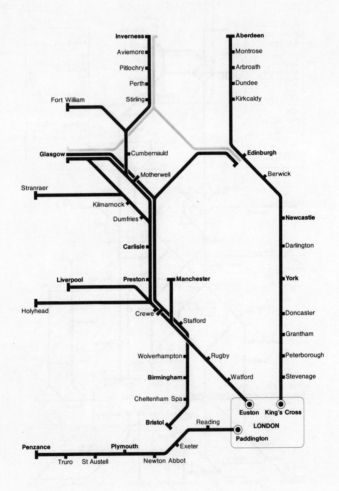

Inter-City sleeper services

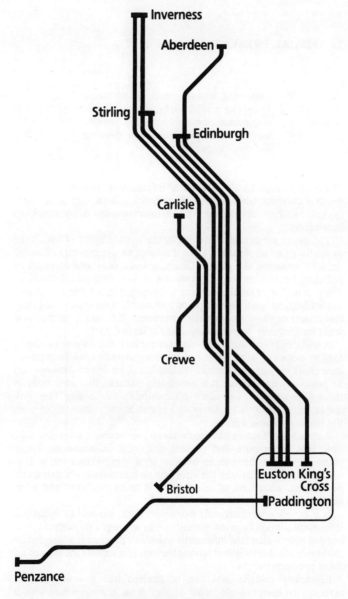

The Motorail network 1986

Answering queries; making decisions; processing routine tasks; graphs, charts, pictograms; visual planning control boards; visual presentation at meetings and conferences

Pictorial presentation of statistical information enables people to grasp a complex body of facts more quickly than they could from spoken, written or printed figures unaccompanied by graphical illustration.

The major advantage, therefore, of the visual display of data is the immediate impact it makes, since it affords an opportunity of seeing the total situation at a glance. Charts, graphs, diagrams on paper or planning boards, can rapidly convey a great variety of information. They can, for example, set out a progression of facts within a particular time span (line graph or bar chart), pinpoint existing facts (pie chart) or show a comparison between what was estimated and what has actually been accomplished (Gantt Chart).

A well designed chart with bold lines or clear colours is attractive to look at as well as being immediately informative but, while an up-to-date chart may be an extremely valuable aid, an out-of-date one can be positively misleading. It is absolutely essential that somebody in the office should have clear responsibility for seeing that any displayed material is regularly and systematically maintained with the latest available figures.

A number of factors have to be taken into account when deciding how best to prepare and present graphical information. Visual planning systems have to be built up to suit individual needs. It is necessary to consider why the information is required, whether it can be charted, what kind of information is to be conveyed and what methods of display are readily available.

It is possible to chart only numerical data; general or imprecise information must be given verbally or in writing. For example, it is not possible to chart the information that one product is selling better than several others without having the exact figures for the sales of all these products.

Extremely volatile data can be charted but it would almost certainly be better to use visual display units in conjunction with a computer to keep track electronically of a continually changing situation. However, it is easy to make manual adjustments when information alters infrequently. Between these two extremes there is a vast quantity of business information which might require updating. Movements such as travel schedules of sales representatives, shipping of goods and transportation of materials by lorry might effectively be displayed on control boards.

Easily adaptable visual planning techniques are being used increasingly for monitoring and controlling all kinds of work in business and industry and this has led to a considerable variety of useful display devices and equipment becoming available on the market.

ANSWERING QUERIES

A customer telephones to ask what is the despatch date of his latest order. When this information is given to him instantly, he will no doubt be impressed with the firm's efficiency. When the chairman asks for last week's production figures for a specific item, a quick look at the production chart will provide an immediate answer. The manager asks 'Who's away this week?' and the holiday rota chart will give the exact staffing position.

MAKING DECISIONS

A display of past and present figures in clear diagrammatic form can have definite implications for the planning of future policy. Data must be conveyed in a precise and highly organised way, otherwise vital information may be missed and bad decisions could be made. Charted data must always be accurate, relevant and easily assimilated.

PROCESSING ROUTINE TASKS

In the office or factory, visual presentation can be used for daily routine operations of such essential work as production scheduling, vehicle loading, sales planning etc.

GRAPHS

Most graphs are used as a means of making comparisons. When compiling them the following general principles should be observed:

> an explicit overall title or heading must be given
> both axes must be clearly and methodically annotated and the scale indicated
> if necessary, a key showing the line formations or colour coding should be displayed.

Single line graph   In Figure i the time scale (in months) is on the horizontal axis. The amount of sales (in thousands of pounds) achieved by the end of each month, is plotted on the graph and the points joined by straight lines.

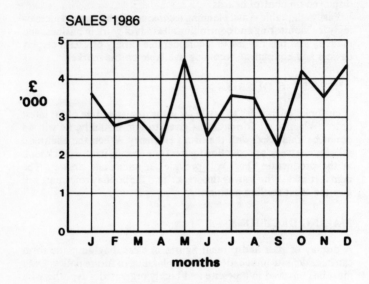

Figure i: Single line graph

Multi-line graph   When more than one variable is used, the line formations must differ. In Figure ii, a continuous line, a broken line and a dotted line have been used. Alternatively, different colours could be used.

CHARTS

Bar charts, using individual bars, can be displayed either horizontally or vertically. They are excellent for giving comparative figures month by month or year by year. A horizontal bar chart can also be used to indicate the sequence of events covering a project from start to finish.

Horizontal bar chart   See Figure iii.

Vertical bar chart   See Figure iv.

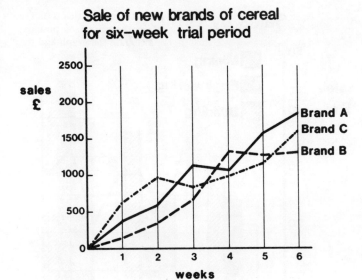

Figure ii: Multi-line graph

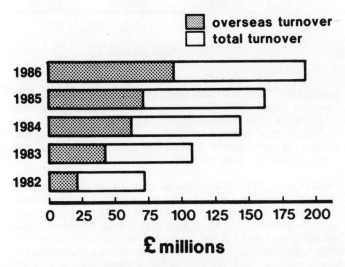

Figure iii: Horizontal bar chart

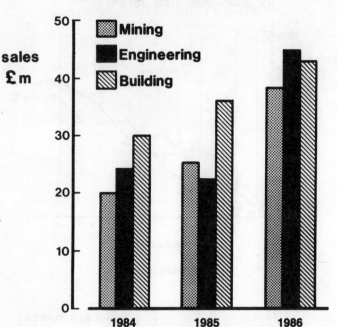

Figure iv: Vertical bar chart

Histogram   This is a specialised form of bar chart, used to show frequency distributions. The vertical bars in Figure v represent classes within the distribution and the area of the bar is proportional to the number of frequencies in each class. No space is left between the bars (unless, of course, there happen to be no members of staff within a particular grouping eg 60–65 years).

Gantt chart   A Gantt chart is used to show a comparison between what was forecast and what has actually been accomplished.

In Figure vi three jobs A, B and C have been started at the same time. Completion of Job A is scheduled in 5 weeks, Job B in 10 weeks and Job C in 14 weeks. A bar is drawn to indicate the actual amount of the work which has been completed by the end of week 8. Job A has been completed, Job B is a week behind schedule and Job C is two weeks in arrears.

Distribution of ages of Company staff in the United Kingdom

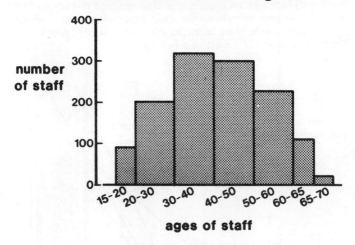

Figure v: Histogram

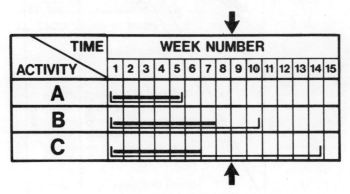

Figure vi: Gantt chart

Break-even chart　　A break-even chart, as in Figure vii, is used to ascertain the level of activity at which a business makes neither profit nor loss – above that point is the profit area and below that point is the loss. It is absolutely essential for some such calculation to be made if a business is to be planned in a rational way. Expenses (which can only be approximate) fall into two types, variable and fixed. Variable (or direct) expenses are those whose amounts tend to vary directly with the volume of production; fixed expenses are those whose amounts remain the same no matter what the volume of production (eg the rent paid for the use of a factory).

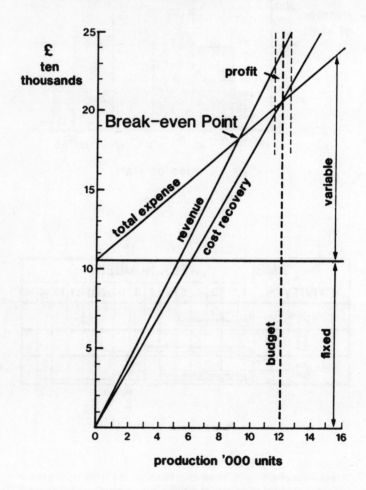

Figure vii: Break-even chart

Z chart It is sometimes useful to be able to show three items of information on one chart, such as the monthly total of sales, the cumulative total and the moving (annual) total (MAT). The resulting chart looks roughly like the letter Z, as in Figure viii, which is how it got its name.

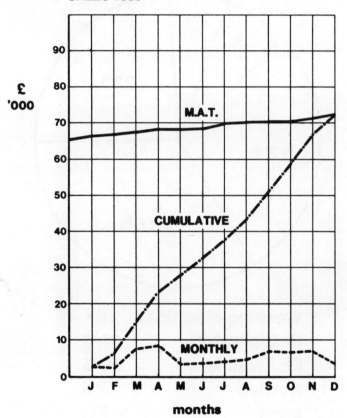

Figure viii: Z chart

Pie chart A pie chart is compiled by dividing a circle into proportional segments. It is used when it is necessary to show the relationship of the parts to a whole. It gives the static position at one particular time; see Figure ix.

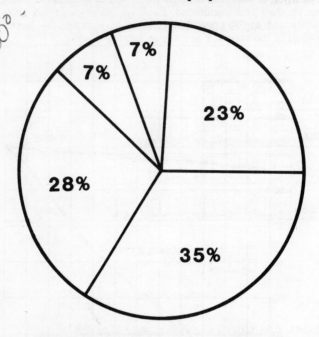

Figure ix: Pie chart

PICTOGRAMS

A pictogram, or pictorial method of display, is represented by symbols or pictures, as in Figure x and is used mainly in the popular presentation of statistical information. To be effective the drawing must be clear and uncluttered. Each symbol represents a given quantity and the larger quantities must be indicated by further drawings of the same size and not by larger drawings.

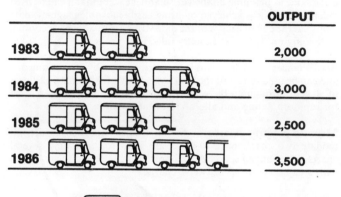

		OUTPUT
1983		2,000
1984		3,000
1985		2,500
1986		3,500

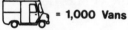 = 1,000 Vans

Figure x: Pictograms

VISUAL PLANNING CONTROL BOARDS

A good visual planning control board system should:
> be designed to fit the special purpose for which it is intended
> be flexible and capable of speedy updating in changing situations
> save time and improve work efficiency
> help in forward planning by giving a comprehensive review of past and present facts and trends.

Sasco Limited*, pioneers in visual planning materials, are acknowledged as a leading firm in this field. They offer a very wide range of planning charts and their carefully designed products are used nationally and internationally. As well as Personal Year Planners and Staff Planners, they will supply control boards designed for all kinds of work.

---

* The address of Sasco Limited is 27 Hastings Road, Bromley, Kent, BR2 8NA

Year Planner   This shows the whole year at a glance and enables appointments to be dovetailed so that last-minute panics or clashing events are avoided. Forward planning can be carried out on the basis of complete and accurate knowledge of all commitments. The best materials to be used for displaying information of this kind are self-adhesive re-usable tapes and shapes of various colours.

Perpetual Year Planner   Planning on the perpetual year planner is the same as planning on the year planner except that it can be used indefinitely. This is achieved by using easily movable magnetic date strips. At the end of each year the date strips are re-aligned according to the day on which 1st January falls.

Staff Planner   This board is designed to show every working day and can be used to record the holidays, absence for training or illness of all staff throughout the year. Magnetic tapes and shapes are used for rapid up-dating and alteration of information.

Mounted Control Boards   Swivel frames, designed to accommodate two charts back-to-back, are ideal for mounting several charts in a confined space. A wall bracket will take up to six frames with a capacity for up to twelve charts.

VISUAL PRESENTATION AT MEETINGS AND CONFERENCES

Sasco also provide considerable opportunities for making a real visual impact, not only in everyday matters, but also at sales and promotion meetings, planning or training sessions and at conferences, with their range of notice and display boards, flip charts and easels, workboards and colorbords. A colorbord is a lightweight, magnetic, easy-to-clean whiteboard which is used with dry-wipe pens, magnetic letters and numbers and self-adhesive symbols.

Most large conference centres are fully equipped with all types of display media and some have experienced consultants and technicians offering advice and help in making the greatest possible impact with aids and equipment such as overhead projectors, slide and film projectors, video and television equipment. All these have a part to play in presenting and communicating information.

USEFUL GENERAL REFERENCES

RAILWAY STATIONS (Enquiries)
London Region
Cannon Street, Charing Cross, London Bridge,
   Victoria, Waterloo — 01-928 5100
Euston, Marylebone, St Pancras — 01-387 7070
Fenchurch Street, Liverpool Street — 01-283 7171
King's Cross — 01-278 2417
Paddington — 01-262 6767
Eastern Region
York — 0904 25671
Scottish Region
Edinburgh — 031-556 2451
Glasgow — 041-204 2844

PASSPORT OFFICES
Belfast — 0232 232371
Glasgow — 041-3320271
Liverpool — 051-237 3010
London   A–D — 01-213 3344
         E–K — 01-213 7272
         L–Q — 01-213 6161
         R–Z — 01-213 3434
Newport — 0633 56292
Peterborough — 0733 895555

CAR-HIRE NUMBERS
Alamo Rent-a-Car — 01-897 0536
Avis — 01-848 8733
Avis Chauffeur Drive — 01-897 2621
Bri-Car — 01-661 1522
Budget — 01-441 5882
Godfrey Davis Chauffeur Drive — 01-834 6701
Godfrey Davis Europcar — 01-950 5050
Guy Salmon — 01-730 8571
Hertz — 01-679 1777
Jays Carriages (Heathrow)
   Chauffeur Hire — 01-897 2761
   Key Rent-a-Car — 01-897 7777
   Swan National — 01-995 4665
MOTORAIL (Car-carrying Services) — 01-387 8541

(correct at time of going to press)

AIRLINE OFFICES (Reservations)

Air Canada	01-759 2636
Air France	01-499 9511
Air India	01-491 7979
Air New Zealand	01-930 3434
Air UK	01-249 7073
Alitalia	01-602 7111
American Airlines	01-629 8817
Ansett	01-897 4000
Austrian Airlines	01-439 0741
British Airways	01-897 4000
British Caledonian	01-668 4222
British Midland	01-581 0864
BWIA International	01-734 3796
Caribbean	01-493 6252
Cathay Pacific	01-930 7878
Dan Air	01-680 1011
Egyptair	01-734 2395
Finnair	01-930 3941
Garuda	01-434 2591
INFOIBERIA	01-437 5622
Japan	01-408 1000
KLM	01-568 9144
Kuwait	01-935 8795
Lufthansa	01-408 0442
Olympic	01-493 1233
Pacific Southwest	01-409 0814
Pan-American	01-409 0688
Polynesian	01-242 3131
Qantas	01-748 5050
Sabena	01-437 6950
Saudia	01-995 7777
Scandinavian	01-734 4020
South African	01-734 9841
Swissair	01-439 4144
Thai Airways	01-499 9113
TWA	01-636 4090
World Airways	01-734 3411

AIRPORTS AND AIR TERMINALS

London (Heathrow)	01-759 4321

(correct at time of going to press)

Passenger Reservations, Fares, Advance Travel
 Information (24-hour service) 01-897 4000
Passenger Flight Information, Aircraft Arrivals
 and Departures
    London (Heathrow) 01-745 7412
    London (Gatwick) 0293 28822
  Charter Sales and British Airtours (Gatwick) 0293 36321
Luton Airport 0582 36061
Stansted Airport 0279 502380
Birmingham, Elmdon 021-767 5511
Manchester, Wythenshawe 061-489 3000
Scotland
  Aberdeen, Dyce 0224 722331
  Edinburgh, Turnhouse 031-333 1000
  Glasgow, Abbotsinch 041-887 1111
Wales
  Cardiff (Enquiries) 0446 711211
Northern Ireland
  Belfast 0232 229271
Republic of Ireland
  Dublin (Flight Information) Dublin 379900
  Shannon Limerick 61444

CAR FERRY SERVICES

Brittany Ferries (Plymouth) 0705 827701
Hoverspeed (Dover) 0843 595555
North Sea Ferries (Hull) 0482 795141
P & O Normandy Ferries 97 203388
Sally the Viking Line (Ramsgate) 0843 595522
Sealink Car Ferry Services (Victoria Station) 01-834 8122
Townsend Thoresen (Dover) 0304 223000

Coach Services Travel Enquiries,
  164 Buckingham Palace Road, SW1 01-730 0202

LONDON TOURIST BOARD

Victoria Station Forecourt 01-730 3488

LONDON TAXI-CAB RANKS

Central	Moorgate, EC2	01-606 4526
East	Mile End Station, E3	01-980 1433

(correct at time of going to press)

West	Lancaster Gate, W2	01-723 9907
	Kensington High Street, W8	01-937 0736
North	Finsbury Park, N16	01-800 4819
South-west	Harrington Road, SW7	01-589 5242
	Sloane Square, SW1	01-730 2664
	St George's Square, SW1	01-834 1014

There are taxi-cab ranks at railway stations and near most large hotels. There are also:

Radio Controlled Taxis
   Owner Drivers Radio Taxis Service   01-286 4848

ALL NIGHT POST OFFICE

Trafalgar Square, WC2

GENERAL KNOWLEDGE

Daily Telegraph Information Bureau   01-353 4242

EMERGENCY SERVICES (London)

Fire, Police, Ambulance		999
Medical	Middlesex Hospital, W1	01-636 8333
Dental	Daytime: Mon.–Fri. only, 0900 and	
	1330 hrs, Royal Dental Hospital,	
	32 Leicester Square, WC2	01-930 8831
Eye	Moorfields Eye Hospital, EC1	01-253 3411

THEATRE TICKET AGENCIES (London)

Abbey Box Office
   27 Victoria Street, SW1   01-222 2992
Keith Prowse Ltd
   74 Cornhill, EC3   01-283 1841
London Theatre Bookings
   31 Coventry Street, W1   01-839 4471
Premier Box Office
   188 Shaftesbury Avenue, WC2   01-240 2245

(correct at time of going to press)

PRINCIPAL LONDON THEATRES AND CONCERT HALLS
(Box Office telephone numbers)

Adelphi	01-836 7611	Old Vic	01-928 7616
Albery	01-836 3878	Olivier	01-928 2252
Aldwych	01-836 6404	Palace	01-437 8327
Ambassadors	01-836 1171	Palladium	01-437 7373
Apollo, Shaftesbury		Phoenix	01-836 2294
Avenue	01-437 2663	Piccadilly	01-437 4506
Apollo, Victoria	01-828 8665	Prince Edward	01-437 6877
Arts	01-836 2132	Prince of Wales	01-930 8681
Astoria	01-734 4287	Queen's	01-734 1166
Barbican	01-628 8795	Round House	01-267 2564
Cambridge	01-836 6056	Royal Albert Hall	01-589 8212
Churchill, Bromley	01-460 6677	Royal Court	01-730 1745
Coliseum	01-836 3161	Royal Festival Hall	01-928 3191
Comedy	01-930 2578	Royalty	01-405 8004
Cottesloe	01-928 2252	Sadler's Wells	01-278 8916
Covent Garden	01-240 1066	St Martin's	01-836 1443
Criterion	01-930 3216	Savoy	01-836 8888
Dominion	01-580 8845	Shaftesbury	01-379 5399
Duchess	01-836 8243	Shaw	01-388 1394
Duke of York's	01-836 5122	Strand	01-836 2660
Fortune	01-836 2238	Theatre Royal, Drury	
Garrick	01-836 4601	Lane	01-836 8108
Globe	01-437 1592	Theatre Royal,	
Greenwich	01-858 7755	Stratford, E15	01-534 0310
Hampstead	01-722 9301	Vaudeville	01-836 9987
Haymarket	01-930 9832	Victoria Palace	01-834 1317
Her Majesty's	01-930 6606	Westminster	01-834 0283
King's Head	01-226 1916	Whitehall	01-930 7765
Lyric, Hammersmith	01-741 2311	Wigmore Hall	01-935 2141
Lyric, Shaftesbury		Wyndhams	01-836 3028
Avenue	01-437 3686	Young Vic	01-928 6363
Lyttelton	01-928 2252		
Mayfair	01-629 3036	**OUT OF TOWN THEATRES**	
Mermaid	01-236 5568	Brighton, Theatre Royal	0273-28488
National Theatre	01-928 2252	Chichester, Festival	0243-781312
New End	01-435 6053	Oxford Playhouse	0865-247133
New Half Moon	01-790 4000	Stratford-upon-Avon,	
New London	01-405 0072	Royal Shakespeare	0789-295623

(*correct at time of going to press*)

INTERNATIONAL TIME ZONES

Add or subtract the number of hours shown, to correspond with Greenwich Mean Time.

Adelaide	+ 9½	Hong Kong	+ 8	Paris	+ 1
Amsterdam	+ 1	Istanbul	+ 2	Peking	+ 8
Ankara	+ 2	Islamabad	+ 5	Perth (WA)	+ 8
Athens	+ 2	Jakarta	+ 8	Prague	+ 1
Auckland, NZ	+ 12	Jerusalem	+ 2	Pretoria	+ 2
Baghdad	+ 3	Johannesburg	+ 2	Quebec	− 5
Bangkok	+ 7	Kano	+ 1	Rangoon	+ 6½
Beirut	+ 2	Karachi	+ 5½	Reykjavik	− 1
Belgrade	+ 1	Kuala Lumpur	+ 7½	Rio de Janeiro	− 3
Berlin	+ 1	Kuwait City	+ 3	Riyadh	+ 3
Berne	+ 1	Leningrad	+ 3	Rome	+ 1
Bombay	+ 5½	Lisbon	+ 1	Rotterdam	+ 1
Bonn	+ 1	Luxembourg	+ 1	San Francisco	− 8
Brindisi	+ 1	Madeira	− 1	St John's (NF)	− 3½
Brisbane	+ 10	Madras	+ 5½	St Louis (Miss)	− 6
Brussels	+ 1	Madrid	+ 1	Seoul	+ 9
Bucharest	+ 2	Malta	+ 1	Singapore	+ 7½
Budapest	+ 1	Mauritius	+ 4	Stockholm	+ 1
Buenos Aires	− 3	Melbourne	+ 10	Suez	+ 2
Cairo	+ 2	Mexico City	− 6	Sydney	+ 10
Calcutta	+ 5½	Milan	+ 1	Tehran	+ 3½
Canberra	+ 10	Montreal	− 5	Tokyo	+ 9
Cape Town	+ 2	Moscow	+ 3	Toronto	− 5
Caracas	− 4	Munich	+ 1	Tripoli	+ 2
Chicago	− 6	Muscat	+ 4	Vancouver	− 8
Copenhagen	+ 1	Nairobi	+ 3	Victoria	+ 8
Dacca	+ 6	Naples	+ 1	Vienna	+ 1
Dallas	− 6½	New Orleans	− 6	Warsaw	+ 1
Delhi	+ 5½	New York	− 5	Washington	− 5
Dubai	+ 4	Nice	+ 1	Wellington	+ 12
Frankfurt	+ 1	Oslo	+ 1	Winnipeg	− 6
Geneva	+ 1	Ottawa	− 5	Yokohama	+ 9
Hanoi	+ 7	Palma	+ 1	Zurich	+ 1
Helsinki	+ 2	Panama	− 5
Hobart	+ 10

CONVERSION TABLES

The bold figures in the central columns can be read as either the metric or imperial, for example: 1 metre = 1.09 yards or 1 yard = 0.91 metres.

Litres		Pints
0.28	**0.50**	0.88
0.43	**0.75**	1.32
0.57	**1.00**	1.76
0.71	**1.25**	2.20
0.85	**1.50**	2.64
0.99	**1.75**	3.08
1.14	**2.00**	3.52
1.42	**2.50**	4.40
1.70	**3.00**	5.28
1.99	**3.50**	6.16
2.27	**4.00**	7.04
2.84	**5.00**	8.80

Litres		Gallons
4.55	**1.00**	0.22
6.82	**1.50**	0.33
9.09	**2.00**	0.44
11.36	**2.50**	0.55
13.64	**3.00**	0.66
15.91	**3.50**	0.77
18.18	**4.00**	0.88
20.46	**4.50**	0.99
22.73	**5.00**	1.10
27.28	**6.00**	1.32
31.82	**7.00**	1.54
36.37	**8.00**	1.76
40.91	**9.00**	1.98

Kilograms		Pounds
0.11	**0.25**	0.55
0.23	**0.50**	1.10
0.45	**1.00**	2.20
0.68	**1.50**	3.31
0.91	**2.00**	4.41
2.27	**5.00**	11.02
2.72	**6.00**	13.23
3.18	**7.00**	15.43

Metres		Yards
0.91	**1**	1.09
1.83	**2**	2.19
2.74	**3**	3.28
3.66	**4**	4.38
4.57	**5**	5.47

Kilometres		Miles
1.61	**1**	0.62
3.22	**2**	1.24
4.83	**3**	1.86
6.44	**4**	2.48
8.05	**5**	3.11
9.66	**6**	3.73
11.26	**7**	4.35
12.87	**8**	4.97
14.48	**9**	5.59

Centigrade		Fahrenheit
− 18	**0**	32
− 15	**5**	41
− 12	**10**	50
− 9	**15**	59
− 7	**20**	68
− 4	**25**	77
− 1	**30**	86
2	**35**	95
4	**40**	104
7	**45**	113
10	**50**	122
13	**55**	131
16	**60**	140
18	**65**	149
21	**70**	158
24	**75**	167
27	**80**	176
32	**90**	194
38	**100**	212

INDEX